WITHDRAWAL

Popular Literacies, Childhood and Schooling

Popular culture, media and new technologies have an ever increasing influence on the lives of children and young people, yet this is not adequately reflected in teaching and the literacy curriculum. This bold, forward-thinking text offers a clear rationale for the development of curricula and pedagogies that reflect children and young people's out-of-school cultural practices.

By addressing popular culture and new technologies in the context of literacy teacher education, this book marks a significant step forward in literacy teaching and learning. It takes a cross-disciplinary approach, and brings together contributions from some of the world's leading figures in the field. Topics addressed include:

- Children's popular culture in the home
- Informal literacies and pedagogic discourse
- New technologies and popular culture in children's everyday lives
- Teachers working with popular culture in the classroom

This important book clearly illustrates the way in which literacy is evolving through popular culture and new technology, and will be an influential read for teachers, students, researchers and policy-makers.

Jackie Marsh and **Elaine Millard** are both Senior Lecturers in Education at the University of Sheffield, UK. Together, they have directed the ESRC Research Seminar Series, 'Children's Literacy and Popular Culture' (2002–2004).

Popular Literacies, Childhood and Schooling

Edited by

Jackie Marsh and Elaine Millard

Routledge
Taylor & Francis Group

LONDON AND NEW YORK

First published 2006 by Routledge
2 Park Square, Abingdon, Oxon, OX14 4RN

Simultaneously published in the USA and Canada
by Routledge
270 Madison Ave, New York, NY 10016

Routledge is an imprint of the Taylor & Francis Group

© 2006 Jackie Marsh and Elaine Millard, selection and editorial matter;
individual chapters, the contributors.

Typeset in Galliard by Keyword Group
Printed and bound in Great Britain by Antony Rowe Ltd,
Chippenham, Wiltshire

British Library Cataloguing in Publication Data
A catalogue record for this book is available from the British Library

Library of Congress Cataloging in Publication Data

Popular literacies, childhood and schooling / edited by Jackie Marsh
    & Elaine Millard.
        p. cm.
    Includes bibliographical references and index.
    ISBN 0-415-36451-5 (hardback : alk. paper)
    1. Computers and literacy. 2. Computers and children.
    3. Language arts (Early childhood). 4. Education–Effect of
    technological innovations on. 5. Popular culture.
    I. Marsh, Jackie. II. Millard, Elaine.
    LC149.5.P67   2006
    372.6–dc22
    2005015461

ISBN10: 0-415-36451-5
ISBN13: 978-0-415-36451-5

Contents

Acknowledgements   vii
List of tables and figures   ix
List of contributors   xi
Foreword   xvii
ANNE HAAS DYSON

Introduction   1
JACKIE MARSH AND ELAINE MILLARD

PART I
Early childhoods   9

1 Technokids, *Koala Trouble* and *Pokémon*: literacy, new
   technologies and popular culture in children's
   everyday lives   11
   MICHELE KNOBEL

2 Children's popular culture in the home: tracing
   cultural practices in texts   29
   KATE PAHL

3 Mr Naughty Man: popular culture and children's
   literacy learning   54
   PAMELA GREENHOUGH, WAN CHING YEE, JANE ANDREWS, ANTHONY FEILER,
   MARY SCANLAN, MARTIN HUGHES

4 Playing with texts: the contribution of children's
   knowledge of computer narratives to their story-writing   72
   EVE BEARNE AND HELEN WOLSTENCROFT

5   A sign of the times: looking critically at popular
    digital writing   93
    GUY MERCHANT

PART II
Youth and adolescence   **109**

6   No single divide: literacies, new technologies and
    school-defined versus self-selected purposes in
    curriculum and pedagogy   111
    COLIN LANKSHEAR

7   Informal literacies and pedagogic discourse   128
    GEMMA MOSS

8   Making it move, making it mean: animation,
    print literacy and the metafunctions of language   150
    DAVID PARKER

9   Nomads and tribes: online meaning-making and
    the development of new literacies   160
    JULIA DAVIES

PART III
Teachers and schooling   **177**

10 Tightropes, tactics and taboos: pre-service teachers'
    beliefs and practices in relation to popular culture
    and literacy   179
    JACKIE MARSH

11 Assets in the classroom: comfort and competence
    with media among teachers present and future   200
    MURIEL ROBINSON AND MARGARET MACKEY

12 Transformative practitioners, transformative practice:
    teachers working with popular culture in the classroom   221
    ELAINE MILLARD

    Afterword: popular literacies in an era of scientific
    reading instruction: challenges and opportunities   241
    DONNA E. ALVERMANN

    Index   249

Acknowledgements

We would like to thank all of the contributors to this book for their excellent chapters and their attention to deadlines, despite their hectic schedules. It has been a real pleasure working with you. Thanks to all at Routledge for their commitment to and work on the project, especially Alison Foyle and Tom Young. We would also like to express our gratitude and appreciation to all of the teachers we have worked with on issues relating to popular culture and literacy over the years; your inspiring work has informed this agenda and continues to do so. Finally, the chapters in this book are drawn from an ESRC Research Seminar Series on Children's Literacy and Popular Culture, held at the University of Sheffield from 2002 to 2004. We would like to thank everyone who contributed to this enormously rich and challenging seminar series, both speakers and participants; we developed our own ideas enormously through the discussions and debates which occurred and are very pleased to be able to disseminate some of these ideas through this book.

Tables and Figures

TABLES

2.1	Time and space in home and school domains	31
2.2	Affordances and timescales of toys	50
3.1	The metaphorical mappings	64
4.1	Focus group survey responses: reported time spent per week playing computer games by 8–9-year-olds	75
4.2	Comparison of narrative features of *Red Riding Hood* and *Lara Croft* story	78
5.1	Basic principles of onscreen writing	95
10.1	Explanation of wording in Figure 10.1	184
11.1	Age range of the surveyed population: Edmonton and Lincoln	204
11.2	Success stories: percentage of the samples expressing comfort	206
11.3	National similarities: percentage expressing comfort with DVDs in both countries	206
11.4	National differences: percentage expressing comfort with text-messaging in both countries	206
11.5	Percentage of the Edmonton sample expressing comfort with digital games	209
11.6	Percentage of the Lincoln sample expressing comfort with digital games	209
11.7	Lincoln teenage responses to questions about gaming	210
12.1	The research projects	225
12.2	Comparison of the participants' teaching roles and experience	225

FIGURES

1.1	*Koala Trouble* – trouble in paradise	17
2.1	Castle in the *Super Mario* game, drawn by Fatih	37
2.2	Fatih's map of his flat	38
2.3	Later drawing of more complicated *Super Mario* game	39
2.4	Continuation of game shown in Figure 2.3	40
2.5	Final stage of *Super Mario* game	41
2.6	Small-world play on the carpet	43
2.7	*Pokémon* figures on the sofa	44
2.8	Mallard drawing	46
2.9	Indian train	47
2.10	Edward's trains lined up	48
4.1	Leonie's computer game drawing	79
4.2	Tyson's computer game drawing	80
4.3	Planning and recording format for *Lara Croft* narrative	82
4.4	Mary's plan for the *Lara Croft* story	82
4.5	Tyson's plan for the *Lara Croft* story	83
4.6	Tyson's *Lara Croft* story opening	88
5.1	Wendy Knits	99
5.2	My last kitty bed	101
5.3	Pixie and Ivy's black rights slide	105
10.1	Mean ranking of attitudinal statements	183
10.2	Time/space continua	187

Contributors

Donna E. Alvermann is Distinguished Research Professor of Language and Literacy Education at the University of Georgia. She was formerly a classroom teacher in Texas and New York. Her research focuses on youth's multiple literacies in and out of school. From 1992 to 1997 she co-directed the National Reading Research Center, funded by the US Department of Education. With over 100 articles and chapters in print, her books include *Content Reading and Literacy: Succeeding in Today's Diverse Classrooms* (4th edn), *Popular Culture in the Classroom: Teaching and Researching Critical Media Literacy*, *Bridging the Literacy Achievement Gap, Grades 4–12*, and *Adolescents and Literacies in a Digital World*. Past president of the National Reading Conference (NRC) and co-chair of the International Reading Association's Commission on Adolescent Literacy, she currently edits *Reading Research Quarterly*. She was elected to the Reading Hall of Fame in 1999, and is the recipient of NRC's Oscar Causey Award for Outstanding Contributions to Reading Research, the Albert Kingston Award for Distinguished Service, and College Reading Association's Laureate Award and the H.B. Herr Award for Contributions to Research in Reading Education.

Jane Andrews is a research associate on the Home–School Knowledge Exchange Project, which is based at the University of Bristol. Before this appointment, she worked on an ESRC-funded research project investigating classroom assessment of primary Key Stage 1 pupils, developing English as an additional language. Her research and teaching interests are in the area of language education and the achievement of minority ethnic pupils.

Eve Bearne divides her time at the University of Cambridge Faculty of education between research and teaching. Her current research interests are children's production of multimodal texts and gender, language and literacy. She has edited several books about language and literacy and about children's literature. She is currently Immediate Past President of the United Kingdom Literacy Association.

Julia Davies is a lecturer in education at the University of Sheffield, where she is Deputy Head of the School of Education. She teaches on the EdD and MA programmes in literacy and language and co-directs the latter. She began her career teaching English, ultimately running a communications faculty in a large comprehensive school. As well as being director of English within Initial Teacher Education at Sheffield for ten years, she has been actively involved in in-service education courses within UK schools, both locally and nationally. She currently leads a longitudinal study, looking at gendered patterns of behaviour and achievement of pupils aged 11–14 years, funded by the Department for Education and Skills. Her research predominantly focuses, however, on online communities, teenagers' uses of new technologies and the development of new literacy and language skills. She has forthcoming chapters in Kate Pahl and Jennifer Rowsell's *Travelnotes from the New Literacy Studies* and David Buckingham and Rebekah Willett's *Digital Generations*.

Anne Haas Dyson is a former teacher of young children and, currently, a professor of education at Michigan State University, where she teaches courses related to qualitative research methods and language and literacy education. Previously she was on the faculty of the University of Georgia and the University of California, Berkeley, where she was a recipient of the University of California, Berkeley's Distinguished Teaching Award. She studies the social lives and literacy learning of schoolchildren. Among her publications are *Social Worlds of Children Learning to Write in an Urban Primary School*, which was awarded NCTE's David Russell Award for Distinguished Research, *Writing Superheroes: Contemporary Childhood, Popular Culture, and Classroom Literacy*, *The Brothers and Sisters Learn to Write: Popular Literacies in Childhood and School Cultures*, and (with Celia Genishi) *On the Case: Approaches to Language and Literacy Research*.

Anthony Feiler is a lecturer in education (special educational needs) at the Graduate School of Education, University of Bristol. He is currently co-leader of the literacy strand in the ESRC-funded Home–School Knowledge Exchange Project and director of the Literacy Early Action Project (LEAP), an early intervention programme for Reception children and their families.

Pamela Greenhough is a research fellow on the Home–School Knowledge Exchange Project, based at the University of Bristol. She has worked on a series of ESRC-funded research projects concerned with the articulation of home and school learning. Throughout these she has maintained a focus on children's literacy learning.

Martin Hughes is Professor of Education at the University of Bristol. He has written widely on children's learning, particularly in the areas of mathematics and the relationship between home and school. His previous books include *Young Children Learning* (with Barbara Tizard), *Children and Number: Parents and their Children's Schools* (with Felicity Wikeley and Tricia Nash) and *Numeracy and Beyond* (with Charles Desforges and Christine Mitchell). He is currently directing the Home–School Knowledge Exchange Project, funded as part of the ESRC's Teaching and Learning Research Programme. He is also writing a book on homework, with Pamela Greenhough, based on a previous ESRC research project.

Michele Knobel is an associate professor of education at Montclair State University (USA), where she coordinates the graduate and undergraduate literacy programmes, and an adjunct professor of education at Central Queensland University, Australia. Her research at present focuses on the relationship between new literacies, social practices and digital technologies. Michele's most recent book is *A Handbook for Teacher Research* (with Colin Lankshear). She is currently working on a new literacies primer, *Technoliteracies* (with Colin Lankshear and Angela Thomas), as well as co-editing *The Handbook of Research on New Literacies* (with Donald Leu, Julie Coiro and Colin Lankshear).

Colin Lankshear is a freelance educational researcher and writer, based in Mexico, where he is a permanent resident. He is currently a half–time professor of literacy and new technologies at James Cook University in Cairns, Australia, an adjunct professor of education at Central Queensland University, Australia, and teaches short courses in Mexico, Canada and the USA. His current research and publishing focus mainly on literacy and other social practices involving new technologies. He is a member of research teams on projects funded by the Australian Research Council and the Australian government investigating factors associated with low female participation rates in ICT professional occupations and 'Success for Boys', respectively. Recent books include *New Literacies: Changing Knowledge and Classroom Learning* (with Michele Knobel), and *Cyber Spaces/Social Spaces: Culture Clash in Computerized Classrooms* (with Ivor Goodson et al.), and he is joint editor of a forthcoming work, *The Handbook of Research on New Literacies*.

Margaret Mackey is a professor in the School of Library and Information Studies at the University of Alberta in Canada. She has published widely on the topics of young readers and their texts in print and other media; her current research investigates the multimodal literacies of adults in the 18–34 demographic. Her most recent books are *Literacies across Media: Playing the Text* (RoutledgeFalmer, 2002) and *Beatrix Potter's Peter Rabbit: A Children's Classic at 100*, an edited book of essays (The Children's Literature Association and Scarecrow Press, 2002). She is the North American editor of *Children's Literature in Education: An International Quarterly*.

Jackie Marsh is a senior lecturer in education at the University of Sheffield, UK, where she co-directed, with Elaine Millard, the ESRC Research Seminar Series 'Children's Literacy and Popular Culture' (2002–2004). She was an editor, along with Nigel Hall and Joanne Larson, of the *Handbook of Early Childhood Literacy* (Sage, 2003) and is an editor of the *Journal of Early Childhood Literacy*. Jackie is involved in research which examines the role and nature of popular culture and media in early childhood literacy, both in and out of school contexts. Her most recent publication in this field was an edited book: *Popular Culture, New Media and Digital Literacy in Early Childhood* (RoutledgeFalmer, 2005).

Guy Merchant is Coordinator of the Language and Literacy Research Group at Sheffield Hallam University, UK. His current research focuses on children and young people's experience of popular digital literacy – particularly the use of synchronous chat and interactive communication through email. He has published a number of research studies and produces a variety of curriculum materials in the area of primary literacy. As a founding editor of the *Journal of Early Childhood Literacy*, he has a strong interest in the changing nature of literacy and its impact on early childhood.

Elaine Millard is a senior lecturer in the School of Education at the University of Sheffield, and a founder member of the Sheffield Literacy, Language and Culture Research Group. Her main research interests concern the changing patterns of children's literacy practices and preferences and in particular in their relation to gender, social difference and cultural change. She is the author of *Differently Literate: Boys, Girls and the Schooling of Literacy* (London: Falmer Press, 1997) and co-author with Jackie Marsh of *Popular Culture: Using children's culture in the classroom* (London: Paul Chapman/Sage, 2000).

Gemma Moss is Reader in Education at the Institute of Education, University of London. Her main research interests are in the areas of literacy and education policy, including gender and literacy; children's informal literacy practices and their relationship to the English curriculum; how the shifting relationships between policy makers, practitioners and stakeholders are re-shaping the literacy curriculum; and the impact of the new knowledge economy in education. She has directed several ESRC-funded research projects exploring these main themes. She is the author of *Un/Popular Fictions* (1989), a study of girls' romance writing.

Kate Pahl is based at the University of Sheffield, UK, where she teaches on the MA Literacy and Language in Education. Her research is focused on ethnographic studies which examine children's texts as traces of social practices and explore the role of multi-modal and visual literacies in the home. Her publications include *Transformations: Children's Meaning Making in a Nursery* (Trentham, 1999), *Literacy and Education* (with Jennifer Rowsell, Sage, 2005) and she has a chapter in C. Jewitt, and G. Kress (eds) (2003), *Multimodal Literacy* (New York: Peter Lang).

David Parker is Research Director for Creative Partnerships, Arts Council, UK. Formerly, he was Head of Research at the British Film Institute. He has published widely on the relationship between moving image media and literacy, including *Edit;Play* (bfi, 2000) with Julian Sefton-Green and *Analysing Media Texts* (Continuum, 2003) with Andrew Burn. He is currently working with Andrew Burn on a multimodal grammar of the moving image.

Muriel Robinson has been exploring questions related to popular culture and children's literacy development since her PhD, published as *Children Reading Print and Television* (Falmer, 1997), which found that children use narrative in similar ways across media to make meaning from the texts they encounter. In recent years she has become increasingly interested in the ways in which younger children use film, television and other media texts before school. She is currently working in higher education in Lincoln, UK.

Mary Scanlan has experience as a children's librarian and a teacher. She has taught in both key stages 1 and 2 and has maintained an interest in literacy. In 2000, she completed an MEd at the University of Bristol which examined materials used to teach reading in Year 2 classrooms. She is currently employed as a Teacher–Researcher on the Home–School Knowledge Exchange Project, working within the literacy strand.

Wan Ching Yee is a research associate on the ESRC-funded Home–School Knowledge Exchange Project and has a particular interest in ethnic diversity and the home. She has worked on a wide range of cross-sectoral research and evaluation projects from school improvement and teacher research to widening access to higher education for minority ethnic groups.

Helen Wolstencroft is Curriculum Development Adviser for Primary English with Essex LEA. She has been responsible for several research projects into the links between children's understanding of film and writing. Her research work has developed to encompass children's production of multimodal texts, including computer games.

Foreword: why popular literacies matter

Anne Haas Dyson

> Just as there is no fixed content to the category of 'popular culture,' so there is no fixed subject to attach to it – 'the people'.
>
> (Hall, 1981: 239)

In this book, Jackie Marsh, Elaine Millard and their colleagues collectively use this 'old school' medium to thoughtfully explore the very current topic of multiple media – 'popular literacies' and their place in children's lives in and out of school. That exploration is made all the more challenging because the topic is one that eludes easy definition. 'Popular literacies' has something to do with 'popular culture', itself associated in some way with the everyday pleasures of 'the people'. To prepare the stage for the authors to come, I provide a brief orientation, if not a definition, for this 'popular culture', its 'people', and its 'place'. In so doing, I hope to underscore why their work matters. Informing this foray on to the slippery conceptual ground of the 'popular' are cultural theorists with ethnographic compasses, who align themselves, not with 'the' people, but with particular people. The particular people who have guided my own reflective journey into the realm of the popular are young school children, and, as usual, I will need their help to stay grounded.

To begin, popular culture is not a television show, a radio programme, a computer game, or any other media text or form of communication. It is also not a genre, like 'rap', 'sports report', or 'talk show'. If it were so easily objectified, so neatly fixed, it would not pose such complex challenges for educators. Those forms seen as academically useful – like Internet searches – could be incorporated, and others of seemingly dubious worth – like cartoons – could be kept out. The operating principle for schools would be biblical in tone: to everything there is a time and a place and, for the most part, school is not the place for popular culture. (After phonics lessons and reading group comes what? Superheroes, with a pull-out remedial group needing extra help?)

Popular culture, though, is not so easily contained in a physical time and space, and the reason for that has to do with 'people'. As Jenkins et al. (2002) detail, the history of 'popular culture' has been tied up with efforts to contain 'the people' and to distinguish 'them' from 'us' (the academics). The 'them' were initially the romanticized 'folk', the peasantry whose artistry was distinguished from that of the 'intellectuals'. With the rise of commercial culture, the 'them' became the newly literate public – 'the masses'. They were the dupes of vulgar capitalism (like Dickens's cheap newspaper serials). Such products contributed to 'the people's' mindless apathy.

Commercial culture products, their mediated form, and even the cultural labels afforded particular products (like those of Dickens and, indeed, Shakespeare [Levine, 1988]) may have changed, but the designation 'popular' continues in its association with ordinary people and, also, with efforts to distinguish those of 'distinction' (Bourdieu, 1984) from the common folk and, moreover, to distinguish the children of the educated from those 'at risk'. Children who are designated as properly prepared for school should be read the classics of children's literature each night before bed, not, heaven forbid, plopped in front of the video player for the fiftieth replay of *The Little Mermaid*.

But gradually assuming importance in educational thought are the very different ideas of scholars associated with cultural studies (for a review, see Storey, 2001). These scholars have been interested not so much in cultural commodities or texts deemed 'popular' as in what ordinary people do with those commodities. In particular societal circumstances, people use whatever symbolic material is to hand to develop shared meaning-making practices. That is, people produce popular culture by participating actively in making use of cultural commodities – they engage in 'popular literacies', as it were. They retell, discuss, role-play, shift genre, merge characters, and on and on, appropriating and recontextualizing material from commercial texts as they participate in a shared community (Jenkins, 1992; Dyson, 2003). The very fact that cultural products are not regulated by the school makes them amenable to these practices and, moreover, deeply implicated in questions of identity, including those of gender, race, class, and/or style of being – a surfer, a member of the hip-hop generation, a sci-fi fan, a basketball buff, or a video game player.

Thus, if attention is paid to what people do with cultural commodities, 'the people' fragment; they lose their determining article, their 'the', and so does 'the' culture industry. However global the reach of the cultural industries, however familiar Mickey Mouse, Michael Jordan, or Pokémon may be far from their own place of origin, cultural commodities always emerge within local circumstances, interrelated with a configuration of textual experiences and used for particular purposes. The culture industry is not simply a capitalist means for controlling people's minds, nor do people use it as some pure means of self-expression and community organization. Popular culture is a prime site for pleasure, for exploration of possible identities, and for negotiation and struggle (Jenkins *et al.*, 2002).

As just a brief example of the incredibly complex layers of local meaning surrounding references to popular media forms, consider the following interaction:

> The writing period is drawing to a close in Elisha's first grade classroom, a racially diverse classroom in an economically depressed neighborhood. The children are reading their products to each other. Elisha has just read the following text:
>
>> Today I am going to call Marisa and ask if I can come over and we will watch basketball.
>
> Mandisa immediately responds, followed on her (verbal) heels by Brad.
>
> *Mandisa*:   Is there a basketball game today?
> *Brad*:   I have that.

It would take a lengthy ethnography to unravel the complex discursive threads knitted together in this brief vignette. To just hint at the complexity,

- consider that Elisha and Mandisa are African American girls. Writing about popular sports was associated primarily with being a boy in this class, but the African American girls all declared that they liked basketball and, Elisha in particular, that she liked the *Black* basketball players (and she assumed that if I [a White woman] liked basketball, then I liked the *White* players);
- consider Brad's statement about 'having that'. Brad, a White boy, like other children in the class, used writing time to participate in a practice that could be called 'plans to play at somebody's house'. The children wrote plans (for the most part, never-to-be-enacted plans) about going to play at somebody's house (see Dyson, in press). For the boys, a prime planned activity was playing video games; among the games the boys planned to play was one named for the National Basketball Association. Boys knew the names of games whether or not they had them or were allowed to play them. Planning to get together to play video games was a cool thing for the guys to do. Elisha was going to a friend's house to *watch* basketball; Brad could *play* it (in cyber space) because he owned the game (or so he declared).

In the local context of this classroom's language life, the media material of popular sports was appropriated as material to maintain, resist and complicate assumptions about human relations. Similarly complex vignettes could be constructed about varied kinds of cultural texts in educational sites, but all would depend on the existent societal structures, the available and/or valued commercial materials, and the spaces children find for their own agency.

It is this embeddedness that makes it impossible to keep popular culture 'out' of school. For it comes 'in' in the imaginations, social sensibilities and textual experiences of students themselves. Popular culture may be there in the cracks of the curriculum, as children play, joke, sing and retell familiar narratives from commercial texts. It may be evident as well in official curricular space, whether or not teachers approve, in what and how children write. During writing centre time, Ashley, five years old, wrote a boxed letter 'S' on the T-shirt of his drawn Superman and then wrote his own name across Superman's chest, boxing his 'S' as well; this young child, just figuring out the written system, was so pleased to share a letter with the beloved superhero (from Dyson, 1982). Jameel, six years old and homeless, constructed a visual pun, merging cartoon dialogue bubbles and drawn air bubbles for a singing fish; underneath the singing fish, on a stapled-on paper strip, were the words of an announcer who would take the singing fish to the streets (the stapled strip was actually a 'pocket' for the money donations that would surely follow (from Dyson, 1993)).

The vignettes could continue indefinitely, but the authors in this collection have their own vivid illustrations of how children and youth use the resources of popular literacies to explore and express their social being and cultural identities. Moreover, their work collectively raises questions about the pedagogical challenges and benefits of teachers explicitly taking advantage of children's experiences with popular literacies. What if, for example, teachers asked children to translate the narrative language and structure of one kind of media text (an adventure computer game, for example) to another (a print-based text, for instance)? Moreover, if teachers were to make such plans, would the popular literacies children drew on still be 'popular', or would they themselves mutate into the standard or correct forms of particular commercial texts?

There are still more provocative questions inspired by these authors. What if popular literacies enter into the hierarchical ordering of school knowledge? Will literacies most amenable to the school's use (like participating in electronic mail or contributing to interactive websites) become an assumed part of 'the children's' experience and, thus, an assumed resource for school learning? What would happen, then, to children without, say, computers in the home, like Elisha and her peers? Would popular literacies become differentiated into new ways to identify lacks in the 'at risk'? And finally, given that popular literacies are so embedded in issues of identity, how can teachers help children critically interrogate dominant images of gender, race, or sexuality without destroying their fun – or having children tune school out, so to speak?

Such difficult questions. So difficult that older generations of educators, like me, may be tempted to leave their exploration to the young. We may assume, too simplistically perhaps, that younger teachers may be more comfortable with the media and more pedagogically inventive as well. But the authors of this collection have something to say about this issue as well. Young teachers are situated in particular local circumstances, with varied material and experiential resources – it will not be possible to offer the young a simple prescription for the use of popular literacies. With their own memories of 'unpopular' schooling, teachers, young and old, may lack confidence and be in urgent need of professional support in an area in which educational establishments themselves have misgivings.

There is much work to be done by all educators on these issues of popular literacies in young lives. I hope that the collective efforts of Marsh, Millard and their colleagues inspire, not universals about 'the people' and 'popular culture', but localized considerations of children's, youth's and teachers' engagement in popular literacies and with how that engagement could productively enter into and help transform schooling itself. To end with another quote from Stuart Hall (1981: 239), who may have had it from Rhett Butler: 'That is why "popular culture" matters. Otherwise, to tell you the truth, I don't give a damn about it'. However, you and I are in luck, dear readers. For Marsh, Millard and their colleagues know too why popular culture matters.

REFERENCES

Bourdieu, P. (1984). *Distinction: A social critique of the judgment of taste* (R. Nice, Trans.). Cambridge, MA: Harvard University Press (original work published 1979).

Dyson, A. Haas (1982). The emergence of visible language: Interrelationships between drawing and early writing. *Visible Language*, **16**, 360–381.

Dyson, A. Haas (1993). *Social worlds of children learning to write in an urban primary school*. New York: Teachers College Press.

Dyson, A. Haas (2003). *The brothers and sisters learn to write: Popular literacies in childhood and school cultures*. New York: Teachers College Press.

Dyson, A. H. (in press). School literacy and the development of a child culture: Written remnants of the 'gusto of life'. In D. Thiessen and A. Cook-Sather (eds), *International handbook of student experience in elementary and secondary school*. Dordrecht, The Netherlands: Kluwer Academic Publishers.

Hall, S. (1981). Notes on deconstructing the popular. In R. Samuel (ed.), *People's history and socialist theory* (pp. 227–239). London: Routledge & Kegan Paul.

Jenkins, H. (1992). *Textual poachers: Television fans and participatory culture*. New York: Routledge.

Jenkins, H., McPherson, T. and Shattuc, J. (2002). Defining popular culture. In H. Jenkins, T. McPherson and J. Shattuc (eds), *Hop on Pop: The politics and pleasures of popular culture* (pp. 26–42). Durham, NC: Duke University.

Levine, L. (1988). *Highbrow/Lowbrow: The emergence of cultural hierarchy in America*. Cambridge, MA: Harvard University Press.

Storey, J. (2001). *An introductory guide to cultural theory and popular culture* (3rd edn). Harlow, Essex: Pearson Education.

Introduction

Jackie Marsh and Elaine Millard

The chapters in this book were initially presented at a number of international research seminars, part of a series entitled *Children's Literacy and Popular Culture*,[1] which was funded by the Economic and Social Research Council in the UK.[2] The aim of the series was to develop understanding about the role and nature of popular culture in children's schooled and out-of-school literacy lives. Over the last few decades, there has been a steadily increasing number of scholars working across disciplines in the field of children's literacy, popular culture and education. These include researchers interested in pedagogy (Nixon and Comber, 2005; Dyson, 1997, 2002; Millard, 2003; Marsh and Millard 2000; Robinson, 1997; Vasquez, 2005), linguistics (Merchant, 2001), media, technology and cultural studies (Buckingham, 1998; Carrington, 2005; Davies, 2003; Luke and Luke, 2001; Sefton-Green, 1998) and those concerned with the influence of home and out-of-school interests on school interactions (Pahl, 2005). While there is a growing body of published work which seeks to define the new turn in children's understanding of alternative forms of meaning-making (Dyson, 2002; Kress and Van Leeuwen, 1996, 2001), there is a need to focus more directly on the ways in which popular culture relates to children's out-of-school literacy practices. However, as well as understanding how popular culture is used and transformed within home and peer groups, there is a corresponding need to understand the nature of popular culture and its influence on children's school work. It has been claimed that children are finding the literacy practices of school increasingly arid and meaningless (Hilton, 1996) or divorced from the practices of their communities and cultures (Corrigan, 1979; Marsh and Millard, 2000; Nagle, 1999). Further, there are suggestions that the current incorporation of new literacies into schooled practices may only work to render them both ineffective and irrelevant as forms of communication (see for example Lankshear's (1997) comments on the use of email as a school exercise). Research has been undertaken in classrooms that has focused on the potential that popular culture has to motivate children and orientate them towards schooled literacy practices (Alvermann *et al.*, 1999; Dyson, 1997, 2002; Marsh, 1999, 2005; Marsh and Millard, 2000). This work has sought to address the anxieties which are frequently expressed by commentators about the damaging influence of popular culture: its addictive qualities (Storkey, 1999); its potential to displace book-based reading practices (Neuman, 1995); its inhibition of socialization (Tobin, 1998); its negative role modelling through the perpetuation of oppressive cultural stereotyping (Gilbert, 1991); and its collusion with commercial interests to turn children into undiscriminating consumers (Adorno, 1975; Postman, 1983; Kline, 1993). The chapters in this book contribute to the ongoing debate as they explore the interface between in- and out-of-school worlds and, in doing so, raise a number of questions for future research, practice and policy in this field.

The book is organized into three distinct parts. In the first section, authors address younger children's early experiences in homes and schools and explore the way in which experiences in the home in the first years of life are imbued with a range of popular cultural forms that are often marginalized in educational settings. In the first chapter, Michele Knobel outlines the experience of two young boys who make productive use of the wide range of technologies available to them and embed them into their semiotic and social practices in meaningful ways. Knobel provides a wealth of evidence which suggests that very young children are competent users of a range of technologies, and she presents a serious challenge to those who seek to impose what she terms as 'school-centric literacy learning and technology uses' on young children without due recognition of this prior experience and expertise. In the second chapter, Kate Pahl offers further insight into young children's cultural worlds in the home by drawing from her longitudinal ethnographic study of three boys. She demonstrates how they weave together a range of experiences in their daily play and textual production, drawing from popular culture, media and family narratives to create complex and playful texts. She suggests that by welcoming in and encouraging the texts made at home, teachers would gain an understanding of children's 'ruling passions' (Barton and Hamilton, 1998). The authors of the third chapter are co-researchers on the ESRC-funded Home–School Knowledge Exchange Project based at the University of Bristol, UK, and they also focus on the out-of-school experiences of children as they move across modes and media. The team consider the varied communities of practice in which children engage, as the site of learning shifts from home to school, and propose that educators need to look closely at the way in which children reappropriate texts from one context to another. If this process is ignored or marginalized within the classroom, then, they suggest, children's 'nascent understandings about how (some) literacy "goes"', the literacy embedded within popular culture, are not recognized or built upon.

In Chapter 4, Eve Bearne and Helen Wolstencroft provide a telling account of work undertaken in one classroom which aimed to develop the kinds of pedagogical practices promoted in the previous chapter. They recount how a class of primary children recast the traditional tale of *Red Riding Hood* as a computer game narrative (based on *Lara Croft*) and trace the varied knowledge the children had of the affordances of written and computer game narratives through a close analysis of their stories. There are significant differences, of course, between off- and onscreen writing, and this is the focus for Guy Merchant's chapter. Merchant explores key aspects of digital writing, arguing that most children's apprenticeship to digital writing occurs through informal learning in out-of-school contexts. These experiences needed to be embedded in meaningful ways in the classroom and Merchant provides examples of school projects which have drawn upon children's emergent understandings of onscreen writing and enabled children to display their considerable knowledge of this mode. In the first part of the book, therefore, authors have sought to delineate young children's expertise and knowledge across a range of media, have outlined how central popular culture, media and new technologies are to many children's lives and have offered insights into classrooms in which these experiences are embedded in productive pedagogies (Lingard, 2005) that build on children's everyday experiences. These chapters emphasize the productive nature of children's encounters with popular culture and view these texts as one of many kinds in children's extensive repertoires.

In the second part of the book, the focus shifts to teenagers and their literacy lives in both schooled and out-of-school contexts. As students progress in their education, their experiences and practices of literacy may seem to be set on increasingly divergent paths, leaving schooling looking decidedly outmoded and unrepresentative of the wider communities they inhabit for both work and leisure. The first chapter in this section, by Colin Lankshear, explores a number of themes which thread throughout the book. Lankshear argues that, far from assuming that a significant digital divide exists for learners between their in- and out-of-school experiences, we need to look closely at the lives of children and young people in order to discern what it is that each domain offers them and how the domains relate or do not relate – indeed, whether they *should* relate at all. He suggests that what might be of more significance is a consideration of those activities which are self-selected and determined and those which are demanded by educational institutions; for authenticity is an important factor in any literacy event. This critique of some of the arguments made for the use of popular culture in the curriculum is taken up in Gemma Moss's chapter. She draws from the work of Basil Bernstein in her analysis of the nature and affordances of schooled and informal literacies and argues that the transfer of informal practices into the structured school curriculum is problematic because of the different construction of knowledge in these domains. However, despite a certain scepticism about what can be learned from the out-of-school interests she researched, she acknowledges a need for change to a school literacy curriculum that seems increasingly out of step with practices and interests of many of its current students.

Whatever the context, therefore, we would argue that teachers need to understand the developing literacy practices of those they teach and be able to deploy appropriate resources and strategies to support and motivate their learning. The remaining two chapters in this section demonstrate how educators might begin to incorporate children and young people's out-of-school interests in meaningful ways, ways that address some of the concerns held by those educators who worry that adults might colonize children's culture, or use it in simplistic ways to create a platform for attainment in schooled literacy. David Parker reports on a project in which teenagers created animated films based on a comic horror novel. Among other things, the project aimed to identify ways in which engagement with the same story across different media might enhance understanding of narrative. Parker argues that the project highlighted clear correlations between literacy and the grammar of moving-image media, but that the quality of explicitness was what made moving-image media distinct and developed the young people's understanding of narrative. This project drew from the pupils' out-of-school experiences of moving-image media in valuable ways and allowed them to transfer and transform knowledge from one domain to another. As Parker indicates, this kind of work involves a consideration of the learning and teaching strategies used as much as curriculum content. In the final chapter in this section, Julia Davies examines the *processes* that teenagers engage in as they participate in informal, online communities and considers how far these processes should be a part of classroom pedagogy. Davies analyzes the way in which participants in an online community cultivate their 'communities of practice' (Lave and Wenger, 1991) and outlines the sophisticated techniques and strategies used to support, police and challenge new and established users. She argues that schools could usefully embed some of these principles into the curriculum, rather than locate technologies within established pedagogical traditions which do not take account of new ways of learning and communicating. The chapters in this second section, therefore, have explored a number of critical issues pertaining to the crossover between school and out-of-school literacies and, whilst they offer varied perspectives, all emphasize the need for careful reflection on the principles which should underpin the task of developing 'culturally relevant pedagogy' (Ladson-Billings, 1995) and curricula.

In the final section of the book, the chapters turn to consider the challenges posed by this task for pre- and in-service teachers and teacher education. In the first chapter in this section, Jackie Marsh discusses data from a longitudinal project which explored pre-service teachers' attitudes towards and their use of popular culture in the curriculum. Many of the student teachers involved in the study expressed a desire to draw on children's popular culture and media in their teaching, but did not implement this for a wide range of reasons, some of which are explored in this chapter. One of the key barriers to such work was the lack of role models to draw upon, given that most of the students had not experienced the use of popular culture, media and new technologies during their own time as school pupils. In the next chapter in this section, Muriel Robinson and Margaret Mackey proffer a more hopeful vision of the future, as they suggest that as students become more confident and competent themselves with a range of new technologies, they may feel empowered to embed them into their teaching. Robinson and Mackey explore the outcomes of a survey conducted with two groups of student teachers in England and Canada which explored their own uses of new technologies and they outline a varied and interesting picture which has implications for future development. Their work emphasizes the importance of a context in which new competencies are developed, showing that personal need and easy access to new technologies is more important than age in determining what is taken up and what is ignored by teachers. However, effective change will only occur through recognition of teachers' needs in relation to professional development. In the final chapter, Elaine Millard reflects on the work of six teachers in England, all of whom have been successful in embedding children's cultural practices in meaningful ways in the curriculum. She identifies those factors which have helped these practitioners to challenge normative discourses and to create affirmative spaces for pupils within their classrooms. Millard stresses the need to allow teachers professional autonomy and the freedom to claim ownership of the curriculum; without this, teachers may feel overly constrained and unable to consider ways of drawing from and building on pupils' 'funds of knowledge' (Moll *et al.*, 1992) in the classroom.

Finally, Donna Alvermann offers an Afterword which looks towards the kinds of changes needed if schools are to offer a curriculum which is relevant and meaningful to pupils. Her focus is directly on the USA, but what she has to say is highly relevant to educators across the globe. This chapter creates a vision of the future which moves beyond arguments for and against the use of children's cultural resources in the classroom to a space in which it is acknowledged that curricula and pedagogy *have* to be rooted in the everyday if they are to offer pupils the skills, knowledge and understanding needed for the cultural, social, political and economic milieu in which they are located. One of the key questions now is not whether or not this needs to happen, but *how* it can take place. Whilst the chapters in this book do not offer a quick fix for these questions of import, they do present a range of reflections and insights which can inform future theory, policy and practice in the field. As we stated at the beginning of this introduction, these chapters were presentations in a series of international research seminars which sought to explore the relationship between popular literacies, childhood and schooling; whilst this seminar series is now complete, the themes it addressed and the issues it explored are still very much in focus and likely to be of increasing importance as we move ever more steadfastly into the technological and culturally complex world of the twenty-first century.

NOTES

1 For further details of the series, including papers and bibliography, see: http://www.shef.ac.uk/literacy/ESRC/seminar_series.html
2 Grant number: R451265240.

REFERENCES

Adorno, T. (1975) Television and the patterns of mass culture. In B. Rosenberg and D. Manning White (eds.), *Mass Culture: The Popular Arts in America*. New York: Macmillan.

Alvermann, D.E., Moon, J.S. and Hagood, M.C. (1999) *Popular culture in the classroom: Thinking and researching critical media literacy*. Newark, DE: International Reading Association and the National Reading Conference.

Barton, D. and Hamilton, M. (1998) *Local Literacies: Reading and Writing in One Community*. London: Routledge.

Buckingham, D. (1998) *Teaching Popular Culture. Beyond Radical Pedagogy*. London: UCL Press.

Carrington, V. (2005) New textual landscapes, information and early literacy. In J. Marsh (ed.), *Popular Culture, New Media and Digital Literacy in Early Childhood*. London: RoutledgeFalmer.

Corrigan, P. (1979) *Schooling the Smash Street Kids*. London: Macmillan.

Davies, J. (2003) Weaving magic webs: Internet identities and teen Wiccan subcultures. Paper given at presented at ESRC Research Seminar Series, Children's Literacy and Popular Culture, University of Sheffield. Accessed at: http://www.sheffield.ac.uk/literacy/ESRC/seminar1.html, November 2004.

Dyson, A.H. (1997) *Writing Superheroes: Contemporary Childhood, Popular Culture And Classroom Literacy*. New York and London: Columbia University Teachers College Press.

Dyson, A.H. (2002) *Brothers and Sisters Learn to Write: Popular Literacies in Childhood and School Cultures*. New York: Teachers College Press.

Gilbert, P. (1991) *Fashioning the Feminine: Girls, Popular Culture and Schooling*. London: Allen and Unwin.

Hilton, M. (1996) *Potent Fictions: Children's Literacy and the Challenge of Popular Culture*. London: Routledge.

Kline, S. (1993) *Out of the Garden: Toys and Children's Culture in the Age of TV Marketing*. London: Verso.

Kress, G. and Van Leeuwen, T. (1996) *Reading Images: The Grammar of Visual Design*. London: Routledge.

Kress, G. and Van Leeuwen, T. (2001) *Multimodal Discourse: The Modern Mode of Contemporary Communication*. London: Routledge.

Ladson-Billings, G. (1995) Towards a theory of culturally relevant pedagogy. *American Educational Research Journal*, **32** (3), 465–91.

Lankshear, C. (1997) *Changing Literacies*. Buckingham: Open University Press.

Lave, J. and Wenger, E. (1991) *Situated Learning*. Cambridge: Cambridge University Press.

Lingard, B. (2005) Socially Just Pedagogies in Changing Times. Paper presented to International Sociology of Education Conference, London, 3–5 January.

Luke, A. and Luke, C. (2001) Adolescence Lost/Childhood Regained: on Early Intervention and the Emergence of the Techno-subject. *Journal of Early Childhood Education*, 1 (1), 91–120.

Marsh, J. (1999) Batman and Batwoman go to School: Popular Culture in the literacy Curriculum. *International Journal of Early Years Education*, **7** (2), 117–31.

Marsh, J. (ed.) (2005) *Popular Culture, New Media and Digital Literacy in Early Childhood*. London: RoutledgeFalmer.

Marsh, J. and Millard, E. (2000) *Literacy and Popular Culture: Using Children's Culture in the Classroom*. London: P.C.P.

Merchant, G. (2001) Teenagers in cyberspace: an investigation of language use and language change in Internet chatrooms. *Journal of Research in Reading*, **24** (3), 293–307.

Millard, E. (2003) Transformative Pedagogy: Towards a Literacy of Fusion. *Reading, Literacy and Language*, **37** (1), 3–9.

Moll, L.C., Amanti, C., Neff, D. and Gonzalez, N. (1992) Funds of Knowledge for Teaching: Using a Qualitative Approach to Connect Homes and Classrooms. *Theory Into Practice*, **31** (2), 132–41.

Nagle, J.P. (1999) Histories of success and failure: working class students' literacy experiences. *Journal of Adolescent and Adult Literacy*, **43** (2), 172–85.

Neuman, S. (1995) *Literacy in the Television Age: The Myth of the TV Effect*, (2nd edn). Norwood, NJ: Ablex.

Nixon, H. and Coomber, B. (2005) Behind the scenes: Making movies in early years classrooms. In J. Marsh (ed.) *Popular Culture, Media and Digital Literacy in Early Childhood*. London: Routledge.

Pahl, K. (2005) Narrative spaces and multiple identities: children's textual explorations of console games in home settings. In J. Marsh (ed.) *Popular Culture, New Media and Digital Literacy in Early Childhood*. London: Routledge/Falmer.

Papert, S. (1994) *The Children's Machine: Rethinking School in the Age of the computer*. New York and London: Harvester Wheatsheaf.

Postman, N. (1983) *The Disappearance of Childhood*. London: W.H. Allen.

Robinson, M. (1997) *Children Reading Print and Television*. London: Falmer.

Sefton-Green J. (ed.) (1998) *Digital Diversions, Youth Culture in the Age of Multimedia*. London: UCL Press.

Storkey, A. (1999) *Media Addiction: Children and Education*. Movement for Christian Democracy, discussion paper 99/4 London: Mayflower C.

Tobin, J. (1998) An American Otaku: or this boy's virtual life. In J. Sefton-Green (ed.), *Digital Diversions, Youth Culture in the Age of Multimedia*. London: UCL Press.

Vasquez, V. (2005) Resistance, power-tricky and colourless energy: What engagement with everyday popular culture texts can teach us about literacy and learning. In J. Marsh (ed.) *Popular Culture, Media and Digital Literacy in Early Childhood*. London: Routledge.

Part I

Early childhoods

Chapter 1

Technokids, *Koala Trouble* and *Pokémon*: literacy, new technologies and popular culture in children's everyday lives

Michele Knobel

INTRODUCTION

Interest in the extent to which very young children's prior-to-school and out-of-school literacy practices can and do cross over into formal education contexts is well established. For example, the fields of family literacy and emergent literacy have long dominated early childhood research and publications, and proponents within each field have had much to say about supporting young children's literacy development in ways that maximize their potential to be successful readers and writers once they begin school. However, one limitation within these fields is the *orientation* generally taken towards young children's home and community lives and literacy practices. In both fields, existing, conventional school literacy conceptions and practices often are used to shape what counts as effective scaffolding of and interventions in young children's literacy development prior to formal schooling.

What has been less attended to, but is rapidly gaining ground as a recognized field of research focus, is the literacies young children aged birth to eight years actually *are practising* in their prior-to-formal-schooling and out-of-school lives and which in many ways can be more sophisticated and 'mature' than those prescribed for them as 'developmentally appropriate' in formal school or school-like settings. In particular, studies of young children's engagement with new digital technologies such as computers, the Internet, email, mobile phones, video games and other digital and screen media at home are providing fruitful insights into the degree to which conventional school literacies grounded in developmental models of early reading (and writing) may no longer provide sufficient guidelines for early childhood teachers in planning effective literacy learning experiences for their young students.

This chapter presents two cases of young boys who not only make use of the new technological and cultural resources available to them at home, but take up these resources in ways perhaps not intended by the original producers of these resources (e.g. by software companies and trading card publishers). Both cases make important points about how these two young boys engage with these resources, how deeply embedded within meaningful practices these resources are, and how both boys ably and confidently appropriate and enlarge the social meanings and possibilities of new technologies and popular culture within their everyday lives. The chapter concludes with a discussion of the implications that young children's take-up and 'making over' of new technologies have for formal literacy education and pedagogy.

TECHNOKIDS, LITERACY AND NEW TECHNOLOGIES

Recent studies are showing that young children – especially middle-class children – are beginning to use computers, the Internet, mobile phones and other electronic gadgets at younger and younger ages (Arthur, 2001; Hutchby and Moran-Ellis, 2001; Marsh, 2005). A 2003 study, for example, commissioned by the Henry J. Kaiser Family Foundation, surveyed, via random phone dialling methods, more than 1,000 parents across the USA about the new media uses of their children aged six months through six years. The findings suggest that very young children are using a range of new technologies, and very often using them independently. Survey data show that approximately 30 per cent of the children in the survey have played video games (with 3 per cent of the children aged less than two years having done so). One in ten of all children in the study had their own video game console in their bedroom (Henry J. Kaiser Family Foundation, 2003: 4, 7).

The study pays particular attention to young children's computer use and reports that almost half of the children in the study (48 per cent) have used a computer, almost one-quarter (23 per cent) of them have loaded their own CD-ROMs, and 12 per cent have asked for specific websites while surfing the Internet. One of the more intriguing findings of this study was that more than half (56 per cent) of those children aged four to six years have used a computer by themselves (i.e., without sitting on a parent's lap, etc.) and 17 per cent of children in this same age group have sent an email message with or without the help of a parent (ibid.: 4, 5). The Foundation also reports data that show 27 per cent of the children in the study aged six months to three years have used the computer without direct guided assistance (ibid.: 5).

These findings resonate with a growing body of research conducted in a range of countries (e.g. Downes, 2002; Holloway, and Valentine, 2003; Kankaanranta and Kangassalo, 2003; Livingstone and Bober, 2004; Marsh, 2005). Indeed, children born in the 1990s and 2000s (in economically 'developed' countries) have captured popular imagination by dint of being born into a world where they will never have personal memories of a life prior to digital devices and networks. These children are often referred to *en masse* 'in the media and education research literature alike' as the 'Nintendo Generation', the 'Digital Generation', 'Cyberkids', 'Millennials', 'NetGenners' and other similar terms. This fascination with a group whom I'll call 'technokids' plays out in interesting and sometimes contradictory ways in literacy education studies. At least three dominant mindsets can be identified in the research literature:

(a) new technologies enhance learning and it is therefore important to document and evaluate the effects of new technologies *on* technokids and their literacy development in order to better support children's success as readers and writers;
(b) new technologies are flashy and seductive, and technokids are in danger of being *too* attracted to new technologies; in fact, new technologies and new media are intrinsically harmful to young children's language, social and physical development, and new technology and media use should be highly curtailed and strictly surveilled;
(c) technokids involve themselves in a range of social and technological practices when using new technologies and it is important to document what these practices are in order to inform and further enhance effective classroom literacy pedagogy.

Each of these mindsets is discussed briefly below.

(a) Tracking the effects of new technologies on technokids and their literacy development

Ever since the 1960s, when computers were first used within compulsory education, there has been strong investment in their potential to enhance learning in general, and literacy learning in particular. Much of the research on young children, literacy learning and new technologies to date has tended to target specific hardware items and software programs and their effects *on* the child (cf. Labbo and Reinking, 2003; Kamil *et al.*, 2000; Kamil and Lane, 1998). Researchers operating from this mindset tend to focus for the most part on the positive (and sometimes negative) impact that technology can have on reading comprehension, growth in phonemic awareness, peer tutoring and collaborative text production, and authoring skills (Lankshear and Knobel, 2003a).

(b) Technokids and the dangers of electronic media

Other researchers working in the area of early childhood and new digital technologies argue that technokids need to be protected from the dangers of computers, the Internet and electronic toys in order to avert a range of social and developmental troubles caused by digital media (cf. Grossman and Degaetano, 1999; Healy, 1998; Levin, 1998; Montgomery, 2002). Arguments in this camp focus on the potential of new digital technologies to generate developmentally *inappropriate* experiences for young children. These inappropriate experiences include 'bad' language models which promote 'stunted' language development, the 'over-predetermination of play' where electronic toys are viewed as removing important creative and imaginative possibilities from children's play, the promotion of violence and antisocial behaviours, diminished time spent playing outside and correlated increases in child obesity levels, diminished time spent reading books, and so on. From this orientation, technokids need to be protected from using new technologies too much.

(c) Technokids and their literacy and digital technology practices

This mindset argues for the importance of examining the ways in which very young children are taking up and using new technologies and media within their self-selected everyday social and literacy practices (Lankshear and Knobel, 2003a; Marsh, 2002, 2004). Much of the driving force behind this mindset has been advocating on behalf of children for wider recognition and valuing of these new literacy and social practices in reaction to narrow, 'schoolish' orientations that privilege particular and normative language and literacy uses, even with respect to very young children. In many ways, this third mindset defines itself in contradistinction to the two mindsets discussed above. For example, from the position of this third mindset, much of the research into the effects new technologies can have on young children's literacy development is grounded in narrow and monolithic conceptions of literacy as something comprising discrete encoding and decoding skills that can be fine-tuned or strengthened via applications of new technologies. Or, with respect to the second mindset, pundits who warn of the likely dangers to be encountered when using new technologies at too young an age are seen, from the position of this third mindset, as promoting erroneous and patronizing constructions of children as passive victims of 'manipulative and dangerous media discourses' and are not paying due attention to children's abilities to construct socially meaningful literacy events and learning experiences using a range of toy-types and technologies (Marsh, 2002: 133).

In addition to offering direct challenges to long-standing claims concerning what counts as 'developmentally appropriate' literacy learning resources, this third mindset has sparked new research which suggests that many young children are not so much 'using' new digital media and technologies as 'making them over' in ways not necessarily intended by their original developers. For example, young Japanese schoolgirls use their camera phones to take snaps of handwritten notes to send to classmates because it's quicker than text messaging, very young children act out and elaborate on the plots of CD-ROM storybooks (including 'clicking' on different toys to make them 'move'), etc. One fruitful way of looking at this 'making-over' phenomenon is provided by Lee Sproull and Sarah Keisler (1991). Sproull and Keisler make a useful distinction between first- and second-level effects in explaining how technologies are taken up and used by people. First-level effects are the planned or anticipated benefits to be had from using a technology as a *resource*. Thus, the anticipated first-level effects of using a mobile phone include being able to make and receive calls while on the move, store frequently used phone numbers on the phone's SIM card, access address and phone directory services, and so on.

Second-level effects are changes that occur within the *context* of social practices as a result of people actually *using* new technologies. For example, mobile phones have impacted directly on the social fabric of countries around the world (e.g. mobile phones mean it's impossible to be 'late' for social gatherings in the traditional sense because meeting times are now more about converging on a place at a fluidly negotiated time, rather than setting a fixed time and place beforehand). Mobile phones have also been instrumental in the development of written dialects (e.g. text messaging language), have generated the expectation that someone who has a mobile phone will always be available to talk or text message, have changed how we interact with the people around us while 'on the mobile', and have shaped fashion and design. Second-level effects are thoroughly social in nature because they depend directly on contexts of use (rather than tools or resources alone) and involve social *practices*, where practices are socially recognized ways of doing and knowing that enable us to achieve some goal or purpose. Second-level effects very often set up a dynamic feedback loop, too. Using a new-technology device or application as a resource stimulates changes and innovations within the contexts of its use, which acts back on subsequent uses of the device or application as a resource, which, in turn, act on and further change the resulting context of use, and so on. For example, the boom in affordable mobile phones for young people saw them customizing their phones in a variety of ways, including producing new ring tones using audio software on their computers. This popular practice has spawned a whole new industry dedicated to creating and selling ring tones for mobile phones that last year earned $US 3.5 billion (*New York Times*, 2004). This effect now means that one's 'cool quotient' is measured in good part by the uniqueness of the ring tone on one's mobile phone – which in turn urges on the customized ring tone industry to produce ever more imaginative and attention-grabbing ring tones.

Studying the second-level effects of young children's new technology uses and the contexts in which this use takes place is readily extended to include a focus on popular culture and literacy practices, as we shall see in the two vignettes presented later in this chapter. Construing digital technology and literacy resources as having first- and second-level effects fixes attention on *practices*, rather than on texts *per se*, and on meaning-making and socially meaningful activity within these practices.

TWO TECHNOKIDS, AND THEIR LITERACY, TECHNOLOGY AND POPULAR CULTURE PRACTICES

The cases of Brian and Alex offer early childhood educators useful insights into how two young children have enlarged upon the new technology, literacy and popular culture resources in their own lives. Popular culture artifacts and practices are invoked here almost by default because they comprise seamless dimensions of the contexts of use in which these two young boys engage with new technologies. The case of Alex is drawn from the mid-1990s, when access to the Internet and a range of software applications at home was only just beginning to gain momentum. The case of Brian was reported more recently. Despite the time gap between the two cases, and their different geographical locations in the world, there are resonances between both boys' literacy experiences, their uses of new technologies and their popular culture practices, that are worth examining closely as part of weighing up the implications of technological second-level effects and associated social practices for early childhood education.

(1) Alex and *Koala Trouble*

Alex was five years old and living in Brisbane, Australia, when he first collaborated with his father on building a website (Lankshear and Knobel, 1997). The heart of his website, *Alex's Scribbles – Koala Trouble*, comprises a series of 13 stories produced by Alex from 1996 to 1999 about Max, a koala, and the adventures Max has with his mother and friends (Balson and Balson, 2001).

The *Koala Trouble* texts are simple narratives requiring readers to solve problems encountered by the characters within the story by clicking on appropriate image-mapped hypertext links (e.g. clicking on a bough helps Max back up into a tree he has fallen out of, or clicking on a stick helps Joey, his friend, out of the lake). The website came about because Alex and his older sister were given an Internet connection for Christmas (at the time, few families in Australia had home Internet access), but Alex rarely logged on even though he was a very competent Internet surfer. His father, Scott Balson, noticed and asked why; Alex explained that he couldn't find anything on the Internet that was interesting for young kids. Scott, himself a webpage designer, suggested that Alex do something about that by creating his own website which he could share with other children his own age.

The stories about Max were Alex's idea, with input from Scott on each new storyline. Alex produced the images for each text by freehand first, using a storyboard layout to structure his narrative. Then each cell in the storyboard was carefully redrawn in black ink outline on a separate piece of paper. With his father's help, Alex scanned each page into digital format, and used a rather sophisticated graphics program (i.e. Autodesk's *Animator Pro*) to add colour and text (see Figure 1.1). Working together, Alex and Scott used HTML editing software to produce the web pages. Much of this technical work was initially done by Scott. Alex did more of it as time went on.

Koala Trouble received 60,000 national and international hits or visits in the first two months after its online launch in 1996. 'During 1997 *Koala Trouble* had reached an estimated audience of *1,000,000 kids of all ages* since it first went up on the Internet. By 1999 that number was closer to two million' (original emphasis; Balson and Balson, 1999: 1). Early in 2005 *Koala Trouble* had registered over five million hits in total, even though the website itself had not been updated substantially from the end of 1999. *Koala Trouble* has been given numerous prestigious awards and accolades, and Alex and Max have received email correspondence from children and adults all around the world (aged from three to 95 years). These letters are often imaginative and creative: adding episodes to Max's adventures (e.g. Max goes scuba diving); or relating how Max is currently there with the email writer, curled up on a bed or hiding in bookshelves and toy bins.

Figure 1.1 Koala Trouble – trouble in paradise. Source: www.scribbles.com.au/max/koala4.html

The majority of the emails are sent by young children and clearly signal these children's understanding of email as a medium of direct, personal communication. For example, Elana, aged three and a half years, sent this message (with the help of an adult):

Date: Sun, 26 Jan 97 11:15:21 -0800
To: alex@gwb.com.au
Subject: (no subject)
We found Max on Mama's and Ati's bookshelf. He said that he was very well. We told him to go home because his friends were missing him. He'll be there soon.
Love from Elana. Age three and a half.

Laura, aged four years, with the help of someone older, sent a message in French and English to Alex telling him they have bears instead of koalas in the Pyrenees.

Date: Mon, 06 Oct 1997 19:53:16 +0200
To: alex@gwb.com.au
Subject: (pas d'objet)
BONJOUR ALEX.
JE M'APPELLE LAURA. J'AI QUATRE ANS. J'HABITE DANS LES PYRENEES, DANS LE SUD DE LA FRANCE. CHEZ MOI IL N'Y A PAS DE KOALA, MAIS IL Y A DES OURS, MAIS PLUS BEAUCOUP. (Hello, Alex. My name is Laura and I'm a four year old little girl. I live in France, In the Pyrenees. In my mountains, there are no koalas, but there are bears, but very few which is a shame.)
See you later, Alex.

Emily is four years old and after reading one of the stories about Max and his friend Sarah the goanna, wanted to know what a goanna was:

Date: Sat, 13 Jun 1998 08:05:32 -0400
To: alex@gwb.com.au
Subject: What is a goanna?
Dear Alex,
Hi, my name is Emily. I am 4 years old. I have just finished reading one of your fun stories. One of the characters was called a goanna. I have never heard of such an animal. Can you describe it?
Sincerely yours,
Emily C.
(Source: All three email texts are taken from www.scribbles.com.au/ max/kids/fav.html; accessed 21 March 2004. Used with permission)

These emails and countless others like them testify to the quality of the narratives on Alex's website. Alex himself made use of the Internet and a range of software in ways most likely not anticipated by Internet service providers and software developers in those days of adult-dominated online spaces. Alex and his father appropriated a range of new technology practices which at the time they began the website were used mostly by businesses and university groups. By creating a 'kid space' on line, Alex ended up producing an extremely popular resource for other children (and for adults) to enjoy and use themselves. His website became a place for young children to post information about their own country, to ask real questions, to comment on the stories, to imagine themselves into the adventures of Max, the koala, and his friends, or to simply say 'hello' to Alex and to thank him for his stories within the context of using the computer and Internet in their own homes and in collaboration with adults there. Some of the second-level effects of his website included a 'world tour' taken by Max in 1998, where he 'visited' two schools in the USA. The students who hosted Max became actively involved in creating their own koala adventure stories to post on line and to use offline as reading and writing resources in their own classrooms.

(2) Brian

Research from the past decade suggests that, in contrast to a significant number of early childhood teachers in developed countries, many parents of young children from a range of socioeconomic classes are to quick to recognize the value to be had by bringing popular culture practices and new technologies together at home (Downes, 2002; Green *et al.*, 1998; Marsh, 2003). For example, James Paul Gee (2004), working in the USA, describes how five-year-old Brian's parents are key participants in Brian's literacy learning at home, and how this literacy learning organically includes a range of resources drawn from popular culture and computer game culture.

By the end of Gee's study, Brian had completed Grade 1 and was reading at a fifth-grade level even though he had not been able to read when he began Grade 1. Gee attributes much of Brian's reading prowess to *Pokémon* and a range of new technologies and text resources, arguing that the texts made available through *Pokémon* collector cards, the *Pokémon* video games Brian played, the books he read at home, and the Internet websites he read provided him with just the right kinds of challenging texts he needed to become a proficient reader.

Brian was passionate about *Pokémon* and used his Nintendo Gameboy – a handheld video game console and screen – to play *Pokémon* video games. According to Gee, these games were surprisingly complex and Brian also needed to be able to read a large amount of dialogue between characters, as well as character descriptions and their polysyllabic names, their attack strategies, and other characteristics (as an interesting aside, media analysts themselves point out that the marketing hype surrounding *Pokémon* has actually masked much of its underlying complexity (Scholder and Zimmerman, 2003). Gee recounts how, to begin with, Brian's mother would read aloud the dialogue and character descriptions appearing on screen and in the manual. She and Brian learned together how to play the video game by discussing and working through it step by step. Brian's passion for all things *Pokémon* extended beyond this game to include the *Pokémon* collector cards, *Pokémon* figurines, *Pokémon* books and *Pokémon*-related websites. Gee argues that these various texts, coupled with Brian's keen interest in the '*Pokémon* universe', both 'motivated him to want to read and taught him how to read' (Gee, 2004: 25).

Gee acknowledges that Brian had a good first-grade teacher who also helped Brian become a proficient reader. However, Gee also points out that the texts and practices with which Brian was engaging at home were noticeably more sophisticated than the texts and practices he had access to in his classroom. Gee provides two random examples of the kinds of texts Brian was reading when he read *Pokémon* character cards or *Pokémon*-related websites:

Description: Kadabra relies on a strong mind rather than a powerful body to win. It can send out waves of mental energy that cause headaches at close range.

Description: Experts believe that Alakazam's brain is as powerful as any supercomputer. Its incredible psychic abilities back up that belief.

(Source: www.pokemon-cards-and-pokemon-pictures.com/evolving.html, in Gee 2004: 26)

In order to make sense of the *Pokémon* universe, Brian needed to understand the concept of 'evolving' and what that meant in relation to *Pokémon* creatures. Building on Gee's example above, Kadabra are actually an evolution of Abra – who are psychic creatures able to teleport out of trouble. Alakazam are in turn an evolution of Kadabra. Thus the evolution chain runs from Abra, to Kadabra and on to Alakazam, with each character having increasingly complex powers. Similarly, Brian also needed to understand the role of classification in distinguishing between different types of *Pokémon* (e.g. *Pokémon* can be 'psychic', 'electric', 'rock', 'grass', etc.) and their attendant attributes (e.g. psychic *Pokémon* have strong mental powers, rock/ground *Pokémon* have little resistance to water *Pokémon*). These are all rather sophisticated understandings; nevertheless, Gee also points out that Brian did not regard his *Pokémon*-related literacy practices as learning, but as *playing*.

Gee discusses how the *Pokémon*-related texts that Brian was reading and discussing at home as part of his participation in the *Pokémon* universe were in many ways affording Brian an apprenticeship in reading and writing in specialist language forms that was not available to him at school. Many of the text forms employed within the *Pokémon* universe, and exemplified above, are similar to academic language proficiencies valued in schools. This includes abstraction, cause and effect reasoning, the use of evidence to support claims, and so on.

Gee underscores the importance of Brian working collaboratively with his parents and how being a member of a particular family impacted directly on his reading.

> Brian's reading connected to Pokémon was fully embedded in his interactions with both parents, interactions that were not defined as learning, but as playing and being socialized into his family. [Literacy learning] is caught up in all the social and emotional valences of the child's early socialization in life as a member of a family of a certain type.
>
> (Gee, 2004: 26)

It can be argued that Brian's literacy practices within the *Pokémon* universe – aided and abetted by his parents – were in a very real sense second-level effects to be had from a particular and interest-driven marriage of popular culture and new technologies. Learning to read not only competently, but far in advance of his chronological age, by means of engaging with *Pokémon* video games, Internet sites and character profile cards, was most likely not a feature deliberately built into these popular culture texts and electronic artefacts. It is clear from Gee's account that Brian found the world of *Pokémon* to be compelling and pleasurable and that learning to read was really a by-product of his interest in and dedication to *Pokémon*.

IMPLICATIONS FOR EARLY CHILDHOOD EDUCATION

Developmental models of early reading posit that all children move through three main stages as they become independent and proficient readers. In broad brushstrokes, these stages are generally recognized as: logographic reading, followed by alphabetic reading, and then orthographic reading. To put this another way, developmental theories of reading argue that children first attend to reading all sorts of 'textual clues' in making sense of text, including pictures, icons, colours, text format, font size and type, etc. Children next attend to sound–letter relationships when decoding words, and by the third stage they are able to pay attention to more complex groups of letter and sound combinations, and to syllables, affixes, derivations, word meanings and so on in decoding a text. Developmental models continue to have a significant impact on early childhood classrooms, and reading resources are often carefully 'levelled' (e.g. by counting word syllables and dividing them by the number of sentences in the text, etc., in order to identify a text's 'decodability' level) and matched to young students' 'reading ages' as calculated by norm-referenced tests. Two of the chief limitations of this conception of early reading are its part-to-whole focus on written language proficiency and the foundational assumption that language itself is a fixed system that is independent of social practices. Both assumptions are problematic for a number of reasons. For example, developmental models of early reading still do not sufficiently account for children who are able to read independently but who do not recognize every letter of the alphabet (Routman, 2003). And developmental models of early reading certainly do not account for young students who are able to read complex texts associated with passionate interests but who struggle with reading school texts (cf., Vazquez, 2005). The *Pokémon* universe, for example, constitutes a system of 150 base character names, sixteen types of *Pokémon*, two additional *Pokémon* that a given *Pokémon* can evolve into, with each *Pokémon* having roughly eight attack skills out of hundreds of possible skills (Gee, 2004: 8–9). Gee argues that this is a significantly more complex system than the forty-four phonemic sounds and twenty-six letters of the alphabet that young children are expected to master in their first year of schooling (or earlier), yet few children he has spoken to within the context of his ongoing research – regardless of their cultural heritage, their families' socioeconomic status, or their school-assessed 'reading age' – have had trouble becoming proficient participants within the *Pokémon* universe.

Even when formal education recognizes the importance of popular culture and new technologies in young children's lives, assumptions about what 'counts' as developmentally appropriate software, activities and content often constrain the quality of the experiences that can be provided by such resources. The kinds of social interactivity built into and growing out of Alex's online *Koala Trouble* stories and Brian's passionate engagement with *Pokémon* websites contrast with much of the online fare currently available for young children. The UK's National Grid for Learning (www.ngfl.co.uk), for example, includes specific website recommendations for young children but does little to provide them with access to truly interactive websites that promote meaningful engagement with new technologies, texts and their contexts of use. The National Grid for Learning, or 'Grid' for short, is a government initiative designed to help raise education standards by providing teachers, students, education institutions and various community groups with access to information and communications technologies. The bulk of the websites recommended for young children by the Grid's portal website, however, comprise simple 'click-and-advance' stories, alphabet and item-matching exercises, and print-and-complete worksheets with little to no problem solving or imagination required (see Lankshear and Knobel, 2003b). Some of these websites are spin-offs from popular television shows, which suggests there may be opportunities for young children to appropriate at least some of these texts into meaningful 'universes' of practice of their own, although the relatively low-level, skills-based nature of the actual activities themselves also suggests that any appropriation is likely to be short-lived and have minimal impact.

Alex's website, in contrast, is a truly interactive space, where children can send emails to Alex that are motivated by interest, if not delight, and participate vicariously in Max's adventures by imagining and writing about additional adventures he has. It is also a context in which reading Alex's stories is not interrupted by phonics drills, read-and-retell prompts, and instructions to print and colour pictures of Max. Brian, using the Internet almost ten years after Alex, does not make distinctions between websites for kids and websites for older *Pokémon* fans and weaves his new technology uses, figurines, playing cards and *Pokémon*-related interactions with his parents into a seamless whole. The secondary effects accruing from this context of use include his ability to read more and more complex and abstract texts, which in turn enables him to engage in more and more complex play within his *Pokémon* universe. And, according to Gee, this more complex engagement with games, texts, figurines etc. has led to Brian choosing to play more complex and cognitively challenging non-*Pokémon* computer games.

However, not all early childhood educators are kindly disposed towards new technologies and many appear to dismiss young children's new technology uses as serious contexts within which to practice 'being literate' – especially, for some reason, where children from low-income families are concerned. Leonie Arthur (2001), for example, interviewed a large number of early childhood teachers for an Australian project that focused on early literacy practices and low-income families. She found that most of the teachers she interviewed tended to regard young children's engagement with digital technologies as a 'problem' with respect to enabling adequate literacy development. For example, Arthur reports one teacher commenting with ill-concealed disapproval that:

> Mum makes a big deal and 'Oh, he can write his name', but it turns out to be on the computer. When he comes in to do it here he has no idea. He might [hand]write an M.
>
> (Arthur, 2001: 299)

In addition, 20 per cent of the teachers interviewed by Arthur espoused deficit views of home literacy and popular culture practices, claiming, for instance, that 'not a lot happens at home' and 'when they come to us [at four years of age] they are 4 years behind' (Arthur, 2001: 299). It seems unlikely that teachers like these would make available spaces in which young children can engage with and become proficient in even the first-level effects of using new technology and popular culture resources, let alone develop these uses into a rich range of second-level effects in the manner of Alex and Brian. Interestingly enough, Alex's father, Scott, recounted in a 2002 interview how little notice Alex's teachers at school have taken of his website and of his digital technology know-how. This did not seem to bother Scott so much – he gave the distinct impression that he assumed the spaces of innovation Alex was able to access at home would more than compensate for his school experiences. It may well be a different story, however, for parents who are not able to afford or find similar kinds of access to innovative, digital technology practices for their children at home or in their community.

Without a doubt, cases like those of Brian and Alex argue for a general rethinking of what constitutes 'developmentally appropriate' resources and literacy experiences for young children. For example, Alex worked closely with his father to become fluent in using a broad range of sophisticated software applications such as *Animator Pro* and HTML editing software, along with adult-oriented hardware such as a scanner and its software interface, and an adult-sized mouse. The written texts on the *Pokémon* game cards Brian collected and played with were certainly not printed in large-type font or single-syllable, easily 'decodable' words. The video games he played were not designed to drill him in alphabet letters or numeracy facts, but were cumulatively complex, and cognitively demanding (i.e. as play progressed, the computer game itself, for example – and not just the content of the game – became *more* complex and challenging). Both young boys challenge the assumptions underlying the development and purchase of 'kidified' or infantalized versions of 'educational' software that are often lockstepped and unchangeable in nature. For example, in the *Crayola* series of image-generating software, children can only 'colour' default objects with a limited palette of colours or set textures that come with the software and cannot add their own. There is little scope here for developing a sequence of stories like those Alex created about Max the koala.

Anecdotal evidence and a growing body of research evidence indicate that early childhood educators need to work hard at keeping up with young children and their technology and literacy practices. For example, a recent study conducted in the UK found that 400,000 children aged between five and nine years have their own mobile phone (Wireless World Forum, 2003). The growing trend towards mobile communication devices for young children will no doubt usher in a second wave of concerns for early childhood educators (e.g. writing and spelling development issues, issues concerning the content of spoken language interactions, mobile bullying). At the same time, the second-level effects likely to accrue from young children's mobile phone use and their long-term engagement with social and Internet networks that are always 'on' and always available promise to be significant. If children's and young people's current mobile communication device and Internet uses are anything to go by, then the technokid generation is likely to be completely at home with a range of cycles of first- and second-level effects that include navigating attention economies on line (and off); establishing and using trust-based and 'civic' reputation networks; participating within distributed affinity or interest spaces on line and off line; being mobile and always available; and engaging in other new and emerging social practices that involve digital technologies and new communication media (cf. Ito, 2003; Knobel and Lankshear, 2004; Lankshear and Knobel, 2003b; netgrrrl ☆ (12) and chicoboy26 ☆ (32), 2002; Plant, 2001; Rheingold, 2002).

CONCLUSION

The cases of Alex and Brian remind early childhood educators to engage seriously with the meanings and effects produced within social practices that involve young children in using new technologies before imposing school-centric literacy learning and technology uses on children, or dismissing innovations in literacy practices and popular culture artifacts and practices as having 'negative' effects on learning. Alex and Brian also remind educators that young children are active participants in and direct contributors to popular culture and their own literacy learning and use by way of new technologies and a range of social and family practices. Of course, not all popular culture and new technology uses necessarily engage young children in complex literacy events and practices – but many of them do, and carefully examining what young children are actually *doing* with the new technologies, popular cultures and literacies in their everyday lives will enable their teachers more effectively to understand what these children are capable of and how to best support their literacy learning and use.

Alex and Brian are not isolated cases (cf. Marsh, 2005), but both show what can happen when young children are supported in their contextualized uses of new technologies that involve them in experimenting with and 'making over' new technologies in meaningful and confident ways. Becoming fluent readers and writers is often a happy by-product of such approaches, which in many ways keeps literacy in its proper scale and proportion in relation to what it means to know and do something well.

REFERENCES

Arthur, L. (2001). Popular culture and early literacy learning. *Contemporary Issues in Early Childhood*. 2(3): 295–308.

Balson, A. and Balson, S. (1999). *About Koala Trouble. Alex's Scribbles*. www.scribbles.com.au/max/about.html (accessed 13 August 2001).

Balson, A. and Balson, S. (2001). *Alex's Scribbles – Koala Trouble*. www. scribbles.com.au/max (accessed 13 August 2001).

Downes, T. (2002). Children's and families' use of computers in Australian homes. *Contemporary Issues in Early Childhood*. 3(2): 182–196.

Gee, J. (2004). *Situated Language And Learning: A Critique of Traditional Schooling*. New York: Routledge.

Green, B., Reid, J. and Bigum, C. (1998). Teaching the Nintendo Generation? Children, computer culture and popular technologies. In S. Howard (ed.), *Wired Up: Young People and the Electronic Media*.

Grossman, D. and Degaetano, G. (1999). *Stop Teaching Our Kids to Kill: A Call to Action Against TV, Movie and Video Game Violence*. New York: Crown.

Healy, J. (1998). *Failure to Connect: How Computers Affect Our Children's Minds, For Better or Worse*. New York: Simon & Schuster.

Henry J. Kaiser Family Foundation (2003). *Zero to Six: Electronic Media In the Lives of Infants, Toddlers and Preschoolers*. www.kff. org/entmedia/loader.cfm?url=/commonspot/security/getfile.cfm&PageID=22754 (accessed 17 March 2004).

Holloway, S. and Valentine, G. (2003). *Cyberkids: Children in the Information Age*. London: RoutledgeFalmer.

Hutchby, I. and Moran-Ellis, J. (eds) (2001). *Children, Technology and Culture: The Impacts of Technologies in Children's Everyday Lives*. London: Routledge.

Ito, M. (2003). A new set of social rules for a newly wireless society. *Japan Media Review*. March 13. 1–4. www.ojr.org/japan/wireless/1043770650.php (accessed 14 March 2003).

Kamil, M., Intrator, S. and Kim, H. (2000). The effects of other technologies on literacy and literacy learning. In M. Kamil, P. Mosenthal, D. Reason and R. Barr (eds), *Handbook of Reading Research: Volume 3*. Mahwah, NJ: Lawrence Erlbaum. 771–88.

Kamil, M. and Lane, D. (1998). Researching the relation between technology and literacy: An agenda for the 21st century. In D. Reinking, M. McKenna, L. Labbo and R. Kieffer (eds), *Handbook of Literacy and Technology: Transformation In a Post-Typographic World*. Mahwah, NJ: Erlbaum. 323–42.

Kankaanranta, M. and Kangassalo, M. (2003). Information and communication technologies in Finnish early childhood settings. *Childhood Education*. 79(5): 287–292.

Knobel, M. and Lankshear, C. (2004). Planning pedagogy for i-mode: From flogging to blogging via wi-fi. *English in Australia*. 139: 78–102.

Labbo, L. and Reinking, D. (2003). Computers and early literacy instruction. In N. Hall, J. Larson and J. Marsh (eds), *Handbook of Early Childhood Literacy.* London: Sage. 338–54.

Lankshear, C. and Knobel, M. (1997). Different worlds: Technology mediated classroom learning and students' social practices with new technologies in home and community settings. In C. Lankshear, *Changing Literacies.* Buckingham: Open University Press. 164–87.

Lankshear, C. and Knobel, M. (2003a). New technologies in early childhood literacy research: A review of research. *Journal of Early Childhood Literacy.* 3(1): 59–82.

Lankshear, C. and Knobel, M. (2003b). *New Literacies: Changing Knowledge and the Classroom.* Buckingham: Open University Press.

Levin, D. (1998). *Remote Control Childhood? Combating the Hazards of Media Culture.* Washington, DC: National Association for the Education of Young Children.

Livingstone, S. and Bober, M. (2004). *UK Children Go Online: Surveying the Experiences of Young People and their Parents.* London: Economic and Social Research Council.

Marsh, J. (2002). Electronic toys: Why should we be concerned? A response to Levin and Rosenquest (2001). *Contemporary Issues in Early Childhood.* 3(1): 132–8.

Marsh, J. (2003). Early childhood literacy and popular culture. In N. Hall, J. Larson and J. Marsh (eds), *Handbook of Early Childhood Literacy.* London: Sage. 112–42.

Marsh, J. (2004). The techno-literacy practices of young children. *Journal of Early Childhood Research.* 2(1): 51–66.

Marsh, J. (ed.) (2005). *Popular Culture, New Media and Digital Literacy in Early Childhood.* London: RoutledgeFalmer.

Montgomery, K. (2002). Digital kids: The new online children's consumer culture. In D. Singer and J. Singer (eds), *Handbook of Children and the Media.* New York: Sage. 635–50.

netgrrrl ☆ (12) and chicoboy26 ☆ (32) (2002). What am I bid?: Reading, writing and ratings and eBay.com. In I. Snyder (ed.), *Silicon Literacies.* London: RoutledgeFalmer. 15–30.

New York Times (2004). Tingalingalingaling! *The New York Times.* January 18. www.nytimes.com/2004/01/18/opinion/18SUN2.html (accessed 18 January 2004).

Plant, S. (2001). *On the Mobile: The Effects of Mobile Telephones on Social and Individual Life.* Report prepared for Motorola. www.motorola.com/mot/doc/0/267_MotDoc.pdf (accessed 27 June 2003).

Rheingold, H. (2002). *Smart Mobs: The Next Social Revolution.* Cambridge, MA: Perseus.

Routman, R. (2003). *Reading Essentials.* Portsmouth, NH: Heinemann.

Scholder, A. and Zimmerman, E. (eds) (2003). *RE:PLAY: Game Design + Game Culture.* New York: Peter Lang.

Sproull, L. and Kiesler, S. (1991). *Connections: New Ways of Working in the Networked Organization*. Cambridge, MA: MIT Press.

Vazquez, V. (2005). Resistance, power-tricky, and colorless energy: What engagement with everyday popular culture texts can teach us about learning, and literacy. In J. Marsh (ed.), *Popular Culture, New Media and Digital Literacy in Early Childhood*. London: RoutledgeFalmer.

Wireless World Forum (2003). *mobileYouth 2003*. London: Wireless World Forum.

Children's popular culture in the home: tracing cultural practices in texts

Kate Pahl

INTRODUCTION

The setting is a family literacy class in a large two-form-entry primary school in London. This class brought together parents and children to work on activities and games to support literacy. I was co-teaching this class, which encouraged parents and children to compose together at home and in the class. I began to collect texts by the children as part of a long-term study of children's literacy practices. One mother, Elif, was shy and quiet, and her son, Fatih, a five-year-old Turkish child, liked to draw but had been taken out of the classroom as he had been disruptive to other children. However, Fatih used the resources in the family literacy class and started to enjoy making meaning within the class. Often, we would encourage the children to draw with their parents. One day, Fatih came into the classroom which two small pennant-shaped flags, drawn in red, and coloured both sides in red, with an image of a star, using rolled-up card and paper. He showed these to me. I asked him what they were. His mother said that they were football flags. Later, I realized that the flags reflected Fatih's interest in his football team, Galiteceri. The flags were made of card and coloured red and white. When I studied them, I realized that they showed a resemblance to the Turkish national flag, as the star and the moon could be seen on the flags. They reflected both the practice of watching football and Fatih's interest in Turkey as his cultural identity.

By attending to both the form of the sign, its materiality, and the making of it from card, to realize the sign 'Turkish flag' and its meaning as a cultural marker of identity, I was able to trace the practices behind Fatih's text. Fatih had made this flag at home, but at school he was not seen as achieving. I was interested in what Fatih brought to this text and how his interest had dominated the making of this sign. Kress's notion of *interest* is paramount when considering what motivates children to make such powerful texts (Kress, 1997). By interest, Kress means what the child brings to the text, the motivation to make the text. In this vignette, Fatih's interest had structured the making of the text, and infused the sign with his own specific focus on football.

TEXTS AS TRACES OF PRACTICE

When children make texts within school settings, whether drawing, writing or other visual or linguistic texts, they draw on their cultural resources to do so. Teachers work with these resources, and create positive spaces where children can take from cultural material – 'stuff' – from many different contexts, to make meaning. Children's popular culture, as evidenced by the studies in this volume, is a rich vein for teachers to tap when they work with children on literacy. While many teachers are keen to support children's text-making using material from home, little is known of children's home-produced texts. What can studies of children's textual practices in the home tell us in order to support children's meaning-making in school?

In this chapter, I draw on research looking at children's text-making in three London homes, focusing particularly on children's multimodal texts produced in response to popular culture. I ask what these texts tell us in relation to children's writing practices in school. What kinds of texts do children produce at home? How are they different from texts produced at school? I consider children's text-making to be multimodal, that is, I argue that children make texts from all kinds of 'stuff', drawing on their visual and linguistic resources to do so (Kress, 1997). For example, a child might tell a story through drawing, an oral discussion, or through writing. At home, children have been observed creating multimodal texts in natural-istic settings as part of a general pattern of activity within the home (Kenner, 2000; Kress, 1997).

How are home-produced texts to be described and in what theoretical context? One way in is to consider time and space in the home domain, as contrasted with space and time in the school domain (Table 2.1). The term *domain* comes from Barton and Hamilton's insight that there are many domains of literacy: school, home or workplace (Barton and Hamilton, 1998). The domain of home is one such specific space. Home practices are informed by cultural meanings and inherited patterns (Douglas, 1991; Bourdieu, 1990). Table 2.1 makes sense of these different domains in relation to time and space.

I consider how timescales in homes differ from timescales in schools. For example, a child may return to a theme, such as *Pokémon*, over and over again, or return to a theme, such as Thomas the Tank Engine, but in a different context. A toy train can connect up with the Thomas the Tank Engine craze, as well as link to a long-term family story of a model train built by a grandfather. In this example, the long-term memory lies within the text along with the train. School timescales are heavily dependent on curricula, school terms and classroom structures. Home timescales depend on such things as shared memories, practices, ways of doing things, mealtimes and living arrangements, as well as cultural and religious activities. Different timescales are also attached to different objects within the home. In order to analyze this, I draw on Lemke's analysis of the different timescales that accompany semiotic activity, and how particular artefacts are associated with longer, or shorter timescales (Lemke, 2000). Lemke described how a Samurai sword, with a century of accumulated meaning, meant something different from an ordinary sword, in the context of Japanese cultural practice (ibid.).

Table 2.1 Time and space in home and school domains

	Home domain	School domain
Timescales of child's meaning-making	Often structured in relation to practices such as bedtime, playing PlayStation, watching television, narratives from parents and grandparents	Structured around curricula, lesson plans, terms, school day
Spatial affordances of child's meaning-making	Spatial possibilities include small toys, bedrooms, play on carpets, moving around home	Structured around possibilities of classroom outside space and artefacts such as pencils and paper

I also look at space. Research on children's bedrooms (Mitchell and Reid-Walsh, 2002) has considered children's views of popular culture through using children's photographs. Drawing on children's images of their toys, they argue that children create visual spaces using photographs in which to view and explore their relationship to popular culture (ibid.). Part of their discussion includes an analysis of children's bedrooms and what these offer children as cultural text-making spaces. In each of the homes I studied, bedrooms were salient for the making of meaning. Particular spaces have textual possibilities. In all three of the bedrooms I visited, a carpet depicting a road and streets had been bought for the child, who then used this for small-world play.

Spatial affordances can also lie within objects. Van Leeuwen and Caldas-Coulthard have similarly considered the spatial affordances of particular toys and considered what these offer a child (Van Leeuwen and Caldas-Coulthard, 2004). Spatiality in homes can be linked to particular sites, such as bedrooms, living rooms, coffee tables, sofas and so on. It can also be linked to children's own awareness of sites of play. These could be linked to key objects, such as the PlayStation console, or the television.

In this chapter, I look at how children's multimodal texts reflect the practices within the home. Walking into any person's home, one is immediately struck by the objects within it. Photographs on mantelpieces, toys, arrangements within rooms and the structure of the home can be observed, reflecting the interests of the participants. I called the list of the things in the home an *inventory*. By making an inventory of these things, I could discern, sedimented within children's texts, traces of that inventory. The concept of an inventory leads to a discussion of culture. Culture can be seen as an active process of meaning making, a verb (Street, 1993). Cultural stuff, found within homes, can be listed and sorted as an inventory. Traces of this inventory can be found within children's texts. I discovered in my study that objects, stories and practices from popular culture were inscribed within text-making, and, as Dyson has described in her recent study, it took a while to untangle these different discursive threads and see what specific influences lay within children's multimodal texts produced at home (Dyson, 2003). Many of the objects within the home reflected children's interests. Pyjamas were inscribed with crazes, such as *Pokémon*, as were curtains, duvets and home decoration. Furnishings and bedrooms took on a textual function, as the arrangement of space reflected the ruling passions of the household (Barton and Hamilton, 1998).

How can research illuminate our understandings of children's text-making? In this study, I was able to collect texts from three London homes for a period of two years. By making repeated visits, every two weeks, and becoming acquainted with the family's routines and practices, using an ethnographic methodology, I began to see how the children's practices were inscribed into text-making. These insights proved helpful when looking at children's texts made at school. In some cases, the content of my field notes illuminated the content of children's texts. In other cases, the observations gave meaning to texts that otherwise I would not have understood.

What I observed was the way in which a repeated practice, such as playing *Super Mario*, became inscribed into a series of drawings, which then took on textual meanings of their own. For example, an early drawing by Fatih, a five-year-old Turkish boy, included a representation of Super Mario alongside a representation of a bird, another interest of his. Particular practices, such as playing *Crash Bandicoot*, a console game, could generate a number of different iconic textual representations. Children used the way games were structured to describe particular narratives.

Cultural practices from one particular game or genre of game could be found mixed within children's texts with another. *Super Mario* exit signs appeared alongside *Crash Bandicoot* boxes. Games-playing generated other kinds of representational strategies, such as a visual description of levels. Texts using a level-based structure were different kinds of texts from the sequential, narrative texts children tended to be encouraged to produce in the school domain.

When I considered how practices in homes could be found in children's texts, I then developed a theory that practices within homes sedimented within children's texts. This led me to look closely at how repeated practices in the home, such as getting out particular toys at particular times, or playing a particular console game, could be seen inscribed in children's texts.

THE STUDY

Three homes were chosen for the study. In each home there lived a five–six-year-old boy. These were:

> Fatih, five, and his mother Elif
> Sam, six, and his mother Parmjit
> Edward, five, and his mother, Mary.

One of the criteria for selecting the small sample was evidence of disjuncture between home and school. Two of the three in the sample had experienced some exclusion from school. The occupations of the parents included teacher, teaching assistant and student at the local English language college. All the parents were single parents, although in some cases this status changed during the study and parents found new partners. In two cases, the housing was local authority, in one case, the family's housing was ex-local authority.

All the parents cooperated positively with the research. I became a friend-like figure, who was interested in the children, and listened to the narratives of the mothers. I visited over two to three years, took field notes and photographs, visited classrooms and other places where the children were making texts, and was able in each case to build up a detailed picture of the children's lives at home. The ethnic backgrounds of the families varied. One family, Fatih and Elif, was Turkish. One, Sam and Parmjit, was British born/Indian, and Mary was born in India but came to England when she was ten, defining herself as English.

The study was ethnographic, and longitudinal. The use of ethnography enables meanings to be slowly understood, in the context of a long-term relationship with the field. By drawing on the perspectives of the families I researched, I could consider how their perspectives could be brought to bear on the data I collected. They became part of the research, as I did. I worked on both 'insider' and outsider' perspectives, understanding that I myself changed the data by being in the field, and interpreting the meanings within that context (Hall, 1999). By recognizing that I both shaped interpretations of meaning and was working with my respondents' interpretations, I tried to put the two together and see what I could learn from the families. In doing so, I was able to situate the texts children gave me within a complex web of family practices. My field notes situated the children's texts and gave them a context.

THE DATASET

Here I give details of the texts I collected at home.

Fatih: 207 drawings collected, produced at home
Edward: 86 drawings collected, produced at home
Sam: 25 texts collected, produced at home.

Sam also made models, which I did not take away, so many of his texts remained at home. Instead, he photographed them with a camera. In addition, I made regular field visits, gave the children a disposable camera to use at home, and visited the children in classrooms and after school clubs. I conducted several ethnographic interviews with the mothers of the children, and used a tape recorder in order to find out about the text-making of the children in more detail.

Textual evidence from homes looks very different from school-based texts. Text-making occurs in naturalistic settings, in contexts which may or not be explainable to the researcher. I relied on field notes to situate text-making, and recognized that texts could have links to a number of different practices. Social practices in homes gathered meaning over time, and were structured by ways of being which families build up in connection with wider cultural meanings and narratives. For example, the month-long time of Ramadan indicated the presence of particular cultural practices in one home. Halloween dictated another set of practices in another home. The World Cup had a similar powerful effect on a third home. When I visited, the time of the year, the cultural context and the space within which the meaning making occurred all affected what happened to children's text-making.

Much of the text-making I observed was incidental to my visits. Some, however, was generated in response to my visits, as children were keen to show me what they had drawn. Text-making, however, did seem to occur in response to playing console games, and engaging in play. In that sense, children's drawings reflected the interests of children. The children's texts included, for the purposes of the research, photographs by children, particular arrangements of toys, drawing, model-making and oral and written language. I understood children's texts to be multimodal, that is, they drew on a number of different modes to make meaning. These could include oral, gestural and verbal modes. I recognized that children's text-making could be ephemeral, and much of what was produced was destined to be thrown out. Tissue paper was a popular medium, as was greaseproof paper, lined paper, bits of card, boxes and modelling material.

The material I discuss here includes photographs taken by children in response to a disposable camera I introduced toward the end of the first year of fieldwork. I also discuss data from the beginning and the end of the fieldwork period. Because the families came from different cultural backgrounds, these will necessarily come into the analysis. Artefacts placed in glass cabinets, pictures on walls, television programmes watched, rituals and practices in the home – all seeped into text-making.

WAYS OF THINKING ABOUT CHILDREN'S TEXTS AND POPULAR CULTURE

When considering children's text-making at home, a number of key points come to the fore. These can be summarized as follows:

1   Children's text-making at home is often hybrid. That is, a character from a console game may be drawn along with a favourite animal or a logo from another cultural context.
2   Children's texts cross sites, and while they may be made at home they can surface at school.
3   Children recontextualize material from one site to another, and in the process of recontextualization, produce new cultural material.
4   Children's texts at home are multimodal, that is, children orchestrate different semiotic resources in an ensemble to make meaning (Kress, 1997).
5   Children's texts made at home have longer and different timescales attached to them than texts at school.
6   Children draw on particular spatial affordances, such as size and rigidity, when arranging toys and creating texts at home.

CASE STUDY I: THE SPACE OF PLAYSTATION IN FATIH'S TEXTS

In the first case study, I consider how playing a console game at home alters the way in which children's text-making is structured. One question rarely asked of children's engagement with popular culture is, how do these phenomena alter the way in which children engage with texts? For example, the way many console games are structured requires that children move through a series of levels, each higher than the last. These levels can be seen sequentially as a set of stages. The following examples come first from Fatih's early drawings, when he was five and started to play *Super Mario* games. The drawings were produced in the context of field visits in his home in the evening.

Fatih's home was a small local authority flat, on a busy road in North London. His living room had a television, which could be plugged into a games console. Fatih liked to play console games with his brother, Hanif, and his cousin. He was so keen to play his mother regulated his playing on occasion (interview, April 2001). When I visited, I noticed that Fatih was excited by playing *Super Mario* on the games console. This console game consists of a character, Super Mario, who has to go through various stages and levels in order to win. Fatih played it sitting on his living-room floor, with a hand-held console attached to a television. He often played in a group, with his cousin, and talked as he played. Fatih described to me how he didn't know how to play at first, and then he came to the castle, and then moved through the stages.

> *Fatih*:   When I was five years old I didn't know how to do these. I come to the castle and I come to the boss and he was on a boat and I went into . . .
>
> (Field notes, 4 December 2000)

Fatih conceived of the journal of Super Mario as a journey up a staircase. He described it in words, but also in the drawing, reproduced as Figure 2.1, which he had produced before my visit.

Figure 2.1 represents a castle, with steps leading up to it; the castle is the eventual goal. The text describes the journey Super Mario makes to get to the top. This text represents the game as a series of steps, and the stages are not drawn separately. Fatih's interest in playing *Super Mario* continued throughout the visits. I also visited Fatih in his classroom, and learned that in his classroom he was doing map-making. A drawing he produced two weeks later with his older brother, Hanif, was of his flat (Figure 2.2).

This was a crumpled piece of paper on which Fatih has drawn the rooms in the flat. Fatih proceeded to describe the map to me using his index finger, while I taped his description. He described the text as being 'my house' and described the process of doing the map game. During his description, Hanif commented on the programme he was watching. This turned out to be *Space Jam* (see Dyson, 2003 for a longer description of the movie *Space Jam*).

Hanif's comments are included; however, he wasn't in the conversation, but was watching the television. Fatih stood beside the map, his index finger pointing out the journey he made as he spoke. We both looked at the map drawing while he described this journey.

> *Fatih*:   This is the . . . this is the . . . door . . . that[1]
> *Hanif*:   Oh we have the CD still.
> *Fatih*:   The the outside door . . . to come inside
> *Kate*:   Yeah . . .
> *Hanif*:   Oh I can't do it.
> *Fatih*:   And this is my room . . . and these Xs are . . . (1.5) if you fi– If you have to look look up . . . look through these Xs . . . These

Figure 2.1 Castle in the *Super Mario* game, drawn by Fatih.

two are my bed and that's the <u>road</u> and we have to check under the . . . carpet road . . . and . . . (1.5) if we see something <u>there</u> we will be the <u>champion</u> and we go out . . . if there's nothing there . . . we go there and that's the <u>toilet</u> . . . and that's // // the back of the toilet . . .

Hanif: // Oh, there is *Space Jam* //

Fatih: and there's a X there . . . there's nothing in there and you go <u>out</u> and that's the <u>sink</u> and you go like <u>that</u>, and you go in <u>here</u> my mum's room, and you check in the fringe and there . . . uh if there's nothink you lift up the . . . uh fr . . . you lift up the pillows and there's nothing in there you go <u>out</u> and you look at the <u>kitchen</u> (coughs) you look through the <u>carpet</u> . . . and there's

Figure 2.2 Fatih's map of his flat.

nothing in there you look here ... nothing in there and look
here ... something in there and ... you get ... and you will be
the champion.

(Taped discussion 18 December 2000)

The map text was a way of navigating the process of becoming the
champion. Elif, Fatih's mother, however, pointed out that the little dumb-
bells at the top of the map, by the words 'finish' and exit', were icons
from the *Super Mario* game. Later research from games-playing informants
suggested the boxes in the drawing took their form from the game *Crash
Bandicoot*, which Fatih was recorded in field notes as playing with his
cousins.

The map could be said to be linked to conventional notions of map-
making, which Fatih was learning at school; also his drawings of his house

at school, which I collected, did correspond to the drawing in this text. However, the key feature of the map is that it is a sequential journey, to find something. Each room has to be searched before the player wins. In this, the map, like a console game, yields its treasure only when the player has gone into every room. This is a feature common in games where the player has to search for things before moving on to the next level.

This form of narrative is a specific feature of console games, yet is not drawn upon in school narratives. Fatih drew, a year later, a series of drawings depicting different stages in the now more complicated *Super Mario* game he was playing (see Figure 2.3).

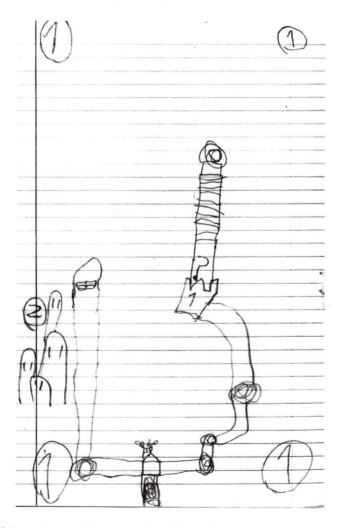

Figure 2.3 Later drawing of more complicated *Super Mario* game.

These were numbered, and showed a series of stages, with a corridor linked by circles. Here, the images are seen as sequential, and move in numeric order. In the second drawing the journey is continued (Figure 2.4)

The drawings seem to be a way of representing sequential games, with circles being the resting points. At intervals, Super Mario's head can be seen. Stars also punctuate the drawing. Fatih's final drawing (Figure 2.5) shows the battle at the end of the game, indicated by the black circle encircled with lines.

Figure 2.4 Continuation of game shown in Figure 2.3.

Figure 2.5 Final stage of *Super Mario* game.

In this drawing, the castle can also be seen, but the stages have been divided up, and the drawings are separated out. This was a way of developing an awareness of level. The concepts of levels of game, of different stages, numerically ordered, informs and structures Fatih's text-making. The practice of playing a particular game has sedimented within his texts, and he has tried to make sense of his 'reading' of playing the game (Kress, 1997). Kress describes reading as an act of sign-making, an interpretative and representational process (ibid.: 64). Fatih has developed an interpretation of the game and then represented it anew within a set of texts. In Fatih's texts spatiality is developed in relation to the particular possibilities within games-playing and then is represented in a particular way within texts.

CASE STUDY 2: SPATIAL AFFORDANCES OF OBJECTS

In the next example, a child drew on the spatial affordances of a group of objects to create small-world play on his bedroom floor and in his living room. The objects were small models of *Pokémon* creatures and other small toys, which the child, Sam, used to orchestrate a narrative. Sam was interested in the spatial possibilities that floor space in his bedroom offered him. I gave him a camera, and he used it to take shots of his bedroom floor, while conducting a running commentary. The commentary related to the semiotic possibilities of the objects Sam moved about on the carpet, and then converted into an oral discursive account of small-world play.

Here is Sam's running commentary of his small-world play on the carpet in his bedroom, which I noted down as he took photographs:

> Charizard and Charmeleon are getting an ice cream. Blastoise is in the pond he went over the track and into the aeroplane. Electrobuzz and Blastoise are talking. The one in the aeroplane is Blastoise. Blastoise and Electrobuzz they look good.
>
> (Sam takes a photograph)
>
> In the water are the water *Pokémons* – Poliwhirl. Ceedra's got out. He's tired of being in the water. He's lying down. I am going to draw a sunset over that photo (of Charmeleon and Charmender). Blastoise is getting angry with Poliwhirl. The train has stopped suddenly and this one's sunk. They've just bashed together the motorbike now bashed over there. Electrobuzz is watching there. He's over there. He fell into the pond.
>
> (Field notes, 9 May 2000)

In order to analyze this episode, I drew upon van Leeuwen and Caldas-Coultard's concept of the affordances of particular kinds of toys (van Leeuwen and Caldas-Coulthard, 2004). These toys were small, and are rigid, but can be moved around. They come from a number of different worlds, including Woody from the film *Toy Story* and several *Pokémon* creatures, as well as small cars, trains and farm animals. Here, Sam is drawing on a hybrid medley of toys to create a narrative in his bedroom. He is drawing on the *Pokémon* toys, but, in addition, he placed them within a 'setting' from a different timescale of play – that of small-world play with trains and cars. Figure 2.6 shows the 'action shot' Sam did while making his commentary. Note how it is positioned from a floor angle, and shoots the characters from below.

Figure 2.6 Small-world play on the carpet.

Sam's meaning-making used the house as a backdrop for his textual arrangements. Later photographs showed Sam's photograph of his *Pokémon* figures, made from modelling material, positioned for the camera, hidden inside the 'caves' of his front-room sofa (Figure 2.7).

Here, the spatial affordance of the sofa lends itself to the idea of 'cave'. Rather than interpret the sofa as 'space for sitting', the sofa has been re-interpreted by Sam as being a possible site for a *Pokémon* scene. The resulting image shows his figures set against a backdrop of cushions.

Sam's house became a site in which his *Pokémon* objects could be displayed and gathered together in different ways. Sam's mother finally allowed Sam to make a collection of small objects in a glass cabinet, where they were displayed as in a museum.

CASE STUDY 3: TIMESCALES OF OBJECTS

I've always liked gore. I've always been changing my subject. When I was a baby I liked wheels, then I liked Thomas the Tank Engine, then I liked Robots, I liked Space then I liked *Pokémon* through seven and a little bit of eight, then I'm into Warhammer now I've moved on from the rest of my – I was getting bigger all those eight life years.

(Sam, 20 November 2001)

Figure 2.7 Pokémon figures on the sofa.

Sam's account of his 'ruling passions' all 'those eight life years', caught on tape during a field visit, gives an image of a person whose identity in practice has shifted in relation to his cultural interests. These interests shifted alongside the growing Sam.

In the study, the children reacted to the cultural stuff around them in relation to their growing selves, and some items were 'left behind' in their attempt to grow through them. In an interview with Sam's mother, Parmjit, she describes this process:

> The one thing he doesn't go near of course is the Thomas stuff, but I think in a way maybe he overdid it and he now feels rather embarrassed about it. For example I don't know when you first came, but for example he still had the Thomas curtains, and that was partly because I couldn't afford and I couldn't be bothered, and I just thought they're nice blue we'll keep 'em, and I think in a way he'd outgrown it and then it was like mummy it's babyish so he gets quite . . . negative and then I've got quite shirty and say look, I don't care that you think it's babyish now but at the time you loved it, you know, and you might be in complete denial that you ever played with Thomas but the fact is for four or five years you really liked it and that's fine and we'll leave it there.
>
> (Taped interview, 11 April 2001)

The practice of responding to a child's interest by 'themed' home decoration is common in many households. All the households in the study responded in some way to this trend, for example, through duvet covers, pyjamas, bedroom furnishings such as a carpet depicting a 'road' and drawings of houses and trains for pretend play. However, there was inevitably a problem when the child's interest waned. A child may continue to wear his *Pokémon* pyjamas long after he has stopped trading cards. Part of this was the parents' inevitable desire to save money. All the households in the study existed on low incomes, and struggled to keep up with the demands of the children for items to reflect their ruling passions. This struggle between accommodating the child's interests and keeping within what is possible was common to all the homes in the study. The families in the study had this feature of accommodation to the child's 'interest', which had a negotiated quality. Elif, Mary and Parmjit all allowed their children to have items in their homes which reflected their children's cultural interests, but also restricted them when the household needed to 'tidy up' or to extend space.

Objects in the home carried family memories and stories. Sometimes these objects were placed together with objects that children were interested in. One example is Edward's train texts. Edward was interested in collecting small model trains. His collection was placed in a glass cabinet in the front room. It included a figurine of the 'Mallard', a famous English train, and a handmade figurine of a train with no identifying characteristic. In an early field visit, I collected an image of the Mallard train which Edward had drawn (Figure 2.8).

However, this train had a different timescale when linked to family history. In this field visit, I had sat down on the family settee, in their front room, and was given a picture of a train by Edward, who was then five. My notes record that he said of the picture,

> 'This is a Mallard train'. Mary explained – 'he likes trains, so we got him all of these'. 'These' were a collection of trains done as miniature figurines. I looked at 'Little Wonder' and Edward produced for me 'The Flying Scotsman'. Edward knew all their names. 'They come with a book – you can send off for it.' The book was called *Legendary trains*. 'Edward sits and reads it for hours', said Mary.

> (Later on in the field visit)

> Mary told me a bit about herself. Her family come from 'all over' – 'They built the railways in India – they came from Ireland and went over there to build the railways. People think my name 'C____' is my married name but it is my real name.'

> (Field notes, 23 March 2000)

Figure 2.8 Mallard drawing.

The Mallard train was linked together with a train which had belonged to Mary's father and made by her grandfather. In this bit of data, Edward is taking some photographs of the Indian train and the Mallard train (see Figure 2.9):

Kate:	This is the grandfather's train [i.e. Edward's grandfather's train].
Mary:	This is my dad's one, yeah, he worked on the railway in India and he used to make models.
Edward:	Most of the trains in there are, and actually what I got is models, before we used to collect them, now there's no more left because I got all of them so now there's only one left and that's the one I still got. It was the one it was the one it was the Bugton P 11 and its like this train, yeah, and its got like this where it goes and it keeps going down and like your going and like it's a bend and you going straight and you down and up.
Mary:	Where was this?
Edward:	In a book. You know the side then I couldn't see that side so I just took the front now do the other side.
Kate:	How old is that?

Figure 2.9 Indian train.

Mary:	He died when he was seventy odd, he died when he was seventy, thirty years ago.
Edward:	My mum's dad gave me this to one year ago and its um…
Mary:	Can you see the whole train?
Edward:	…thirty nine…I can't see the back
Mary:	My dad said he loves trains that much he'd appreciate it more than him keeping it so he gave it to him last year.

(Transcript, 7 June 2001)

Edward here linked the interest he had in trains and collecting with his grandfather's train, which was displayed in a glass cabinet in the front room. The original train, made by Mary's grandfather, operates as a momento of the family history of building the railways in India. Mary described a complex family history, involving a grandfather from Warwickshire and two relatives from Ireland on both sides, plus an ancestor in the West Indies. These narratives resonate with the colonial history of that period. However, the focus of the discussion was the train. This focus was carried over into her grandfather's model of a train. Edward was given this, as part of his enthusiasm for trains. The family then framed the interest in trains partly through Edward's passion for collecting, and partly in their focus on their family history.

Edward's passion for trains, including Thomas the Tank Engine, the Mallard and his grandfather's train, links to long-term family memories. Behind this interest in trains lies a complex family history, which, like the

Samurai sword, is imbued with long-term family meanings. Toys in the home may appear to be 'just toys' or they may, like Edward's Mallard train, mean more to the family. The inventory of traces is layered with meanings in relation to the toys scattered around the home.

Edward enjoyed lining up his toys and photographing them (Figure 2.10). In this example, Edward has lined up his 'Thomas the Tank' trains, in the same way that he lined up and photographed the Mallard and his grandfather's train. The link across the different kind of trains is specific to the cultural family history of migration that accompanied the depiction of the trains.

THE INVENTORY OF TRACES

In the homes, I followed the inventory of toys and tracked the way they were used, from being in a box, out of the way, to becoming a 'display', to becoming part of play. Toys occupied a contested space within the home. After the child had used them for play, they would then be reclassi-fied as 'mess' by the mothers. This process, from play to mess, was evident in the words and actions of the mothers when talking about their children's play.

Figure 2.10 Edward's trains lined up.

The home becomes the site for both display and play. The playing with toys is momentarily turned into sediment, and is disrupted for a new practice, the receiving of visitors. Because homes have to accomplish a multitude of tasks, including receiving visitors, amusing children, providing food, and displaying and upholding cultural processes, the way of doing things in the home, or the *habitus* (Bourdieu, 1990), is crossed with a variety of different strands and the traces of each process can be followed, sometimes literally, across the front-room carpet floor. The semiotic sediment that made up the family's *habitus*, its dispositions, was crossed with many voices. When I entered a home, I would note these voices, from the Arsenal, to pet-keeping to Thomas the Tank Engine, as the family's texts layered these meanings.

The inventory of toys supported the making of culture as, 'an active process of meaning making...'(Street, 1993: 25). In order to explore the cultural models behind the three children's meaning-making, I looked at their play, and the inventory of toys that supported the play. I came to realize that, behind the construction of texts, lay a complex set of cultural accretions and sediments, each layering and building up one over the other. The text, as a manifestation of the *habitus*, betrayed its own sedimentation. Repeated visits to each of the households elicited this sort of complex cultural data, and it became apparent that a text could have many different cultural processes lying behind it. This gave the children's texts an inter-textual quality. They also became a record of a number of lived 'ruling passions' (Barton and Hamilton, 1998).

While I observed families in their homes, cultural models such as a console game were recontextualized. Practices such as playing console games were carried over into different ways of making meaning, and then fell into semiotic sedimentation. One key aspect of this process was iteration. All the children returned again and again to cultural forms they were interested in, altering them subtly in each textual rereading, enabling sedimentation to be observed within the home. It was a process which involved the construction of meaning, and a repeating patterning of meaning.

As an example, Parmjit described how her son's relationship to toys was in itself iterative:

> ...and also because he's not really a toy toy child, we don't you know buy a whole load of things, so actually I've done very little throwing out, and it's interesting that its all there, and then he what he'll do is he'll go back to it, but then as I said he does it on a different level, which is really kind of nice for me because that's why I always feel bad about throwing his things away...
>
> (Interview, 11 April 2000)

Parmjit's description of how her son returns to his toys, but on a different level, could also apply to how the children created texts within the home, sometimes returning to them, or constructing the same text again, but with a new development within it. The struggle Parmjit expressed between Sam's need to 'move on' and his need to return to things is here resolved through the concept of returning to things 'on a different level'. Like the different levels in console games, children explored the same subject through text-making over and over again. In this way, text-making sedimented and then supported accrued meaning.

CONCLUSION

When thinking about how children used material from popular culture in their text-making, I have considered how the timescales associated with the object and text-making interacted. For example, the small-world play on the carpet could be located within a timescale of about two years, which was the timescale of the play. Also, the spatial affordance of the small object made the play possible.

In Table 2.2 I have put together the affordances of toys together with the timescale of objects in relation to children's popular culture and literacy. When objects had been placed on the grid, I have considered the relationship between the timescale within which the object had been placed and the kinetic affordance of the object. Van Leeuwen and Caldas-Coulthard have begun to develop a systemic network of kinetic design, which includes the categories rigid/non-rigid, flexible/articulated and deconstructable/

Table 2.2 Affordances and timescales of toys

Type of object (from inventory)	Timescale of using/ playing with toy (observed)	Kinetic design, or affordance of toy	Text-making observed	Practice observed
Pokémon figurine	2 years	Small rigid plastic object can be used in small-world play	Oral narrative describing the play	Small-world play on the carpet
Train figurine (Thomas the Tank Engine)	From aged 4–8	Small plastic object linked to others. Used as part of play in front room (photograph)	Photographic image of toys lined up	Visiting Thomas the Tank Engine centre. Talking about trains including Mallard, Indian train

non-deconstructable (Van Leeuwen and Caldas-Coulthard, 2004). I worked with these categories when considering how toys were used in the home.

The question of space and time can therefore be considered in relation to whether either is salient at one particular moment. One observation is that when space is salient, a different kind of meaning-making occurs than when time is salient. This consideration has been explored by Marsh (2004) in a recent paper, describing the different affordances given to children when working in a medium where space was salient (moving-image media) as opposed to a medium where time was salient (narratives) (Marsh, 2004). Time and space were salient in moving-image media narrative, whereas time was less salient in still images and Marsh considered the implications of these for schooled literacy (ibid.).

When looking at children's text-making in the home, I considered the affordance of particular objects and artefacts in relation to time and space. I considered how toys offered certain affordances for play. I also considered how certain objects provided a longer timescale to children. I found that objects which held meaning beyond the timescale of the activity, such as Fatih's bird, embedded within his *Super Mario* text, or Edward's Mallard train, reappeared more frequently within homes, but were often blended with objects and narratives from children's popular culture, such as Thomas the Tank Engine.

What I would argue is that fine-grained ethnography in homes produces a way of seeing children's interaction with popular culture in relation to their *habitus*, the detailed strategies and practices of everyday life. This understanding creates a frame which enables an analysis of how timescales interact with these practices and strategies. Edward's Mallard train and his Thomas the Tank Engine arrangements existed on one timescale, connected to his enthusiasm for the Thomas stories and a train collectors' manual. The discussion about his grandfather's train existed on a different timescale, that of his mother and grandfather. I focused on the material semiotic affordances of the objects children drew on to create hybrid textual meanings within homes. Children's popular culture, the objects, games and activities strewn across the front rooms, like Dyson's voice-strewn streets she invoked, are spaces where children mix and blend different objects, drawing in their cultural inventories to produce new texts (Dyson, 2003).

What do we take from this in relation to children's popular culture and literacy? We can focus on the *timescales* attached to an object – how long it is played with, and whether it links to a longer household narrative or is localized to a specific game. This can create the idea of 'bricolage', that is, the placing of hybrid objects and artefacts alongside each other (Merchant, Chapter 5, this volume). The objects were played with and represented in texts in very different stages of interest. Some objects were infused with meaning, and saturated with a number of different meanings. Particular toys offered particular types of semiotic affordances. For example, trains could be lined up. Small objects could be manipulated on a carpet, or placed under a cushion. The objects which attached themselves to children's popular culture had different resonances in relation to existing narrative structures within the home. They were absorbed, played with and discarded. I would argue that this was invisible meaning-making, often counted as 'mess' and forming hard-to-tidy-up miscellaneous piles within that, but offering rich semiotic possibilities which could be used by teachers within the school domain.

The data here were gathered by close ethnographic observation of children's meaning-making in the home. By drawing on the features of these instances, such as Fatih's use of levels to make representations of the games, his work with maps to develop his own game, Sam's placing of objects in new terrains to create imaginary scenarios and Edward's interest in trains as part of his family heritage, we can identify immediate possibilities for classroom discussion and writing. Literacy teachers can use these experiences within the classroom to work on content area literacy, filling their classrooms with the meanings and experiences children bring with them, and celebrating their differing cultural resources.

NOTE

1 Transcription conventions:___ indicates emphasis, (1) indicates time in seconds of pause, // indicates overlap in talk.

REFERENCES

Barton, D. and Hamilton, M. (1998) *Local Literacies: Reading and Writing in One Community*. London: Routledge.

Bourdieu, P. (1990) trans. R. Nice, *The Logic of Practice*. Cambridge: Polity Press.

Douglas, M. (1991) The Idea of a Home: A Kind of Space. *Social Research*. 58 (1), 287–307.

Dyson, A.H. (2003) *The Brothers and Sisters Learn to Write*. New York: Teachers College Press.

Hall, C. (1999) Understanding Educational Process in an Era of Globalization: The View from Anthropology and Cultural Studies, in E.C. Lagemann and L.S. Shulman (eds.) *Issues in Educational Research*. San Francisco: Condliffe Jossey-Bass Publishers, pp. 121–156.

Kenner, C. (2000) *Home Pages: Literacy Links for Bilingual Children*. Stoke-on-Trent: Trentham Books.

Kress, G. (1997) *Before Writing: Rethinking the Paths to Literacy*. London: Routledge.

Lemke, J.L. (2000) Across the Scales of Time: Artifacts, Activities and Meanings in Ecosocial Systems. *Mind, Culture and Activity*, 7 (4), 273–90.

Marsh, J. (2004) Moving Stories: Digital Animation in the Nursery. *Paper presented at Digital Generations Conference, IoE, July 2004*.

Mitchell, C. and Reid-Walsh, J. (2002) *Researching Children's Popular Culture: The Cultural Spaces of Childhood*. London: Routledge.

Street, B.V. (1993) Culture is a Verb: Anthropological Aspects of Language and Cultural Process, in D. Graddol, L. Thompson and M. Bryam (eds.) *Language and Culture*. Clevedon: BAAL and Multilingual Matters.

Van Leeuwen, T. and Caldas-Coulthard, C. (2004) 'The Semiotics of Kinetic Design', in D. Banks (ed.) *Text and Texture – Systemic–functional viewpoints on the nature and structure of text*. Paris: L'Harmattan, pp. 355–83.

Chapter 3

Mr Naughty Man: popular culture and children's literacy learning

*Pamela Greenhough, Wan Ching Yee, Jane Andrews,
Anthony Feiler, Mary Scanlan and Martin Hughes*

In this chapter we draw on data from the Home School Knowledge Exchange Project[1] to look at ways children may be developing unschooled literacy knowledge from their experiences with popular culture texts. The first part of the chapter is based on a video of a story-creating event, made by one of our project families. The unfolding creation and the surrounding conversations allow us insights into the children's emergent literacy understandings, particularly with respect to narrative. For a view of the knowledge children may be developing about character, we turn to an interview with a child where attention was focused on the cartoon series *The Simpsons*. We then consider the learning evident in these examples in terms of two major metaphors – acquisition and participation (Sfard, 1998). Finally, we discuss the implications of our observations for literacy learning in school.

Our first exploration centres on a video made for the project by a family living in Cardiff. There are two children in the family – Luke (a 'target' child directly involved in the research[2]) and Rhian, his sister. At the time of the video, Luke is aged six years and one month and Rhian is a couple of years older. The children live in a large, stylish terraced house with their mother and Welsh-speaking father. They both attend a Welsh medium school where the curriculum is delivered wholly in Welsh during the first few years. Luke does not write often at home. He prefers to 'be active' and spends hours out in the garden practising penalty kicks. Today, as the video shows, his mother tries to get him writing by suggesting that he could draw up a fantasy football team that he and his friends would like to play. Luke, however, is not interested and holds up his hand in a stop gesture. He then announces 'A Little Naughty Man'. In answer to his mum's surprised question, 'What is a little naughty man?', he draws and cuts out a little man with a triangle hat. He is helped throughout by his sister who, for example, draws some dots for him to join up to make the triangle for the hat. He says it could have a string on it and be a puppet. His mum, still trying to get him writing, suggests that he could make a list in his book (some lilac A4 sheets folded and stapled by his dad) of the things he would like to take on holiday or the things he would like to do at the weekend. But Luke wants his Naughty Man to be in the book and, with the help of his sister, sticks the cut-out on the front page with sellotape.

During the following 30 minutes, Luke fills the book with pictures and occasional captions as he tells the story of Mr Naughty Man. It is a violent story. Mr Naughty came across the sea, saw diamonds and stole them, punched a man, lifted him up and 'throwed' him in a bin. He pushed a policeman down the stairs and made him bleed, took a gun out of his pocket and shot him and the policeman died. At this point the story takes a supernatural turn as Luke draws a picture of a graveyard with Mr Naughty rain coming down which punches and kills people. On the story goes. Luke announces that Mr Naughty is clever and that he could walk through walls. He is wholly engaged in his narrative. When his mother makes suggestions that could lighten the story, for example, 'When's Mr Nice Guy going to appear, then?', he refutes her ideas.

Luke: There's no Mr Nice Guy (slapping the table), OK, (blows
          a raspberry), (laughs), {...}[3] it's my story, not yours

When his mother suggests it is getting late and he should stop, he begs to be allowed to do 'just one more page'.

Luke's composition is surrounded by conversation mostly between his mother and sister. The conversation often takes the form of a commentary between them on what he is doing. In the following excerpt, his mum's writing agenda starts to surface but Rhian heads off any potential criticism by referring to a literary exemplar for the form of picture-story being used.

Mum: You haven't written any words in there, Luke, [{...}
Rhian: [Is it just going to be a picture book?
Mum: [just doing pictures
Rhian: ['cos I've got a picture book of Santa Claus and it's got little
          speech bubbles and it says in the.. it's.. you.. I can tell that
          Santa Claus doesn't like Christmas because the bubbles say
          'Uh-oh, not some snow'.
Mum: Oh yeh, that's {em}
Rhian: [He says 'Oh no, more {slippery}..'
Mum: [I know the book you mean
Rhian: [but the {...}
Mum: [He's a grumpy Santa Claus, isn't he?
Rhian: Yeh

When Luke's mum leaves the scene from time to time the story construction continues, with Luke's sister playing a strong supporting role, sometimes suggesting ideas but also acting as immediate audience, modelling response to the story.

> *Luke*: Wherever you hide, he (Mr Naughty Man) knows straight away
>
> *Rhian*: Aw, is there any way you can hide so that he doesn't know? Is it.. is there something like an invention you have to build and he can never see you
>
> *Luke*: Well, if you hide in a dark closet, very dark, [you'll die
>
> *Rhian*: [you'll be scared, will you be s.. If you hide in dark.
>
> *Luke*: You'll die.
>
> *Rhian*: You'll die.
>
> *Luke*: In this story, you'll die.
>
> *Rhian*: [{so you have to come out}
>
> *Luke*: ['cos Mr Naughty spies {live} in dark. And when you go in there
>
> *Rhian*: So, wherever you hide.. and if it's dark where you hide, there's a spy hiding in there to kill you. Aw. (To the camera and the imagined audience behind it) So you'd better keep your lights on (little laugh) just in case he comes to your house and one of his spies catch you...Don't worry, it's just Luke's story (reassuringly).

From his mother, he hears rather more negative reactions: 'Oh no, Luke, it's a horrible story', when the policeman dies. Eventually, Luke reaches a point where he is prepared to write 'the end' on his story but he states his intention to write another scary story the next day.

> *Luke*: Another one, tomorrow it's going to be another.. another scary story.
>
> *Rhian*: Aw.
>
> *Mum*: Aw blimey, Luke.
>
> *Luke*: {Sorry},
>
> *Rhian*: [He might change
>
> *Mum*: [{You're} going to be a horror writer when you grow up.
>
> *Rhian*: He might be.. he might change his mind tomorrow, he might have a good day and think I like flowers, and start writing sweet things.

CHILDREN'S KNOWLEDGE

Throughout the construction of the story and the conversation surrounding it, we can see evidence of the children's emergent literacy understandings and the way they are being developed, especially in relation to narrative.

Plot

One area concerns plotting. The way the story will end is a recurring theme in the talk, as a 'happy ending' is seen (by the females) as a way of relieving the unremitting darkness of the story. Luke's mum presents a view of the happy ending as normative, a view that Luke challenges with a single word.

> *Mum*:   He hasn't finished yet, there'll be a happy ending, though.
> *Rhian*:   I hope.
> *Mum*:   I'm sure that.. because usually the good guys win, don't they, not the bad guys.
> *Rhian*:   Yeh, Scooby Doo, they capture the person who dresses up like a ghost.
> *Luke*:   Titanic.
> *Rhian*:   Oh, Titanic (reconsidering).

Robinson and Mackey have observed that:

> It is striking how much the research about television/film and print literacy works on the assumption that these operations represent discrete categories, when ... much of children's early textual experience washes across media boundaries.
>
> (Robinson and Mackey, 2003: 134)

We would also observe that the knowledge that we see enacted in writing and being built in talk also traverses media boundaries. The endings, for example, which are called upon in the argument above are drawn from film (or life) and a TV cartoon series, while being brought to bear upon a story represented in static pictures and print. Robinson (1997) has suggested that it is narrative that is the driving force that transcends boundaries.

In addition to the talk about endings in general, there are references to features which seem to link up with the scary-movie genre in particular. At one point Mr Naughty Man is dead and 'nasty blood is coming out of him'. In true scary-movie style, Luke then announces 'but he wasn't dead'.

> *Mum*:   I thought it was going to be a nice little pirate adventure, and then Luke does a horrible story about killing and death and..
> *Luke*:   (announcing) Mr Nasty Man[4] wasn't dead.
> *Mum*:   Oh no.

As we know, in this genre, the end is not the end. An awareness of plot twists and things not being as they seem is also evident.

Luke: [The goodies.. the goodies stole money (Turns page)
Mum: The goodies steal the money?
Luke: Yeh
Rhian: That means they're going to turn into baddies now and the bads are going to turn good and the goods are going to turn bad (little laugh).
Luke: No.
Rhian: Or have the goodies stole the money to put back?
Luke: [If I tell you
Rhian: [where it's meant to be
Luke: I'll spoil the story.

We might also note in this context the way the setting underscores the plot. Luke takes a convention, which is widespread amongst his peer group, of drawing faces on the sun and raindrops and imbues it with greater potency as it becomes Mr Naughty rain that joins in with the action (cf. as in both horror stories and *King Lear*). Additionally, the scariness is increased as there is no apparent escape from the horror, since the rain is magic and can go through things.

Intertextuality

Another feature we see emerging in the course of the video is the use of allusion. At the start of the following excerpt, the children appear to be trying to strengthen the communicative power of the story within the restrictions of the captioned picture form that Luke is using. Luke has written 'ha ha' and Rhian suggests that adding an exclamation mark will give it greater weight. She then describes the way she, herself, would add to the scariness of such a story (by borrowing Arnold Schwarzenegger's line from *The Terminator*).

Luke: Ha (high-pitched) ha (lower pitch) because he's glad he killed him...
Rhian: Ha ha, ha ha ha (turns it more into a cackle). Do you want to put it like... one of these things (draws an exclamation mark on a separate sheet)... that says he's shouting it?
Luke: (Nods, does exclamation mark on page 7)
Rhian: And making it loud {do you see} {it's going} ha ha ha ha shot you, ha ha.
Luke: Ha ha ha (gives an evil laugh).
Mum: That's a nasty laugh isn't it, that's a scary laugh.

Rhian: Ha ha ha haa (does her own version of scary laugh)...If I did
          one of those story...in one of them I'd write 'I'll be back'
          (fiercely). That sounds quite scary, doesn't it, 'I'll be back'.
Luke: Soon (quite fiercely)
Rhian: 'I'll be back soon to get you'. If he missed a shot and he
          went.. and the man he tried to shoot ran away, maybe
          shouts – 'I'll be back after you soon enough', and makes a big
          laugh again.

Appropriation and recontextualization of symbolic material is a major
way in which authors layer meaning into their texts. See, for example,
Eliot's use of the nightingale (from Greek myth) in the *Waste Land*,
although Rhian's revoicing of 'I'll be back' is likely to be more easily
recognized and probably more successful for many audiences than Eliot's
'jug jug'.

One interesting aspect to the would-be intertextuality in the excerpt is the
seeming likelihood that neither child has watched the original, as indicated
by their joint easy acceptance of the addition of the word 'soon' to the iconic
expression. However, Rhian knows the phrase from somewhere, has picked
up on its currency (possibly from playground games and conversations)
and recognizes it as fitting for action plots. Children will, it seems, utilize
the assets available to them (Tyner, 1998) even when their hold on the
knowledge involved may be quite tenuous.

Rhian's proposed inclusion of 'I'll be back' would seem to underscore
Sipe's (2000) contention that children know that 'stories are *so porous* to
each other that they can be combined, stitched, woven together, and fused'
(p. 85, emphasis in the original). Sipe's statement is made in the context of
an examination of intertextuality in children's oral responses to stories read
aloud to them at school. Mostly, he was concerned with its occurrence in
the interpretation and making sense of the texts, but he also observed
a creative dimension to the connections the children made between stories.
It is this creative element that is relevant when we look at children's own
composing. In her observations of young children engaged in school literacy
events, Dyson (e.g. 1999, 2002) discerns five major types of appropriation
and recontextualization of media material – content, communicative form/
genre, graphic/technological convention, voiced utterance and ideology.
These may be interlinked (as in the excerpt here) where working with one
type, for example a particular genre, engenders another, like a voiced
utterance.

Programme genres

We have already noted above the use of genre features relating to types
of narrative. The video of Luke and Rhian also contained indications of

a feeling for the genre of programmes on television, in particular wholesome children's programmes with a presenter, like *Blue Peter* or *Art Attack*. Rhian seemed to see herself as such a presenter, as we saw earlier, when she spoke directly to the camera and advised children to keep their lights on (because Mr Naughty spies hide in the dark) and followed up with the reassurance that it was only a story. She captured the encouraging tone of a presenter exactly, as was noted in the transcript from time to time, as in the following case, when Luke is drawing Mr Naughty Man for the first time.

> *Rhian*:   And maybe a nose (pointing to her own nose) his dot for the nose. Oh yeh (enthusiastically) he looks good already (all said in the tone of an encouraging adult, possibly the presenter of a children's TV art programme)

She also addressed the audience directly using the second person and involved them interactively by asking them questions. In the following example, Luke and Rhian have just recapped the story for their father in Welsh. As he leaves the scene, the dialogue continues.

> *Luke*:   (Welsh) Everyone thinks it's a nasty...story.
> *Rhian*:   (Welsh) Well it *is*.
> *Luke*:   (Welsh) Does everyone like it?
> *Rhian*:   (Welsh) Yes, it's a very likeable story. (English) It's very scary, isn't it?
> *Luke*:   (Welsh) This..
> *Rhian*:   (addressing an imagined audience behind the camera, in English) I wonder if any of you (emphasis on 'you') think Mr Nau.. Naughty Guy and Mr Nasty Guy is very scary, if he came to your house.. I'd hide under my bed, I wonder what you would do (chuckle).

The use of tag questions among other features of inclusivity is also indicative of the register of this kind of presenter. There is also the gentle mocking of the sidekick or co-presenter (and a paternalistic air), as in the following example.

> *Rhian*:   I hope it doesn't start raining now, Mr Nasty Guys, because we'll explode, but it's just a story so don't worry, everything will be OK, hope you don't get nightmares (to the audience), Luke is silly.
> *Luke*:   So, I'm telling {them} about the story
> *Rhian*:   Come on then, no, it's OK, think everybody at home is really excited, wondering what's going to happen

Luke: (turns the page)
Rhian: (flattens the fold) Is it going to end nicely, or bad?

These examples suggest that children's embedded knowledge of programme genre may be quite subtle and go beyond that which may be uncovered by direct probing (Buckingham, 1993).

Character

Our second exploration is concerned specifically with character. There is very little characterization in Luke's story. Mr Naughty Man is something of a cipher. There is no description of the character other than at the start when we hear about the triangle hat. We are given no understanding as to the character's motivation. He is just, as his name indicates, a representation of badness played out in his actions. Elsewhere in our data, however, we have found that children possess reserves of knowledge of character based on their experience of screen-media stories. These perspectives on character were often elicited as the children talked about the small plastic toys from crackers and cereal packets that we took with us to interviews.

We found that the target children could list the traits of the characters they watched and provide evidence from the characters' actions to back up their judgements. One boy said that Homer Simpson was 'greedy and lazy, greedy 'cos he keeps eating doughnuts and drinking stuff, and he's lazy 'cos he always sits down and never does nothing, he never goes to the {...} for the hotdogs, so Marge has to do it, and he only spins around in his chair when he's at work'. Parveen's description[5] of Homer enlarged on his stupidity.

Parveen: Homer, he loves {Duff}.. beer.
Int: What kind of things does he like?
Parveen: Doughnuts, sleeping in his job ... in his job area, well he likes Duff beer.
Int: Is that a kind of beer?
Parveen: Yeh, it's the beer that he drinks, he loves burping, and the things that he doesn't like.. or who he doesn't like is Mr Burns.
Int: Now, who's he?
Parveen: He's Homer's job officer, and Homer got the job off him, but he's still in his job.
Int: So is Homer quite clever, do you think.
Parveen: He's a quite bit dumb.
Int: Is he, right.
Parveen: He doesn't know nothing, anyway, (little laugh) ... because there was this lady, it was Marge when she was small, she

had like a {drink}, and Homer knocked her over by accident,
and then she started to cry, so then she went.. then she
went to her mum and then Homer said – Sorry, I'll buy you
a new one, and then he said to her.. he said to Apu can I
have one of those drinks Lapsang something and then Apu
said that Lapsang Suchong is a type of Slush Puppies drink,
and then Homer pretended that he knowed and then he
said – I knew that

Parveen's family are Sikhs. Her father describes himself as 'born and
bred' in the UK. Her mother and paternal grandfather moved to
England from India and speak Punjabi most of the time at home.
The family have cable TV and when Parveen's father goes to work in the
evening the choice is between watching the cartoons favoured by the
children in the family or the Asian films favoured by their mother. As we
can see from Parveen's extensive knowledge, the cartoon option must
often win. She could account for why characters behave in particular
ways. In the following excerpt, she recounts the explanation to be found
in one of *The Simpsons* stories for Bart's feelings towards his younger
sister, Lisa.

Int: Right now you said about Bart at the beginning that
        he was a..

Parveen: A bit cheeky and a rude boy and he doesn't like his sister.
        When he was small and he used to like his cot he used to say
        that.. because his mum was having like a baby.. it was
        Lisa who was it, and Lisa needed to have that cot and his
        dad made this scary room for Bart only because he's about
        three years old, it was like a Krusty[6] room, but it was like
        so scary that he wanted to get out but his dad locked him,
        so Lisa had his cot and then when Lisa was downstairs and
        his mum.. his mum was making d.. his mum was watering
        the plants, while his dad was playing.. while his dad was
        chatting to his next door neighbour.. I don't know, I've
        forgot his name, and Bart got Lisa and he said I'm going
        to kill you, give my cot back now, and then he whacked her
        and then Bart got in so much trouble, that he had to stay in
        his room for about 6 hours.

Int: Goodness, and you said his room was a bit Krusty, what..
Parveen: Krusty, yeh.
Int: What, like Krusty the Clown?
Parveen: Yeh, Krusty the Clown.
Int: What was in his room?

Parveen: Well, like scary stuff, like Krusty stuff, like a Krusty wat.. a Krusty alarm clock cos when he wakes up, Krusty gets a big sledge hammer and he bangs it on his arm.

Int: That's his waking-up call is it, so that's a bit scary for a 3-year-old.

Parveen: Yep, he started to cry when he started look.. he was looking at his bedroom. Behind his bed on the wall there was like a poster and it was like all different kind of clowns but then it was so scary...

Int: So does this explain why Bart doesn't like Lisa so much

Parveen: Yeh, because she stole his cot when she was only a newborn.

Since many of the screen characters appeared in series of stories, it was also possible to talk to the children about the way a character might usually behave and the things that they might do that were unexpected. Characters were, therefore, understood as more than one-dimensional. This was especially the case with *The Simpsons*, where the series itself plays with this feature.

Parveen: This is Lisa. She gets sometimes in trouble.

Int: Does she do naughty things, then?

Parveen: Well, once she did because she cheated, well she wanted to go to the toilet and Bart said come to the boys' toilet, so she went in the boys' toilet and she found this boy who's Bart's friend called Nelson and he got the cheat for her maths test and she got them all right, but she didn't want to cheat but she took the paper and she started cheating and she said to herself when she went back home – what have I done, and then she told her teacher that I've cheated, she said to her teacher that.. because her teacher said well done, Lisa, you got them all right, and she said to her teacher I didn't, I cheated and then em.. the principal of Lisa's school, he said to Lisa, what Lisa, you can't cheat 'cos you never ever cheat, you won't do a such a thing like that.

METAPHORS FOR LEARNING

It would appear, then, that children can be learning a great deal from their out-of-school encounters with popular culture texts, especially in respect of narrative and story-making. Much of this knowledge may be largely tacit and enacted in composing, retelling or play. However, understandings may emerge more explicitly in interpersonal contexts involving, for example, disagreement or advice-giving. How might we regard this learning? During recent years, theoretical stances have tended to take either a cognitive or a socially situated view. Sfard (1998) has discerned two metaphors underpinning the theoretical perspectives – acquisition in the former cases and participation in the latter.[7] Her schematic comparison between the two can be seen in Table 3.1.

Although Sfard argued that educational theory would benefit from an adequate combination of both metaphors, we have found the ease with which we can map the individual metaphors onto school and home useful in distinguishing between the two domains (Hughes, 2001). The acquisition metaphor is helpful in understanding the school domain, while the participation metaphor seems particularly relevant to the domain of home. These distinctions also help to delineate the challenges that are posed for home school knowledge exchange (Greenhough et al., 2004).

However, while we would expect the participation (and practices) oriented perspective to be most appropriate when we look at children's learning from popular culture media, we find we are presented with some difficulties. A social mechanism for learning is not precluded in either perspective but in the participation view the interpersonal dimension is primary. Yet, when we look at the children's learning from screen media, much of it would seem to have been accomplished without the coterminous interventions of others. Rather, it is the texts themselves which have taught many of the lessons or afforded the learning. Meek (1991) has written about the literacy lessons children learn from texts – for example, coming to an

Table 3.1 The metaphorical mappings (Sfard)

Acquisition[a] metaphor		Participation[b] metaphor
Individual enrichment	*Goal of learning*	Community building
Acquisition of something	*Learning*	Becoming a participant
Recipient (consumer), (re-)constructor	*Student*	Peripheral participant, apprentice
Provider, facilitator, mediator	*Teacher*	Expert participant, preserver of practice/discourse
Property, possession, commodity . . .	*Knowledge, concept*	Aspect of practice/ discourse/ activity
Having, possessing	*Knowing*	Belonging, participating, communicating

Notes

[a] Sfard suggests the acquisition metaphor underpins a variety of theories from moderate and radical constructivism to interactionism and sociocultural theories since they all focus on the development of concepts and the acquisition of knowledge.

[b] Examples here include the legitimate peripheral participation of Lave and Wenger (1991) and Rogoff's apprenticeship in thinking (1990).

understanding, through reading Anthony Browne's *Bear Hunt*, that fiction makes possible a multiconsciousness. However, since Meek's examples are mostly books, mediation by more capable others is indeed necessary (at least at young ages) to allow the learning to proceed. Screen stories, on the other hand, are able to teach the lessons of 'how it goes' (p. 155) without such mediation. We need theories, then, that allow for the role of the expert or the knower to be instantiated in the text as well as in the activity of others.

We also need to recognize the multiplicity of communities (and practices) that may be represented in encounters with popular culture and their role in learning. Although several may be brought together, a simple example is provided in the intersection of the creating community and the reception community. That these can be different but both accessible to children is graphically illustrated in the Mr Naughty Man event, where Luke aligns himself with the writers and their genre in his attempt at production but learns that response to this stuff can be negative and that the reaction to violence, especially when it happens to good guys, can be contested, especially by older middle-class females. If we are to make the best of the idea of participation, it needs to be viewed as multiple rather than singular. We need a metaphor of participations.

This multiplicity also leads us to consider the constructive nature of children's activity as they build on their experience from one context and employ it in another; moving, for example, from a context of consumption to a context of creation. Rhian uses her knowledge of presenters, gained from watching programmes, when she comes to 'present' her own programme. That the knowledge children are creating is not merely reproductive is demonstrated in her comment about *Scooby Doo*. From repeated watching, she has come to recognize the formulaic aspect of the happy ending in this series (when it is revealed that there is almost always a normal explanation for the apparently supernormal – and scary – happenings). There seems to be an impulse for children to make or create connections across times, places, texts and activities, as we have suggested in the context of mathematics learning (Hughes and Greenhough, 1998). This quality is also evident in the acts of reference which constitute inter-textuality. The generative nature of this drive can be overlooked by those who take too bounded a view of context and cognition or practice.

However, there are difficulties with the acquisition metaphor as well. When knowledge is seen as a permanent trait or possession of the person, account may not adequately be taken of the ways in which knowing or participating may be activated differently according to context. Dyson's notion of reframing (2000) is helpful here in recognizing the fluid and mutually reconstituting nature of knowledge and context. This is especially appropriate when we consider the place of children's media-based learning in the situation of school, which we consider next.

IMPLICATIONS FOR LITERACY LEARNING IN SCHOOL

There is little doubt that many children find popular culture stuff interesting and engaging. Marsh (2000) reported that excitement accompanied the introduction into a nursery of literacy activities related to the Teletubbies, resulting in more children joining in with the activities for extended periods of time. We also saw how riveted Luke was by his story-making. A first argument, then, for creating a presence for popular culture in school relates to its motivating quality. Its potential for playing against the marginalization of children from diverse backgrounds is also raised (e.g. Arthur, 2001).

The fact that many children find popular culture interesting is not, however, seen by all as a reason for its inclusion in the classroom. Smidt (2004), for example, basing her argument on observations of her grand-children, suggests that children's real passions are not the superficial elements of popular culture they appear to be but the underlying schemas that individuals are working on. She illustrates this by reference to her grandson's interest in Beyblades, which she maintains is actually a passion for rotation. She suggests that teachers should know about popular culture in order to recognize what it is that children are really referring to in their play and argues that 'aspects of popular culture should be "owned" by the children and left out of classrooms' (p. 84).

This approach, however, fails to recognize the knowledge that is left out of classrooms by such a stance. This is not the superficial content knowledge of and about popular culture but nascent understandings about how (some) literacy 'goes'. The second argument, then, for the presence of popular culture in school is based on the recognition that children are acquainted with important literacy ideas through their experiences with popular culture. If popular culture is not allowed a place in the classroom, then the possibility of building on these understandings and extending them in school is denied. However, the process of supporting and making the best of them is not always straightforward. Teachers working within the strictures of school can find it a challenge.

> T: I mean we did try.. certainly in the last couple of years we've tried doing some.. you know some children really like cartoons so we tried getting them to do some sort of cartoon writing and things which helped the real low achievers to feel like they could read and write, you know they could pick out bits in comics where it said 'Ow', and things like that, (laughs) but when we tried complete free writing sessions and they were trying to write things like about football matches, it was fairly disastrous because they stopped thinking really about what makes a good piece of writing and just slipped into 'and Beckham passed the ball to Owen, and Owen passed the ball to Beckham, and it went in the net, 2 nil'

(laugh) and they completely lost that ability to think and criticise their own work {...} you know.

PG: That's really interesting, sort of doing the running commentary thing, but not seeing it as a piece of writing.

T: No, no, and the same if they start rewriting a story...if they're doing a story that's from school, and they perceive as a sort of school story, like Goldilocks, they'll try and put in all that rich story language, 'cos they apply what they've learnt in school, but if they're telling you the plot of, you know, the *Scooby Doo* movie or something they went to, it's nothing like as high quality a piece because it's almost like they don't transfer that skill over as much, and that would be the trick, wouldn't it, to be able to marry the two up better.

(Interview with teacher at the start of Year 2)

One problem children face, which is implied in the interview, is that of reproducing texts across formats and modalities, as they try to recreate, for example, a filmic piece as a written story, or a televised event with voice-over as a narrative. As Bearne and Kress (2001) point out, different modes provide different affordances. Children may find it a challenge if they are limited to working in a particular mode. It is also the case that the task of rewriting the tale of Goldilocks heard as a story, expressed in storying conventions with phrases coming ready-made for reusing, is likely to be easier (and more immediately successful, according to school criteria) than rewriting the story of the *Scooby Doo* movie, which has been experienced as a visual entity with no narrator describing the action or the setting, and with only the dialogue being immediately available for replay. Thought needs to be given, then, to the formats and modes that are made available to the children for their compositions and the ways these are judged. Rather than simply writing a story, for example, they may be asked to produce an illustrated script with action directions and written dialogue. Devices such as these can serve to reduce the size of the act of translation from known to created. Children will also be helped when teachers are capable of tuning their ear to the more unusual voices the children are representing and are able to appreciate their successes at capturing tone and phrase. It may be the children's sensitivity to genre stereotypes (of the football commentary, for example) that guides them away from other forms of story language they may sense as unsuitable. Teachers may also need to tune their perception more acutely to the visual elements. Other formats which may allow children to display and apply their knowledge in different ways include creating computer fan pages and making review programmes on video. Fan pages, for example, may have sections such as plot synopsis, best lines, funniest/scariest moments, and reasons for liking characters.

However, we have been arguing throughout most of this chapter that children's encounters with popular culture build their understanding of narrative, and we would hope to see the best being made of this knowledge when it comes to sustained story-making. What may be needed are ways of making the children more aware of what they know so that they can see its relevance to the demands of their writing made by school, and use their knowledge more effectively. One idea implemented on the project, though not designed for this particular purpose, may be helpful here. In one school, children took home shoeboxes and were asked to fill them with items that they thought would stimulate their writing (Greenhough *et al.*, 2005). The children brought in a wide variety of items and generally the impact of the activity on their writing was very positive, although it varied from child to child. The presence of actual things helped some children to structure their writing better. One boy, for example, gained more control over plot. Another child managed an ending, which she had never done before. Other children became more creative. The teacher said of one girl that it was the first time she'd done a piece showing imagination.

The idea of a physical collection can be developed further in ways that help to bring tacit knowledge closer to the surface. The children might, for example, be asked to put together a character box based on a favourite character. The boxes could then be used over time to elicit some of their understandings about characterization. They might be asked to discuss what would be the typical things their character would do, who their character would be friends with, what acting out of character would look like, what might bring about acting out of character, what would be a dilemma for their character. With characters from any story being accepted, all children would, it is hoped, become more aware of what they know and that their knowledge is relevant and valued. This may also provide a context for raising questions about ideology (Marsh and Millard, 2000), but should maybe include all stories represented, not just those derived from popular culture.

In this chapter we have drawn on data from the Home School Knowledge Exchange Project to look at the knowledge and knowing that children may be developing through their out-of-school encounters with popular culture. Our research in children's homes has shown that children from a range of backgrounds share an interest in popular culture, and its appeal for many children is markedly strong. Our evidence also suggests that, through these experiences, children can be developing valuable literacy-related awareness, particularly in relation to narrative and story-making. These observations have raised questions for us as to the ways in which learning is conceptualized. They also encourage us to consider how we might build on the potential of this vernacular understanding within school. Above all, this work points to the importance for children's literacy learning of establishing creative links between school and the fertile worlds beyond.

NOTES

1 The Home School Knowledge Exchange Project is funded by the ESRC (reference number L139 25 1078) and is part of its Teaching and Learning Research Programme. Detailed information about the project can be found on the project website (http://www.home-school-learning.org.uk/) and the TLRP website (http://www.tlrp.org). We are very grateful to the children, parents and teachers who participated in the project and to the LEAs of Cardiff and Bristol for their support.

2 In the literacy strand of the project, we worked with four schools. The project's aim was to develop new ways to exchange knowledge between home and school. This aspect of the work was supported by a teacher–researcher who worked part-time with one class in each school over a two-year period to develop knowledge exchange activities. As part of our evaluation of these activities, six families in each class were selected by stratified random assignment as 'target' families. Parents in each family were approached in the playground or by telephone and asked if they would talk in their homes to members of the research team. All but two agreed and in those cases reserves were included.

Interviews were carried out with parents from these families at the end of the first year, when the children were aged 5/6, and with parents and children at the end of the second year, when the children were aged 6/7. (A small number of children from among the targets were interviewed more frequently and over a longer period to provide more in-depth case studies). The interviews were designed to explore aspects of home literacy learning and to gauge responses to the knowledge exchange activities that were taking place. At the end of each interview we asked the family if they would make a video for us of home literacy events, and left a camera with them for this purpose.

3 We use the following representations in our transcripts:
{…} unclear
[simultaneous speech
[

4 Earlier, Mr Naughty Man got renamed Mr Nasty Man by Luke's mum, who, in recapping part of the story, didn't get things quite right.

5 Parveen was in Year 3 by the time of the interview that elicited the selected excerpts.

6 Krusty is a grotesque character on children's TV as portrayed in the cartoon series. It is a feature of *The Simpsons* that the stories parody both popular culture media influences and the moral panics that can be engendered by these influences. In this story recounted by Parveen, we see the trend for children's rooms to be made over with characters and motifs from popular culture being satirized.

7 We would observe that the terminology used by different authors can be somewhat confusing. Gee (1996), for example, uses acquisition to refer to discourses that are picked up in 'natural, meaningful and functional settings'. This resembles that which Sfard would designate participation. He contrasts this with 'learning', which he uses for the product of teaching which breaks down material into analytic bits (pp. 144–145). This is akin to Sfard's acquisition.

REFERENCES

Arthur, L. (2001) Popular culture and early literacy learning, *Contemporary Issues in Early Childhood*, 2 (3), 295–308.

Bearne, E. and Kress, G. (2001) Editorial, *READING literacy and language*, 35 (3), 89–93.

Buckingham, D. (1993) *Children Talking Television: The Making of Television Literacy*, London: Falmer Press.

Dyson, A.H. (1999) Coach Bombay's kids learn to write: Children's appropriation of media material for school literacy, *Research in the Teaching of English*, 33, 367–402.

Dyson, A.H. (2000) On reframing children's words: the perils, promises, and pleasures of writing children, *Research in the Teaching of English*, 34, 352–367.

Dyson, A.H. (2002) Textual Toys and Compositional Tutus: Studying Child Literacy in the Context of Child Culture. Invited keynote address, ESRC Seminar Series – Children's Literacy and Popular Culture, Sheffield, July. (http://www.shef.ac.uk/literacy)

Gee, J.P. (1996) *Social Linguistics and Literacies Ideology in Discourses*, London: RoutledgeFamer (2nd ed).

Greenhough, P., Hughes, M., Andrews, J., Feiler, A., Johnson, D., McNess, E., Osborn, M., Pollard, A., Scanlan, M., Salway, L., Stinchcombe, V., Winter, J. and Yee, W.C. (2004) Home School knowledge exchange: Activities and conceptualisations. Paper presented at the Teaching and Learning Research Programme Conference, Cardiff, November. (http://www.tlrp.org/dspace/handle/123456789/113)

Greenhough, P., Scanlan, M., Feiler, A., Johnson, D., Yee, W. C., Andrews, J., Price, A., Smithson, M. and Hughes, M. (2005) Boxing clever: using shoeboxes to support home school knowledge exchange, *Literacy*, 39 (2), 97–103.

Hughes, M. (2001) Children learning at home and school. Thirteenth Annual Drever Lecture, University of Edinburgh, May.

Hughes, M. and Greenhough, P. (1998) Moving between communities of practice: children linking mathematical activities at home and school. In A. Watson (ed.), *Situated Cognition and the Learning of Mathematics*, Oxford: Centre for Mathematics Education Research.

Lave, J. and Wenger, E. (1991) *Situated learning: legitimate peripheral participation*, Cambridge: Cambridge University Press

Marsh, J. (2000) Teletubby tales: popular culture in the early years language and literacy curriculum, *Contemporary Issues in Early Childhood*, 1 (2), 119–133.

Marsh, J. and Millard, E. (2000) *Literacy and Popular Culture: using children's culture in the classroom*, London: Paul Chapman.

Meek, M. (1991) *On Being Literate*, London: The Bodley Head.

Robinson, M. (1997) *Children Reading Print and Television*, London: Falmer Press.

Robinson, M. and Mackey, M. (2003) Film and television. In N. Hall, J. Larson and J. Marsh (eds), *Handbook of Early Childhood Literacy*, London: Sage.

Rogoff, B. (1990) *Apprenticeship in Thinking: Cognitive Development in Social Context*, Oxford: Oxford University Press.

Sfard, A. (1998) On two metaphors for learning and the dangers of choosing just one, *Educational Researcher*, **27** (2), 4–13.

Sipe, L. (2000) 'Those two boys could be brothers': How children use intertextual connections during storybook readalouds, *Children's Literature in Education*, **31** (2), 73–90.

Smidt, S. (2004) Sinister storytellers, magic flutes and spinning tops: the links between play and 'popular' culture, *Early Years*, **24** (1), 75–85.

Tyner, K. (1998) *Literacy in a Digital World: Teaching and Learning in the Age of Information*, Mahwah, NJ: Lawrence Erlbaum.

Chapter 4

Playing with texts: the contribution of children's knowledge of computer narratives to their story-writing

Eve Bearne and Helen Wolstencroft

Children now have available to them many forms of text which include sound, voices, intonation, stance, gesture, movement, as well as print and image. Many of these are embedded in children's popular culture and have changed the ways in which young readers expect to read, the ways they think and the ways they construct meaning. Necessarily, then, children bring to their reading and writing a wide and varied array of resources and experience through which they interpret any unfamiliar texts that they meet. There is a problem, however, about how knowledge of the multidimensional texts of popular culture can be acknowledged and honoured in the classroom. Children's cultural capital in terms of text knowledge may not always square with the kind of literacy curriculum on offer in schools. This comes into sharp focus when the popular texts under consideration are computer games.

Games are considered part of child or youth culture, often an unknown type of text from those most in evidence in classrooms. Whilst they may be acknowledged as part of the pupils' out-of-school cultural lives, the topic for conversations among fellow players and perhaps as part of after-school clubs, for the most part, games remain firmly outside the curriculum. A barrier remains, despite the case for games being seen as a valid part of classroom life. Games have been examined as an ideal context for learning of many kinds (Gee, 2003); as valuable cultural capital that can be drawn on to enhance learning (Marsh and Millard, 2003) and as a model for literary study (Burn, 2005). Nevertheless, fears are often expressed about the pernicious influence of computer games and game-playing is compared unfavourably with the perceived benefits of reading books. However, as Margaret Mackey explains, 'children live in a world of many fictions' (Mackey, 2004: 56) and whilst adults need to exercise care about children and their activities, she argues:

> I think we benefit from considering a broader picture, one that does not automatically ascribe all the imaginative virtues to the reading of print and equally automatically assume that fierce powers of social

depravity are a necessary element in the playing of computer games. Before we can begin to think about the implications for teaching, we need to clarify our understanding of what is going on.

(Mackey, 2004: 56)

This chapter is an attempt to add some detail to 'what is going on' by teasing out some of the classroom implications of children's knowledge of computer games, particularly in respect of the writing demands of the curriculum.

The work described here came from a series of lessons which aimed to find out about children's knowledge of narrative text organization drawn from their experience with computer games. After listening to what the children had to say and looking carefully at the work, it would seem that their knowledge of game narratives of different kinds adds significantly to their potential for constructing written narrative texts. This suggests the value of explicit classroom discussion of variations in the structures, purposes and effects of game texts in relation to book texts. The wealth of the children's examples supports Mackey's view that teachers need to find out what is going on: to discover (if they don't already know) how such texts work and to recognize and value the contribution of games to children's potential for handling the literacy demands of school.

THE PATTERNS OF PLAY

There are intriguing variations in the value ascribed to play in relation to learning. Whereas in early years settings there is an unquestioned assumption that play aids learning, as learners grow older a strong distinction is made between what is considered work and what is play. However, engagement with digital texts and technologies is shifting such strong demarcations. Children's playing of computer games often has an element of effort more associated with 'work' (Facer et al., 2003). Whilst it can be used as a description of sporting activity and competitive games of all kinds, in its informal uses, 'play' implies both an inner world of individual imagination and an overt performative element; often, play is a domain where the child is in charge (Smidt, 2003). However, no matter which nuance is invoked – sport, board games, role play in the nursery, for management training or in the playground – play is a regulated activity, even if informally. It involves following some kinds of procedures, patterns or rules. In this way, play can be seen to have a kind of grammar, with expectations and regularities. Many of the children in this study were very familiar with the text grammars of different kinds of computer games. The sections which follow look at how their writing combines the imaginative, performative and regulated aspects of play drawn from their experience of computer game texts.

This project was carried out with a class of eight-to-nine-year-olds in a small village school near a market town in East Anglia. There were 28 in the class – 16 girls and 12 boys. There were five afternoon sessions over a five-week period in the summer term.[1] Several of the pupils have statements of special educational need and several are bilingual. Initial surveys showed that only seven of the 16 girls regularly played computer games, whereas all the boys did. However, most of the girls who did not choose to play games were familiar with them; they simply preferred to spend their leisure time watching television, videos or DVDs, playing with friends, or pursuing other interests. On average, the children who played computer games said they spent about three hours a week on them, some of the more dedicated spending much more time than that, but others choosing to do other things as well as playing on the computer.

The types of games listed in the surveys included: shoot-'em-up; quest, adventure and 'collecting' games; SIMS and similar games where the aim is to create a society and setting (often described as 'God games'); football and racing games; maths, science and literacy games; and war simulations. This suggests a great variety in text experience drawn from computer games since some have a more linear (and 'book-like') sequence than others which depend on choices and hypertextual links. There was no marked difference between games played by boys and girls, although the girls showed a slight preference for society-creating games. These were by no means restricted to the girls, however, with a good number of boys enjoying SIMS and girls noting preferences for quest, adventure and collecting games. As a comparison, their book reading choices (the work was carried out during the height of Harry Potter interest) showed that both boys and girls were avid readers of Rowling. Outside this preference, and in line with other readers of their age, many girls enjoyed reading Jacqueline Wilson and a similar proportion of boys mentioned Roald Dahl as a favourite author.

The aim first of all was to investigate the children's knowledge and familiarity with computer games; most particularly, to see if their experience of computer games texts could contribute to their understanding of the kinds of text structures traditionally taught in schools. Underpinning this was the view that children come to school with a wealth of text experience – capital drawn from their knowledge of popular culture – and a belief that this could be a strength in narrative composition.

WHAT IS GOING ON? THE FOCUS GROUP

After the initial surveys to discover the children's experience of different kinds of computer games, eight pupils (four boys and four girls) were selected as a focus group, who all had experience of computer games (although this was varied) and who represented the range of ages and language experience in the class. Each was interviewed and invited to choose a pseudonym. Distinctions between boys' and girls' responses have only been commented on where there was a noticeable difference.

All eight pupils said they were good at computer games, mostly citing the enjoyment of the challenge and getting to higher levels, creating societies, strategic play or problem-solving and pursuing quests. The most experienced player, who reported playing 24 hours a week (borne out by parents), said that he *was literally into the world* (of the game) *and in my own world*. All the children, except for one girl who was just learning, had been playing for at least three years; the most experienced player since he was three. The boys generally reported spending more time playing each week than the girls (see Table 4.1).

All of the group reported younger and older siblings and parents or caregivers as players (with a balance of females and males), although the most experienced player is the only one in his home who plays computer games. There was interesting variation in the ways that these young players reported learning to play. In some cases they thought that they had learned by a combination of factors, citing:

- family members and friends as key instructors, most often *telling me which buttons to press* and watching more experienced players (five mentions);
- reading the manual or instructions for the specific game (three mentions);
- the computer as teacher: *they tell you what to do* (tutorials with pop-up windows and voice-over) (two mentions);
- trial and error: *I just figured it out as I went along* (one mention).

Table 4.1 Focus group survey responses: reported time spent per week playing computer games by 8–9-year-olds

Name	Boy/Girl	Hours spent per week playing computer games
Mary	Girl	Learning – less than an hour
Leonie	Girl	1–2 hrs
Alicia	Girl	$2\frac{1}{2}$ hrs
John	Boy	4–5 hrs
Selvia	Girl	5 hrs
Joseph	Boy	11–12 hrs
Jonnie	Boy	12 hrs
Tyson	Boy	24 hrs

When asked to describe the difference between a story in a book and a computer game story, most drew a distinction between the moving pictures in computer games and books where there are no pictures so that 'You can let your imagination run wild'. Other responses included:

> They make computer games stories different – you can't carry along with the same story – they do more challenges.

> They sometimes change to make more levels – you don't get the levels in a story ... like in *Lord of the Rings*.

> A story in a book you can only imagine – you can't see ... can't get into it because you can't experience how they're feeling. In computer games you can experience things – what it's like to be in the position of the player.

> I get absorbed in a book – not in computer games.

These responses indicate an implicit sense of the different affordances of game and print narratives and hint at some of the intriguing flow between immersed and engaged playing and reading (Douglas and Hargadon, cited in Mackey, 2004), where *immersion* suggests a full commitment to the world of the text and *engagement* indicates an ability to move in and out of the text world, taking 'an extra-textual perspective on the text' (Mackey, 2004: 53). The ability to be 'in charge' of the game narrative (albeit directed by the game itself) allows the interplay of immersion and engagement which is a strong contributory element to critical reading.

The last question in the interview asked 'If you had to give advice to someone about getting better at computer games, what would you say?' There was a range of responses, but overall responses emphasized reading the instructions, choices and selection, and persistence:

> Read instructions and get familiar with it and take one step at a time.

> Listen to the instructions and read them carefully.

> Try looking at instructions and try to select something like a secret passage.

> Get to know what the choices are ... the choices you can make.

> Keep cool; use your mind and keep trying and trying until you do it.

> Practise and you'll get better at hand/eye coordination.

Discovering a certain amount of 'what was going on' supported our initial sense of the children's substantial experience of the text structures of different kinds of computer games.

TRADITIONAL TALES AND FRAME NARRATIVES

Traditional tales often have predictable narrative structure: someone has to overcome something, often with a little help, and at the end of the story is often in a better position than at the beginning (Bearne, 1996 and 2000; Propp, 1958; Goldthwaite, 1996). However, there is rarely a sequel. We do not hear about the further adventures of Cinderella once she has become a princess, or life in the house made of bricks once the pigs have got rid of the wolf. Frame narratives, on the other hand, are constructed as a series of free-standing short stories integrated into a novel (Mark, 1994). Often the individual adventures are framed by a focus on the central character, who provides the interest of the narrative as a whole. Whilst the frame novel is perhaps the more familiar form, there is a long-standing oral tradition of short stories which make up a continuing narrative: the Hodja stories from the Middle East or Anansi stories, for example. In print form, *Just William* or *Matilda* are examples of frame stories where each chapter follows a similar structure to the 'problem-solving' of traditional tales, but where the individual adventure of the chapter is one in a series which makes up a whole novel. Quest computer games are very like these kinds of frame narratives: the identified central character and the expectations and regularities of the stories provide a good deal of the appeal to young readers and players. Despite criticisms of weak characterization and thin plots (Berger, cited in Marsh and Millard, 2003), quest-type computer game plots are reminiscent of oral and written optimistic and 'youthful' fantasies (Whitley, 2000). Whilst there is a strong element of predictability, each episode presents a problem to be solved, a quest to be followed.

The aim of this series of lessons was to explore continuities between school and out-of-school text experiences. We wanted to look for indications of intertextuality or fusion between different areas of young people's narrative experience (Beavis, 2000; Millard, 2003). We chose a well-known traditional story and a frame computer narrative as the basis for the five weeks' work. Starting with *Red Riding Hood*, the sessions moved on to use a *Lara Croft* narrative as a basis for the children's writing. *Red Riding Hood* was known by all the children so gave a common starting point. As well as familiarity, however, it has some similar features to the *Lara Croft* computer narrative which would be used later. Each has a girl as the central character and each is about a journey with potential hazards requiring some resourcefulness from the protagonist (see Table 4.2). One important difference is that in *Red Riding Hood*, depending on the version, there is the possibility of another character rescuing the girl and, as already mentioned, *Red Riding Hood* is a completed tale. Another difference is that the traditional tale is associated with either a print or an orally told version, whereas *Lara Croft* is familiar through images, most of them on screen. There is also a difference in the ability of the central character to influence events.

Table 4.2 Comparison of narrative features of *Red Riding Hood* and *Lara Croft* story

Narrative feature	Red Riding Hood	Lara Croft computer story
Central character	Unaware of the hazards of the journey	Resourceful and ready for hazards
Task	To take a present to grandma	To solve strategic problems to get artefact/code/message
Oppositional Character (enemy/villain)	Wolf – cunning and devious. Specifically wants to harm central character	Guards – indiscriminately hostile and aggressive. Will harm anyone who attempts to get into the guarded area
Complication	Central character duped by enemy in disguise	Unexpected hazards/ blocked access
Helper(s)	Woodcutter	Electronic devices/ personal resources or skills of central character
Resolution	Closure. Happy ever after	Particular problem solved and new adventure signalled

Where Red Riding Hood is passive, a target for a familiar type of predator, *Lara Croft* is active and resourceful – able to use both her wits and her physical prowess.

In the first session after the surveys were completed, the children were asked to draw a representation of the story of *Red Riding Hood* as a computer game. They later wrote instructions for their game and then wrote the story. Of course, asking children to draw a computer game in the two dimensions of paper somewhat distorts the possibility of finding out their awareness of three-dimensional structures, but even so, their drawings revealed a great deal about their knowledge of the grammar of computer games. In the initial interviews, choice was one of the key features identified by the children's evaluations as providing satisfaction. This is an important difference between the *Red Riding Hood* and *Lara Croft* stories: the traditional tale offers very little choice, except, perhaps, in the route taken through the woods, whereas choice is a key feature of computer narratives.

It was instructive, then, in trying to find indications of awareness of the children's knowledge of differences between the text structures of written and computer narratives, to see how far the children drew on each as they planned their computer game versions of *Red Riding Hood*. There were interesting differences in some of the reflections of games knowledge evident in their plans. In a fusion (Millard, 2003) of the narrative timeline of the traditional tale and the spatial representation possible in a computer game, the children used the interactive linear elements essential to computer games, the language of Internet game cheats and oral interactions with peers, as well as the layouts and structures of the support booklets that accompany each game.

Each plan maintained the traditional story timeline to provide an overarching narrative essential to good game play. On closer inspection, it seems that the children transformed specific elements of the narrative, such as walking through the forest, meeting the wolf or collecting flowers for Grandma to provide interactive levels of game play. Leonie (Figure 4.1) uses a 'collecting' theme to move through the narrative and includes the typical game devices of hidden doors and extra lives hidden in boxes: *Little Red Riding Hood and the woodcutter have to look for the trap door* and *she has to jump on boxes and some have points and lives.* Cut scenes (top left and bottom left) provide the back story at the beginning and end of the narrative.

One of the most curious inclusions in the plans were the small written 'cut scenes', as shown in Leonie's plan, imitating full video scenes intended to provide back stories at the opening of the game, link levels in the narrative and provide a resolution. This device was predominantly used by girls in their plans to add extra detail and orient the narrative. Whilst with such a small sample it is difficult to suggest generalities, the use of written narrative background may reflect the girls' familiarity with cut scenes from video or DVDs.

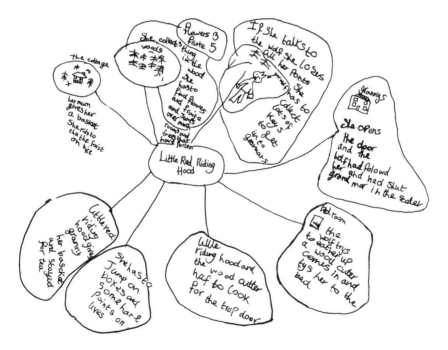

Figure 4.1 Leonie's computer game drawing.

Those children with the greatest understanding of the elements necessary to a games narrative added a range of choices in each level leading to positive or negative consequences. Tyson's plan (Figure 4.2) shows the most sophisticated options for a player at each level, reflecting knowledge gained from considerable personal time spent playing games. On arrival at Grandma's house, the player can either encounter a ghost, which means having to throw stones to save the game character from danger, accruing points for the accuracy of the shot, or take the traditional line of asking Grandma questions about her appearance. However, if one of the questions is incorrectly remembered, the player will *lose powers*.

Throughout all the children's computer game plans, repeated motifs like chases to beat the wolf to Grandma's house, timed challenges, collecting objects to overcome puzzles later in the game, hidden levels and doors, hidden objects, obstacles and problems showed their ability to merge the features of traditional narrative with a game format.

As well as using familiar aspects of narrative structure in their plans, the children drew on the specific language associated with games. Imperative verb commands typical of and specific to games texts were used to describe

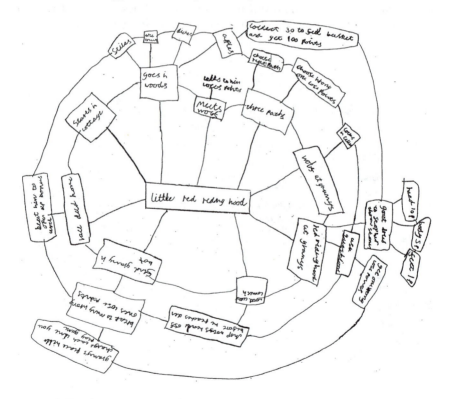

Figure 4.2 Tyson's computer game drawing.

the game play at each level. Verbs such as *collect, get, avoid, kill, jump* could have been drawn from different text sources: walk-throughs or 'cheats' that guide a player through the pitfalls of a game depend on these verbs to enable a player to read and react at speed in a tricky situation. These verbs are also common to oral texts that are part of the social experience of game play. Siblings, friends and older onlookers shout frustrated commands to the player to direct them in their choices or guide them through different levels. Certain games, such as *Sonic Adventures*, have a disembodied voice accessed in training levels or through command buttons that provide similar commands for a lone player. Even with the restrictions of the drawn plan, the children showed considerable grasp of the language and structures of games narratives.

COMPARING STORIES

After they had written their *Red Riding Hood* stories, the class were asked to work in groups with images taken from a *Lara Croft* game. There were ten images in all, which followed varying pathways through the game, requiring the children to make choices based on the visual information in the images. They had to choose a series of images to construct a coherent narrative. The format in Figure 4.3 was used to help them choose and record their choices.

There were two images to choose from for A, then four for B and so on as the narrative branches. The children needed to read the images carefully to identify how they would make choices to develop the story. Figures 4.4 and 4.5 show two different chosen routes through the stories based on image selection. Both provide evidence of games experience, with Mary's use of finding hidden codes and screen-based movement and Tyson's introduction to the narrative with an explicit instruction to 'watch cut scene'.

Evaluations at the end of the sessions showed that almost all the class enjoyed writing their *Lara Croft* narratives more than any of the other activities, indicating the opportunity to choose as an important satisfaction factor. During the activity itself, however, there was some discomfort, particularly from girls, because of a sense of insecurity in knowing how to make these choices. Their unease may, of course, have been related to lack of familiarity with this kind of image-based choice activity, but observations showed that for some it was a matter of lack of knowledge of text structure. Examples of the *Red Riding Hood* and *Lara Croft* narratives show intriguing differences. Some writers, girls particularly, found retelling the traditional narrative as a computer game story an easier task and were much less assured in handling the elements of a visually generated story. Others, mostly boys, although there were some girls, were able to present

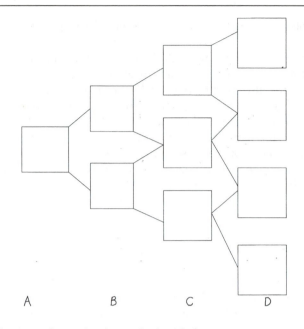

Figure 4.3 Planning and recording format for *Lara Croft* narrative.

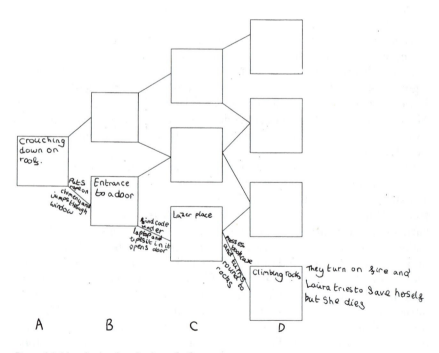

Figure 4.4 Mary's plan for the *Lara Croft* story.

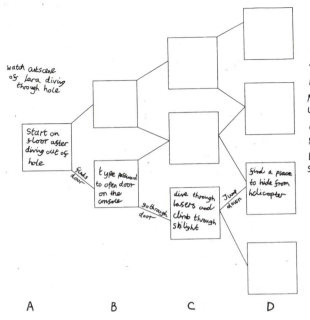

The handwritten text within the figure reads:

watch cutscene of lara diving through hole

Start on floor after diving out of hole

finds door

type password to open door on the console

go through door

dive through lasers and climb through skylight

Jump down

find a place to hide from helicopter

after hiding jump on the helicopters ladder when the pilot doesn't notice. climb up and knock out pilot take parachute and freefall until in right place. pull cord on parachute and fall down safely. run back to manor without being spotted by patrols or choppers

A   B   C   D

Figure 4.5 Tyson's plan for the *Lara Croft* story.

a competent traditional narrative but showed much greater vitality and voice in their stories based on images of the computer game. The following sections give some details of aspects of narrative which were either enhanced or restricted by the source story.

Action, sound and perspective

Overall, the *Red Riding Hood* stories obeyed the conventions of traditional tales, although with some of the flavour of games. One key difference was in the visual, aural and movement elements of the stories. Katy, for example, tells her *Red Riding Hood* story with clear third-person narrative structure:[2]

> Little Red Riding Hood's granny was ill. Her mother had tried delivering some good food to her, but had dropped it all on the way, so she asked Little Red Riding Hood to go and pick up everything she had dropped and deliver them to grandma...
>
> ...She set off to find everything. But first she had a choice, there were three paths but little Red Riding Hood went straight for the middle one. Her first item was an apple, second a cake and her third was a carrot.

Her second story, *The Philosicus Jewel*, based on the *Lara Croft* images, is conveyed through dialogue, including inner speech, giving the reader clues about narrative development through the character's thoughts. She also draws on film experience, with a whiff of *Raiders of the Lost Ark* and a great deal of sound and movement:

> 'Lottie, your mission is to return the Philosicus jewel to King Silomdun, the King of Egypt.' said Shandy.
> 'Yes Sir. I'm ready,' I said. I jumped out of the LFS building, landing in a crouch. I ran across the floor and through a door. There's another door. It won't budge, I've got to crack the code. Mmmm. Ahha. A computer, I wonder what the clue is. It's King Silomdun. Simple. Egypt. Yes!!!
> 'Wow, a laser protected museum. Right. Simple.'

Although Katy uses finding and choosing as organizing elements of her *Red Riding Hood* story, the physical movement of her second story, as well as the move into first-person narrative, provide a more immediate, vital narrative voice. Similarly, Alicia finds the shift towards a visually generated story liberates her to use more dynamic expression. Her *Red Riding Hood* story echoes the expected structure of the traditional tale and the ending is the only place where she uses action verbs to any great extent:

> Once upon a time there lived a little girl. Her name was Little Red Riding Hood. Her name was really Rose. One day her mother said...
> ...The wolf jumped out of bed and chased Rose round the house. The woodcutter heard her screaming and came in and chopped the wolf's head off. Rose let grandma out and they lived happily ever after.

In her visually generated narrative, she uses a traditional opening and ending but this story is much more evocative of the dimensions of a screen-based story:

> One day Jenna Sendell was looking for trouble while she was crouching on a roof. She heard a noise, a rustling sound it was. Jenna jumped down. She had a thick rope in her backpack. She took it out and flung it on the chimney next door. She took hold of it and swung it over and smashed through one of the windows to see if she could find out what the noise was. The noise was a beeping sound coming from a big door next to it there was a laptop...
> ...She looked up and saw a window, She did a double flip and smashed through the window. An alarm went off. Jenna was running because a helicopter was chasing her... [Alicia's ellipsis]

The verbs *crouching, flung, swung, smashed*, the *rustling* and *beeping* and the visual directions, rather like the vectors of visual image, direct the reader's gaze: *next to it, looked up, did a double flip, running because a helicopter was chasing her* all add to the dimensions – and the urgency – of the story.

Although Jane also draws on the visual and movement in her *Red Riding Hood* story:

> ...In the wood there was lots of corners, wide ditches, high stiles, and stones. She loved jumping over the stiles, collecting stones and leaping wide ditches. SUDDENLY! A wolf with pointed ears and a long tail jumped out from behind a tall tree...

she is less successful in shaping her second story. She tries to use familiar narrative devices, as in her opening and use of 'suddenly', but is not comfortable in linking the episodes of the visually generated story:

> Once upon a time in a faraway land there lived an adventurous girl, her name was Meg. She loved going on adventures. One day she was crouching very low on the highest building in London. SUDDENLY she heard a noise, it sounded like a police car coming to capture her. She suddenly got a piece of rope from her backpack and tied a knot in the centre of it, waved it in the air...

In her first story she uses *jumping* and *leaping* and directs the reader's eyes: *from behind a tall tree* and in her second *crouching, waved it in the air*, but she is much less secure in narrative structure. This may reflect her comparative lack of experience with computer games. Her survey responses showed that she only used the computer to carry out activities like *Art Attack* and she indicated that she preferred watching videos and television. Her use of devices like 'suddenly' and the story openings suggest a greater familiarity with told stories or those with a more 'traditional' narrative structure.

Orientation of the narrative

Successful stories have to orient the reader, explaining some of the *where, who, why, what* and *how*. To be able to direct a narrative in this way implies a secure sense of structure: where the story might go and how it will end. One of the key differences between the successful and less successful *Lara Croft* stories was the extent of assured orientation. In some children's work there were noticeable differences between the two stories. In her choice of repetitions, Emma blends the rhythms of traditional narrative with some of the features of computer games:

> ...Whilst she was walking she saw a row of stinging nettles. She had to jump over them. She did. Then there was 6 lakes. She had to swim across, so she did. Then there was 5 trees to climb, so she did...

However, she is much less assured in the visually generated story, seeming unsure of how to string the narrative together:

> One day Jenna was crouching on a high high wall. She suddenly jumped and then ran. Her heavy back-pack slowed her down. Jenna looked in her bag. She had a drink. Then she took out some heavy weights then set off to the street. She is crouching on a roof she was waiting for some guards to go...

John is much more successful. His first story is very game-like:

> Once upon a time there was a girl called Little Red Riding Hood or Ribon for short.
> Ribon's grandma was very ill. So she decided to take a basket of cupcakes to grandma.
> So Ribon took cupcakes to her grandma and she met some obstacles on her way.
> There were spider webs, paths, woodpiles and stiles.
> But the most dangerous of them all was a BIG BAD WOLF!
> Ribon met the wolf and the wolf chase ribbon into his trap. Fortunately for Little Red Riding Hood the wolf had dropped the key...

Like a computer game walk-through he takes the reader through the sequence of obstacles that the character has to overcome and uses upper-case letters to create dramatic tension. His second, visually generated story, however, is even more secure, orienting the reader with a humorous verbal cut-scene prequel:

> After escaping from Luemcets's killer bunny factory our hero has landed on a roof top in China. She must go through the local museum and on the way avoid patrols. Lara slipped into the museum.

John is quite clearly familiar not only with the discourse of the computer game story as shown by his use of 'our hero', but succinctly gives the reader information which fills in the past and signposts where the narrative is going: 'she must go through...and on the way avoid patrols'. These three sentences show very assured narrative direction and control.

Tyson was the most experienced player in the class. His *Red Riding Hood* plan showed a good grasp of the narrative complexities of games structures. In his writing he is also very assured, offering clear cut-scene orientation:

> One sunny morning, Sarah Ravenscroft, also known as Red Riding Hood, was in her cottage. Her mum gave her a basket and told her that the wood was covered in stiles, trees, ditches and apples that she could collect...

The transduction (Kress, 1997) of games motifs to the traditional story is accompanied by aspects of action, sound and perspective:

> Little Red Riding Hood avoided all the obstacles and collected apples all through the wood. Just as she was getting to the three paths she saw a wolf. 'ello girlie', he said but Sarah moved on. 'You ain't goin' nowhere', as he blocked Sarah's path. 'Get lost', as she threw a stone at him. The wolf was dizzy and Red Riding Hood ran on...

Avoiding and *collecting* lead Red Riding Hood *through* the wood until she is confronted by the wolf (with a distinct stereotypical 'villain' accent!), her path is *blocked* and she has to *throw* a stone which results in the wolf being *dizzy*. The choice of language directs the reader to the visual and spatial elements of the episode. The end of this story indicates an interesting merger between the traditional narrative and the frame narrative. Where a traditional tale usually has a 'closed' resolution with no opportunity for another episode, frame stories depend on the possibility of repetition. Tyson provides an 'open' ending to his Red Riding Hood story:

> [the woodcutter] raced Red Riding Hood home and she beat him

blending the traditional tale with the structure of the frame story of a computer narrative.

Tyson's *Lara Croft* narrative has features in common with his *Red Riding Hood*, although it has distinct elements drawn from a computer-game-inspired story. As Figure 4.6 shows, he heads the story *Level 1*, locates it in New York with a specific time and provides a title. These are aspects of screen information which help orientation by visual means.

However, Tyson shows his understanding of the written form by his introduction, orienting the reader skilfully and succinctly:

> After finishing her training, Lara Croft is asked to take a mission to retrieve the jewel of Imhotep from the armed thugs disguised as officers.

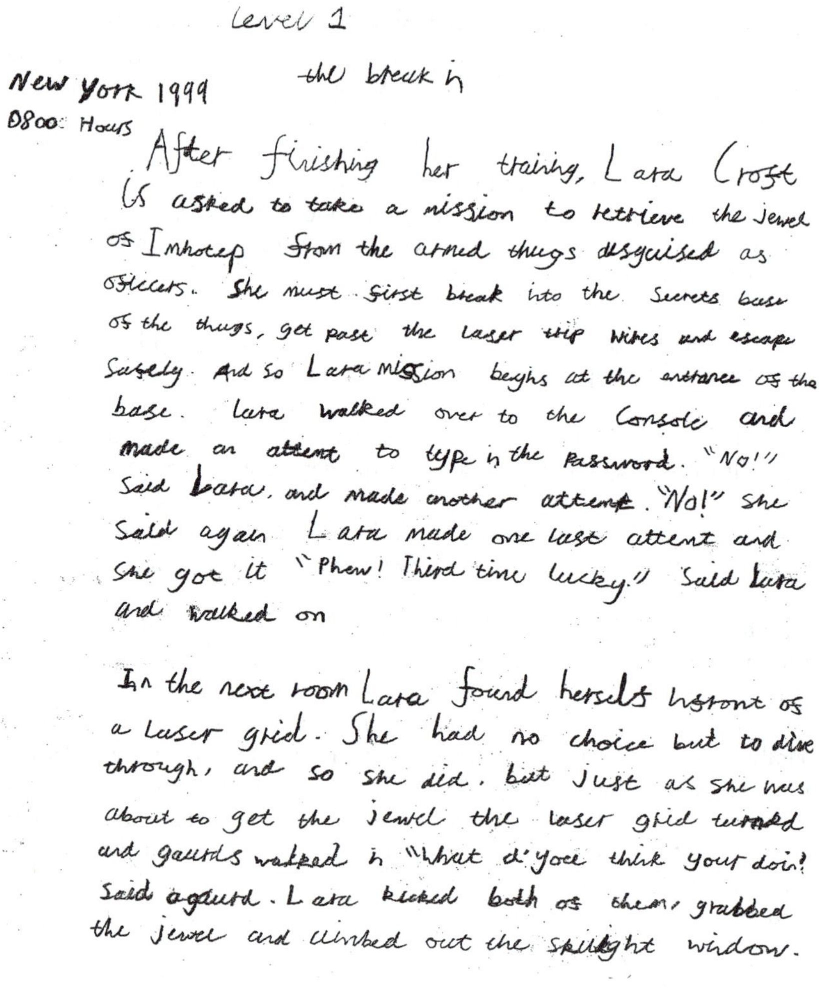

Level 1

New York 1999   ~~the~~ break in
0800: Hours

After finishing her training, Lara Croft is asked to take a mission to retrieve the jewel of Imhotep from the armed thugs disguised as officers. She must first break into the secrets base of the thugs, get past the laser trip wires and escape safely. And so Lara mission begins at the entrance of the base. Lara walked over to the console and made an attempt to type in the password. "No!" said Lara, and made another attempt. "No!" she said again. Lara made one last attempt and she got it "Phew! Third time lucky." Said Lara and walked on

In the next room Lara found herself infront of a laser grid. She had no choice but to dive through, and so she did. but just as she was about to get the jewel the laser grid turned and guards walked in. "What d'you think your doin?" Said a guard. Lara kicked both of them, grabbed the jewel and climbed out the skylight window.

Figure 4.6 Tyson's *Lara Croft* story opening.

She must first break into the secret base of the thugs, get past the laser trip wires and escape safely...

In his use of the 'armed thugs disguised as officers' and the list of the obstacles Lara has to overcome, Tyson puts the reader in the position of knowing just what will be required if the game – and the story – are to be successfully completed. He then shifts the direction of the narrative with a change of tense:

> And so Lara's mission begins at the entrance of the base. Lara walked over to the console and made an attempt to type in the password...

Tyson takes the story forward with an episode which has a very strong similarity to his account of Red Riding Hood's encounter with the wolf: in both cases, the oppositional character(s) are hostile and aggressive. He has forsaken the cunning plausibility of the wolf, who specifically wants to harm Red Riding Hood, for the more stereotypical 'villain' of the computer game story:

> In the next room Lara found herself in front of a laser grid. She had no choice but to dive through, and so she did. But just as she was about to get the jewel the laser grid turned and guards walked in. 'What d'you think you're doin', said a guard. Lara kicked both of them, grabbed the jewel and climbed out of the skylight window...

The end of the story is presented in the open form of a frame narrative with a clear indication of the next episode:

> She then pulled the cord on the parachute and sailed down safely. She ran back to the manor without being spotted by patrols or choppers.
>
> Level 2 The Sea Adventure

Tyson's two narratives are powerful examples of how young writers can use the capital of their popular cultural text experience in classroom work. In a fusion of game text and the classroom requirements for writing narratives, he shows how knowledge of computer game narratives adds energy to storytelling.

SUMMARY

As might be expected, there were variations in the assurance with which different children used their computer game knowledge to construct written narratives. However, their plans and stories showed that a great deal 'is going on' as they merge their home-developed text experience of games with the curriculum requirement to be able to construct a coherent narrative. The computer game 'take' on a traditional story revealed children's ability to draw on sound, location and action to enliven retellings of familiar stories. In the visually generated stories there was much greater use of dialogue, typical of written narratives based on moving-image sources to drive the narrative forward (Burn, forthcoming; McClay, 2002). This may be an amalgam of different kinds of visual text experience from film, DVD, computer game and even comics.

One feature which does seem to reflect computer game experience directly is the intriguing introduction of written cut scenes to orient the reader to the story. Beavis (2001) argues that these aspects of games texts 'teach' narrative structures, using clips to provide narrative plot lines and 'to indicate progress made' (Beavis, 2001: 147). Those children who were less experienced in playing seemed less secure with the structures of quest game narratives, which meant that narrative orientation and development caused more problems. The more assured players were able to move between different media, using their player experience to modify and enliven both their retellings of a given story and their own constructions of a visually inspired narrative. Although the planning activity offering choices of pathways based on images was a little tricky to grasp at first, the children's *Lara Croft* writing showed strong elements of sound, action and perspective or location. In terms of knowledge of different text structures, the writing demonstrated very clearly how children can use the imaginative, performative and regulated patterns drawn from playing computer games to enhance the pace, structure, viewpoint and voice of written classroom narratives.

The work described here suggests the importance of getting to know about children's knowledge of texts drawn from their out-of-school experience. These young writers moved between the textual worlds available in the classroom and at home, integrating their different experiences of oral, written and image-based stories. This suggests the urgency of providing opportunities for children with different home experiences to draw on their varied 'funds of knowledge' (Moll *et al.*, 1992) so that there are opportunities for those whose experience has been largely non-book-based to explore their own interests in school too.

NOTES

1 Our thanks to Jane Brooks and the children in her class, the headteacher and other colleagues in Rickling Green Primary School, Essex.
2 All children's spellings have been corrected but layout and punctuation preserved as in their originals.

REFERENCES

Bearne, E. (1996) 'Myth and Legend: the oldest language?', in Styles, M., Bearne, E. and Watson, V. *After Alice: exploring children's literature*. London: Cassell, pp. 143–52.

Bearne, E. (2000) 'Myth, legend, culture and morality', in Bearne, E. and Watson, V. *Where Texts and Children Meet*. London: Routledge, pp. 183–97.

Beavis, C. (2000) 'Computer games as class readers: Developing literacy skills for the twenty first century', *The English and Media Magazine*, **41**, Spring.

Beavis, C. (2001) 'Digital culture, digital literacies: Expanding the notions of text', in Beavis, C. and Durrant, C. (eds) *P(ICT)ures of English: Teachers, learners and technology*. Wakefield Press, Adelaide, pp. 145–61.

Burn, A. (forthcoming) 'Potter-Literacy – from book to game and back again; literature, film, game and cross-media literacy', in *Papers: Explorations into Children's Literature*, **14**(3).

Douglas, J.Y. and Hargadon, A. (2001) 'The Pleasures of Immersion and Engagement: Schemas, Scripts, and the Fifth Business', *Digital Creativity*, **12**(3): 153–66, cited in Mackey (2004).

Facer, K., Furlong, J., Furlong, R. and Sutherland, R. (2003) *ScreenPlay: Children and Computing in the Home*. London: RoutledgeFalmer.

Gee, J.P. (2003) *What Video Games Have to Teach Us about Learning and Literacy*. New York: Palgrave Macmillan.

Goldthwaite, J. (1996) *The Natural History of Make-Believe*. Oxford: Oxford University Press.

Kress, G. (1997) *Before Writing: rethinking the paths to literacy*. London: Routledge.

Mackey, M. (2004) 'Children reading and interpreting stories in print, films and computer games', in Evans op. cit. pp. 48–58.

Mark, J. (1994) 'The Patrick Hardy Lecture' in *Signal*, No 75 J. Stroud, Glos: Thimble Press, pp. 19–36.

Marsh, J. and Millard, E. (2003) *Literacy and Popular Culture in the Classroom*. Reading: National Centre for Language and Literacy, The University of Reading.

McClay, J. (2002) 'Hidden "Treasure": New Genres, New Media and the Teaching of Writing', *English in Education*, **36**(1): 46–55.

Millard, E. (2003) 'Towards a literacy of fusion: new times, new teaching and learning?', *Reading literacy and language*, **37**(1): 3–8.

Moll, L., Amanti, C., Neff, D. and Gonzalez, N. (1992) 'Funds of Knowledge for Teaching: Using a Qualitative Approach to Connect Homes and Classrooms', *Theory into Practice*, **31**(2): 132–41.

Propp, V. (1958 first translation) *Morphology of the Folktale*. Austin, TX: University of Texas Press.

Smidt, S. (2003) 'Six fingers with feeling: play, literacy and politics', in Bearne, E., Dombey, H. and Grainger, T. (eds) *Classroom Interactions in Literacy*. Maidenhead: Open University Press.

Whitley, D. (2000) 'Fantasy narratives and growing up', in Bearne. E. and Watson, V. *Where Texts and Children Meet*. London: Routledge, pp. 172–82.

GAMES REFERRED TO

Lara Croft Tomb Raider, Computer and Video Games, 2000.
Sonic Adventure, Sega, 1999.

Chapter 5

A sign of the times: looking critically at popular digital writing

Guy Merchant

Screens are the new surfaces for written communication and have rapidly become a ubiquitous feature of everyday life. Screen-based communication is now widely used to establish and maintain relationships, in service encounters, in the routines of work, and in our private lives. In fact, reading and writing with this new technology are deeply embedded in changing social practices – practices which involve the production and consumption of different kinds of texts, and the development of new kinds of relationships and interactions. Access and control of new tools, and the development of specific behaviours, skills and attitudes are prerequisites for participation in these new communicative practices. And, if the screen is the medium of new times, digital writing is the sign of the times. Those children and young people who are growing up with digital technology are often the innovators and adapters, incorporating the new into their lives, or exploiting and adapting it for their own purposes; and yet literacy educators, and others with an academic interest in literacy, are only just beginning to grapple with the changing world of written communication. They are learning that digital writing is an inescapable part of modern life and as such warrants careful critical attention. This chapter identifies some of the main avenues of enquiry in the field of digital writing, focusing particularly on their relevance to those involved in education.

THE TECHNOLOGY OF WRITING

In order to think more critically about the nature of digital writing, it is important to develop an understanding of the relationship between writing and technology. Disentangling the concept of *technology* from everyday uses of the term *new technology* provides us with a useful starting point. The word technology is often used to describe the ways in which we make and use tools to increase our control and understanding of the material environment. Writing itself, by this definition, is a technology, as Vygotsky (1980) observed. He described writing as the production of 'mnemotechnic symbols': a technology for remembering, recording and organizing our social experience. Clearly, in contemporary society, writing is a technology which performs a wide range of personal and social functions and has become an important means by which we represent ourselves to ourselves and construct possible worlds (Kress, 1997).

However, writing is not just a technology in its own right; it is also dependent upon technology for its production. The history of writing is also a history of invention, in which different cultures have developed new materialities for mark-making, experimenting with new tools for writing and new surfaces for writing on (Hannon, 2000). A landmark in human achievement was the combination of paper-binding techniques and the wooden printing block, leading to the production of the world's oldest printed book (the Dunhuang *Diamond Sutra*: AD 868). Here a new technology served the needs of a particular social group and opened up new possibilities in meaning-making and communication.

If we look at the history of writing (Ong, 1982; Sampson, 1985; Sacks, 2003) we can see how it always involves a physical act, a way of leaving a mark on the environment – and this act of mark-making involves skilled use of writing tools. From this point of view, writing has a long and intimate relationship with the technologies of production. Some of the earliest known examples of writing are the impressions of wooden or stone implements on clay tablets. A very different technique is being used in the production of this text, with the gentle pressure of fingers on the alphabetic keyboard of a laptop. None the less, both are physical acts, involving a particular posture and quite specific use of the hands (Wilson, 1998). In fact, the relationship between our hands, the tools we use for writing and the surfaces we write on are very significant in the development of new kinds of writing.

Most screen-based writing uses a keyboard and pointing device (such as a mouse); usually the alphabet is beneath the hands, and the text is displayed vertically in front of the writer. Variations are seen in portable devices such as the Personal Digital Assistant (PDA), which often requires the use of a stylus. In contrast, mobile phone users generally use their thumbs to text, as they work with fewer keys set in close proximity to one another. Mackey (2003) writes about the changing role played by our hands in reading digital texts and clearly we can now see how this is also true for digital writing, as the affordances of new tools suggest new ways of creating and shaping texts through movements of hands, fingers and thumbs (Merchant, 2004).

But it is also the case that digital writing changes the relationship between the writer and the text. The once direct relationship between hand movement and the mark on the page has now been transformed. Although we can touch the screen, or print out our writing, the text is essentially a trace in the digital circuitry, the display a flicker of pixels that merely looks like print on the screen.

Despite these quite obvious changes in the way we write and the writing tools that are used in the modern world, literacy educators and policy-makers have been slow to incorporate digital writing into their discourse. Curriculum documents that inform literacy instruction in the early years of schooling are usually predicated on the assumption that a necessary part of learning to write involves getting to grips with pencil and paper – often in a quite literal sense. But yet it is not hard to imagine a future – particularly in affluent post-industrial economies – in which such writing implements are largely redundant. I have argued elsewhere that learning about the new tools and surfaces of screen-based writing involves the understanding of some quite distinct principles (Merchant, 2005a) which are rarely recog-nized in the early years' literature. Some examples of these are shown in Table 5.1.

It seems, then, that an acknowledgement of the differences between the screen and the page as surfaces for writing and the use of new kinds of writing tools are important for curriculum designers and literacy educators alike. But, clearly, digital writing is also concerned with the creation of quite new textual forms, and it is examples of these that are considered next.

TEXTUAL INNOVATION

Popular uses of digital technology involve the creation and consumption of texts that are radically different from print-based forms. In this section, I review some of these new forms, highlighting their key characteristics. I begin by looking at the highly interactive texts produced in email, chat and SMS (short message service – commonly referred to as texting), before moving on to a consideration of discussion boards and weblogs.[1] This selection is significant because all of these forms are popular, require minimal technical expertise and are dependent on the use of writing. Whether synchronous or asynchronous, together they represent different kinds of digitally mediated interactive written discourse (Ferrara *et al.*, 1991; Werry, 1996; Merchant, 2001).

Table 5.1 Basic principles of onscreen writing

1. The remote principle – *physical actions on a keyboard or similar device control what appears on screen.*
2. The location principle – *letters, symbols or words are selected from the keyboard by touching, pressing, clicking or toggling.*
3. Pressure principle – *the weight and duration of finger/thumb pressure influences what appears on the screen.*
4. Rhythmic principle – *actions combine in rhythmical patterns and combinations to produce or modify text.*

Email is one of the most widely known and used kinds of digital writing. The fact that templates are modelled on the traditional office memo, and that the language used to describe message exchange borrows from the lexicon of the postal service, sometimes obscures the contrasts with analogous print-based communication. In fact, for many people, email has become so commonplace that its particular characteristics can be overlooked. As email comes of age, we see how it serves a wide range of purposes, from institutional control to opportunist marketing, and from everyday social contact to light relief in the workplace. Genres and sub-genres of email continue to proliferate and with them so do the linguistic markers of formality and informality, authority and power.

Most desktop computers and an increasing number of mobile devices provide access to email systems and these enable us to exchange written messages with any other user or user group whose email address is known or available. Email has been described as a 'lean medium' in that message exchange is primarily verbal and there are relatively few options with respect to how our writing is presented on screen (Tyner, 2003). Email correspondence is normally relatively brief. Longer written texts, images and sound are sent as file attachments. So what are the key characteristics of email as a form of digital writing?

First, and perhaps most importantly, email offers us a direct and immediate way of communicating. We can write and send in a matter of minutes – little wonder that the complex processes of folding paper in envelopes, finding postage stamps and locating a postbox have come to be referred to as 'snail mail'. Traditional ways of exchanging written messages are simply slower, they take longer to produce, and longer to deliver. Second, email provides us with a shared communicative space. The email text looks more or less the same wherever and whenever it is accessed. The communicative space is therefore released from the limits of time and place. In this way, email engenders a sense of co-presence (Kress, 2003). Third, email is an interactive medium in which replies are usually expected and often written on the top of the original message (Ferrara *et al.*, 1991). This can lead to a series of interlinked or chained messages which have some similarities to conversations. And, of course, at the press of a key our message can be returned or forwarded to others to include them in our conversation. Finally, like other forms of digital writing, email links easily with other electronic texts. This is partly achieved through the attachment function described above, but also through the use of hyperlinks within the text.

Although the promise of co-presence and rapid message exchange are defining features of email, the medium is essentially asynchronous. This is important, because, despite the immediacy that co-presence suggests, sending an email does not depend on the recipient being on line at a particular moment in time. However, other forms of digital communication do.

Various forms of online chat fall into this category. These highly interactive, synchronous connections, made possible with networked computers and fast connection (such as broadband), have attracted a lot of attention, particularly in the popular form of the chatroom. My own study of teenagers' use of synchronous chat (Merchant, 2001) shows how actual and virtual friendships are sustained and new relationships negotiated through these onscreen communicative practices. Of course, when teenagers are on line they deploy a whole range of new literacy skills (including the use of symbols, hyperlinks and abbreviations), but it is worth reiterating that these are mediated through rapid typing, motivated by a drive to maintain pace, relationship and the conversational flow of synchronous interaction.

Chatrooms are an arena for quite chaotic verbal interaction. This is described by Crystal (2001) as like being at a noisy cocktail party where diverse conversational threads are overheard and often disrupt any sense of discursive continuity. In chatrooms, individual turns are usually displayed on screen in a form that is rather like a dynamic playscript. Chatroom interactions occur in real time, and as a result, securing a turn in the conversation calls for speed and brevity in message production. Users often experiment with word abbreviation and non-alphabetic keyboard symbols. As Werry (1996) shows, these sorts of linguistic innovation can be seen in the synchronous chat of a wide variety of online communities and take place in different language systems. This play with language is seen in other forms of digital writing and is influenced by a range of factors which are explored below.

The key characteristic of chat is the way in which multiple users contribute to a shared textual space. Immediacy and co-presence are essential features. In a chatroom the time is 'now' (regardless of local time) and the communicative space is 'here' (regardless of the global distribution of participants). Although one can lurk in a chatroom, these virtual spaces are essentially highly interactive, and usually include a facility to engage in more focused one-to-one interaction. A particularly interesting feature of synchronous online communication is the way in which writing is used in ways more that are traditionally associated with speech.

There are many similarities between chat and instant messaging (IM). Like chat, IM takes the form of a synchronous online conversation which shows and attributes contributions as they occur in real time. IM environments display the user's contact list and provide information about which friends are on line. In comparison to chatrooms, there are more one-to-one interactions; expert users may work across several windows. Systems like AOLmessenger also allow webcam link-ups; however, despite the multimedia promise, audio messaging is comparatively rare. It is interesting to observe that, for a variety of reasons, the primary mode of message exchanged in chat is still the written word.

SMS, the system that makes mobile phone text-messaging possible, has had a huge impact on communicative practices. Although mobile phone use is highly concentrated and deeply embedded in the social lives of the under thirties, it is by no means exclusively their domain, and patterns of ownership span the adult population and are now pushing down into childhood (Livingstone and Bober, 2004). Whilst this technology has transformed telephone use, it is the add-on feature of text messaging which is of central importance to the discussion of digital writing. The portability of the mobile means that we can send a text message from our phone to another, more or less wherever we are. Whilst other forms of digital writing such as email can be accessed in a wide variety of locations, we still need to be in close proximity to an Internet connection (a cable or hub). Apart from some 'dead areas', where reception is problematic, and the territorial limitation of telephone networks, texting can be done anywhere and anytime.

The particular constraints of this medium are of interest here. Mobile screens are small: a fraction of the size of laptops and desktops, and smaller than most paper formats (such as cards, notepads and post-its). The physical act of writing involves scrolling through the small numeric pad for each letter in order to compose a message, with each screen displaying approximately 160 characters. It's not surprising, then, to recall that the early studies of texting focused on the abbreviations and creative spelling that emerged as users exchanged short messages (Shortis, 2001). The advent of predictive text has clearly had an impact here, and, at the same time, we are witnessing a rapid growth in picture messaging. Yet despite this, the original written form of text messaging remains dominant and is growing in popularity, infiltrating ever new groups at a global level (Herring, 2004). The most fluent text users treat mobile devices as a thumb-controlled technology discovering a new kind of dexterity. Recent news coverage of the 'fastest text-messager' reports James Trusler texting 160 characters in 1 minute 7 seconds – a counter to the arguments that mobile keyboards are in some way unergonomic.

Contemporary messaging technology allows users to make sophisticated choices about whether to talk, leave voice-mail, text or picture message. New sorts of communicative decisions are made, and new sorts of conventions may well arise. Ito (2003), for instance, describes how Japanese teenagers use text messaging as a precursor to phone conversations. She documents the emergence of a new sort of etiquette in which the exchange of text is a bit like a door knock, an invitation to engage in phone talk. In addition to this, it is also quite likely that subtle functional distinctions govern the decision to text or talk, although little work has yet been published in this area. So, for instance, confirming arrangements and cancelling appointments may, under certain circumstances, be more easy to conduct in the written form of a text message.

The distinctive features of text messaging are its speed and brevity, and the ways in which it combines with other modes of communication. Texting is characteristically informal, and normally involves friends and family members. Most texting is a one-to-one communication and acts as an extension to the phone call. After all, to text someone, their details must be in your address book – and the key part of the address is the phone number. However, as mobiles become more popular and more sophisticated, new possibilities emerge. Rheingold (2003) documents how mobiles can be used to coordinate groups or 'flashmobs'. Large retail corporations are poised to develop marketing by text. These are early indications that the essentially private world of texting may not remain that way for long.

The growing popularity of weblogs (or blogs) – relatively simple publishing tools which allow users (often at no cost) to publish on the web – is of particular interest here. Blogs are essentially online journals which are regularly updated, often with fairly brief postings. They have become a very popular form of digital text. In fact, experts estimate that there are literally millions of blogs worldwide (Blogcount.com, 2005) serving the needs of a wide range of individuals and affinity groups. Figure 5.1 shows a page from a knitter's blog: Wendy Knits. This is a fairly typical blog design, with hyperlinks shown along the sidebar.

Clues to the writer's nationality, gender, lifestyle, class and so on are inscribed both in the visual and verbal information of this extract.

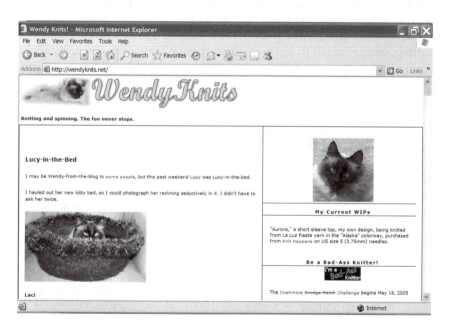

Figure 5.1 Wendy Knits.

Of course, the reader may have been misled, but none the less the author of this weblog has gone to some length to communicate a quite specific identity. At the same time, of course, there is plenty of information that is withheld (other details about the writer's daily life) or simply alluded to.

Blogs, as a form of digital writing, are characterized by a tendency to blend the personal with the public. The similarities with more conventional diary-writing are reasonably clear, but yet to write a blog is a bit like displaying your diary in a shop window, for friends and passers-by to read at their leisure. Here the question of audience is problematic. The language used in blogs tends to be informal or even playful in quality, and topics often blur distinctions between the serious and the frivolous. Although multiple authorship is possible, most blogs are produced by individuals. Readers can usually post comments and in so doing make their contribution to the blog, as in Figure 5.2.

An important aspect of digital technology lies in the ways in which it is used to demonstrate the user's relationship to popular culture. On discussion boards, subscribers' contributions often have the function of providing nuanced orientations to cultural products. We can find discussion boards on an extremely wide range of topics from politics to video-gaming. Discussion boards are typified by multiple use and the text is co-constructed by subscribers who read and reply. The written language can be informal, and playful and conversational threads develop as users interact around emerging areas of shared interest.

Examples of new genres of digital text suggest a need to reconceptualize writing, our approach to learning about writing, as well as our ideas about teaching and using writing in the classroom. In the following section, I identify some of the key characteristics of these digital texts as a reflection on the changing nature of written communication.

RECONCEPTUALIZING WRITING

Innovation in the production and consumption of digital writing shows how traditional relationships between readers, writers and texts are radically changing. Many aspects of writing that were taken for granted in the era of print are now no longer so fixed. A number of academics have provided accounts of these shifts and here I present a synthesis of this work, drawing specifically from Kress's social semiotic approach (Kress, 2003), Lankshear and Knobel's work on new literacies (Lankshear and Knobel, 2003), Prensky's work on the games generation (Prensky, 2001) and Carrington's work on textual change (Carrington, 2004). However, it is important to preface this with the recognition that these changes are not in and of themselves a *result* of technological innovation – for that would be to

My Last Kitty Bed

Wasn't that a poem by Robert Browning? No, that was *My Last Duchess*. Okay, here's my version.

That's my last kittybed standing on the form,
Looking as if it were felted. I call
That piece a wonder, now: my hands
Worked busily a day, and there she stands.
Will't please you sit and look at her?
For I feel as though she's not near felted.
The size of that pictured countenance,
The depth and breadth of its earnest fuzziness,
But to myself it seems to be,
Still a mite too large.
And seemed as if it needed,
Another cycle in the hot water wash.

Okay, so I'm not a poet. I finished the kitty bed last Tuesday, and ran it through three cycles to felt it, then popped it on top of a large cylindrical object (in this particular case my Tupperware pie carrier with a beach towel wrapped around it).

On Friday I took it off its felting form and plopped it on the table to scrutinize it critically. It still seemed a tad large to me. I turned away for a moment, and when I turned back, this is what I saw.

Clearly, the expert pronounces it usable. But just out of spite, I ran it through another wash cycle.

Posted by wendy at March 28, 2005 05:43 PM | TrackBack

Hej Wendy!

There´s a demand here from Sweden to see how well Lucy´s eyes match that new kitty bed. Another photo, please!

Posted by: [sender] on March 29, 2005 10:01 AM

Figure 5.2 My last kitty bed.

subscribe to a form of technological determinism (Robins and Webster, 1999). It is more that new tools for communication have emerged out of a changing social world which places people in different relationships with one another and even engenders an altered sense of who we are (Giddens, 1991). So, communication needs have changed along with the capacity to communicate in new ways. Yet at the same time the power of digital media in general, and digital writing in particular, has begun to reinforce the sense that we are witnessing the emergence of a new social order.

The brief overview of textual innovation given above suggests some of the changes that are taking place. Most obviously, texts themselves are changing. The following trends become quite clear:

- A move from the fixed to the fluid: the text is no longer contained between the covers or by the limits of the page.
- Texts are revised, updated, added to and appended (and often archived).
- Genres borrow freely, hybridize and mutate.
- Texts become collaborative and multivocal, with replies, links, posted comments and borrowing.
- Reading and writing paths are non-linear and epistemology is rhyzomic.
- Multimedia allows for a rich interplay of modes as texts become multimodal.

These trends are established by, and in turn help to establish, new kinds of relationships between writers and readers. This redefinition of the writer/ reader relationship is reflected in:

- a move from the control of the author to the control of the reader;
- ways in which readers can easily become writers;
- textual interaction and collaboration which results in shared authorship;
- the emergence of multiple and diverse affinity groups;
- the new reading paths and writing processes associated with screen-based texts;
- the ways in which identity is contingent: anonymity and role experimentation (or deception) are always possible.

Finally, this results in changing contexts in which:

- a sense of space is shared as the local becomes global;
- the time is now as we inhabit a world of co-presence and synchronicity;
- boundaries between work and leisure begin to blur;
- distinctions between the public and the private are less clear;
- the serious and the frivolous intermingle.

The implications of these shifts are particularly significant and lead me to suggest that documenting the rapidly changing nature of writing now becomes an important challenge for academics and educationalists. Whilst there is a growing body of work devoted to the study of new textual forms such as web pages, blogs and email (Herring, 2004) and some recognition of the significance of digital culture in literacy education (Gee, 2004; Lankshear and Knobel, 2003) there is clearly a need for more detailed research into digital writing and its introduction into educational contexts (Andrews, 2004). Yet this is no easy matter because, as the foregoing analysis highlights, the certainties associated with print-based practices are disappearing as reader and writer positions begin to blur and the fixity of textual objects is called into question.

A DIGITAL APPRENTICESHIP

This brings us to the question of what all this might mean for literacy educators. Whilst it seems fairly obvious that most children are growing up in a textual universe in which digital writing is a pervasive feature, there is little indication of how this experience could be harnessed in school settings. Despite numerous policy initiatives and considerable financial investment, the literacy curricula of English language education systems are still quite overtly print-based. Attempts to technologize classrooms often pay little regard to popular communicative practices. So, for example, in their critique of the National Grid for Learning, Lankshear and Knobel (2003) point out how the initiative failed to come to grips with new possibilities, and the changes in the form and function of literacy that characterize e-communication. Such work, they argue, is unlikely to equip pupils with the sorts of practices and critical perspectives that will equip them for the future at the same time as failing to engage them in the present.

But, despite this, recent studies of young children's use of e-communication in classroom contexts have contributed to a growing understanding of its potential. So, for example, in a recent study, Harris and Kington (2002) report on a case study of ten-year-olds in email contact with employees at a mobile phone factory some 30 miles away from the school. 'Epals' learnt about children's interests and in turn offered insights into the world of work. Teachers involved in the project commented on how they found out more about their pupils when reading the messages they exchanged. A more formal evaluation showed gains in pupil motivation and social skills.

McKeon's (1999) study of 23 children's email interactions with preservice teachers looked at the balance between purely social exchanges and topic-focused exchanges (in this case book-talk). Roughly half of the exchanges of these nine- and ten-year-olds fell in to each category, leading McKeon to speculate that:

> classroom email partnerships may provide students with a new way to learn about themselves as they select information that defines who they are and send it via email to another.
>
> (McKeon, 1999: 703)

From this it seems that e-communication can provide useful opportunities for exploring identity and relationships, while providing a discursive form which depends on purposeful communication with audiences beyond the confines of the classroom.

Merchant *et al.* (2005b) provides further examples of this kind of work through projects which explore the use of digital writing in structured peer-to-peer e-communication, engaging learners in different schools in the construction of a shared knowledge product (Bigum, 2005). In this work children demonstrate authentic engagement with digital writing practices as they move between informal social and topic-focused inter- action. So, for example, here a ten- and eleven-year-old use email to exchange views on their favourite recording artists:

> *Daz*:   . . . my favourite pop band is sclub 8 and I love the black eyed peas album and it is great.
>
> *Hannah*: . . . i have a busted cd and I went to see them on Sunday and I went on stage and they sang happy birthday and I went back stage and meet mcfly have you got sclub cds?
>
> *Daz*:   . . . I have about ten sclub8 CDs and they are brill.

In contrast, these two children (using the names Ivy and Pixie as aliases), whose informal emails have touched on a number of themes, including their enjoyment of fairytales and their growing familiarity with the language of text-messaging, cooperate on a PowerPoint presentation on 'special people'. This idea is proposed in an email from Pixie, an assertive African-Caribbean girl:

> Do u like the idea of putting special people like Martin Luther King and Nelson Mandela

and agreed by Ivy:

> pixie,
>   yes would be a brilliant idea, you could explain about them and why they are special because some people may not understand,
> ivy

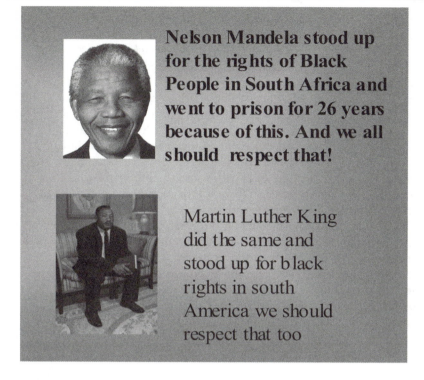

Figure 5.3 Pixie and Ivy's black rights slide.

Figure 5.3 includes images of Nelson Mandela and Martin Luther King and explicit reference to their significance in 'black rights'.

These examples not only show how digital writing can be incorporated into the school curriculum but also how it involves new sorts of communicative practices that begin to challenge dominant discourses about classroom literacy and pedagogy. A common feature of these projects has been the use of informal e-communication, involving pupils in writing activities that do not take place under the watchful gaze of the teacher. This involves more autonomy for young readers and writers as they interact and co-construct texts. However, as the last example shows, collaboration with remote writing partners can be used to produce work that is quite familiar in curriculum terms (such as the theme of 'special people') at the same time as harnessing the multimodal affordances of new media.

As Andrews (2004) observes, many schools in the UK have yet to move beyond a conception of digital literacy as word-processing. Consequently, the use of other kinds of digital writing in the classroom, particularly web-based forms such as blogs and discussion boards, is rare, and for some safety-conscious education authorities, problematic. Yet, at the same time, pioneering schools are beginning to explore the possibilities of a range of new literacy practices, sometimes within the controlled contexts of VLEs (virtual learning environments).

There is plenty of scope for innovative work on the use of new technology with younger writers. Although we are now more familiar with the changing nature of young children's home experience (Marsh, 2003) and the various kinds of understandings about digital writing that they demonstrate in early years settings (Merchant, 2005), we are still a long way from identifying and describing development in digital literacy.

A synthesis of real-world uses of communication technology and the wider curricular intentions of classroom teachers may provide a way forward, but, as Tyner observes, 'There is little consensus about how technology is best infused into learning environments' (Tyner, 2003: 379).

In the meantime, most children and young people are apprenticed to digital writing through informal learning in out-of-school contexts. Given the centrality of e-communication in everyday life and the unevenness of provision, access and use, a failure to embed digital writing in classroom practices may simply perpetuate disadvantage. Alternatively, we can rise to the challenge by accepting the wide-reaching changes in written communication that are taking place and looking for new ways of extending the experience of young writers in school settings.

NOTE

1 Instant messaging is another form of interactive digital writing that is currently enjoying growing popularity. However, in the interests of brevity I have decided to make only passing reference to its key features.

REFERENCES

Andrews, R. (2004) *The Impact of ICT on Literacy Education*. London: RoutledgeFalmer.

Barton, D. (1994) *Literacy: An Introduction to the Ecology of Written Language*. London: Blackwell.

Bigum, C. (2005) 'Knowledge Producing Schools', http://www.deakin.edu.au/education/lit/kps/ last accessed 27 February, 2005.

Blogcount.com (2005) http://www.dijest.com/bc/ last accessed 27 February 2005.

Burnett, C., Dickinson, P., Merchant, G. and Myers, J. (2004) 'Digikids' *The Primary English Magazine*, 9 (4): 16–20.

Cope, B. and Kalantzis, M. (2000) *Multiliteracies: Literacy Learning and the Design of Social Futures*. London: Macmillan.

Carrington, V. (2004) 'The uncanny: digital texts and literacy', paper given at the UKLA International Conference, Manchester, July 2004.

Crystal, D. (2001) *Language and the Internet*. Cambridge: Cambridge University Press.

Ferrara, K., Brunner, H. and Whittemore, G. (1991) 'Interactive Written Discourse as an Emergent Register', *Written Communication*, **18** (1): 8–34.

Gee, J.P. (2004) *What Videogames Have to Teach us About Learning and Literacy*. New York: Palgrave Macmillan.

Giddens, A. (1991) *Modernity and Self-Identity: Self and Society in the Late Modern Age*. Cambridge: Polity Press.

Hannon, P. (2000) *Reflecting on Literacy in Education*. London: RoutledgeFalmer.

Harris, S. and Kington, S. (2002) 'Innovative Classroom Practices Using ICT in England', http://nfer.ac.uk/research/down_pub.asp (last accessed 27 February 2005).

Herring, S.C. (2004) 'Slouching toward the ordinary: current trends in computer-mediated communication', *New Media and Society*, **6** (1): 26–33.

Ito, M. (1995) 'Technologies of the Childhood Imagination: Yugioh, Media Mixes, and Everyday Cultural Reproduction', in J. Kraganis and N. Jeremijenko (eds) *Structures of Participation in Digital Culture*. Durham, NC: Duke University Press.

Ito, M. (2003) 'A New Set of Rules for a Newly Wireless Society', *Japan Media Review* available http://ojr.org/japan/wireless last accessed 25 October 2004.

Kress, G. (1997) 'Visual and verbal modes of representation in electronically mediated communication: The potentials of new forms of texts', in I. Snyder (ed.) *Page to Screen: Taking literacy into the electronic age*. London: Routledge, pp. 53–79.

Kress, G. (2003) *Literacy in the New Media Age*. London: Routledge.

Lankshear, C. and Knobel, M. (2003) *New Literacies: Changing Knowledge and Classroom Learning*. Buckingham: Open University Press.

Livingstone, S. and Bober, M. (2004) *UK Children Go Online: Surveying the experiences of young people and their parents*. London: London School of Economics and Political Science.

Mackey, M. (2003) *Literacies across Media: playing the text*. London: RoutledgeFalmer.

Marsh, J. (2003) 'The techno-literacy practices of young children', *Journal of Early Childhood Research*, **2** (1) 51–66.

McKeon, C.A. (1999) 'The nature of children's e-mail in one classroom', *The Reading Teacher*, **52** (7): 698–706.

Merchant, G. (2001) 'Teenagers in cyberspace: language use and language change in Internet chatrooms', *Journal of Research in Reading*, **24** (3): 293–306.

Merchant, G. (2004) 'The Dagger of Doom and the Mighty Handbag', in J. Evans (ed.) *Literacy Moves On: using popular culture, new technologies and critical literacy in the primary classroom*. London: David Fulton.

Merchant, G. (2005a) 'Barbie meets Bob the Builder at the Workstation', in J. Marsh (ed.) *Popular Culture, New Media and Digital Literacy in Early Childhood*. London: RoutledgeFalmer.

Merchant, G. (2005b) 'Digikids: cool dudes and the new writing', *E-Learning*, **2** (1): 50–60.

Ong, W.J. (1982) *Orality and Literacy: the technologizing of the word*. London: Methuen.

Prensky, M. (2001) *Digital Game-based Learning*. New York: McGraw-Hill.

Rheingold, H. (2003) *Smart Mobs: the next social revolution*. Cambridge, MA: Perseus Publishing.

Robins, K. and Webster, F. (1999) *Times of the Technoculture: from the information society to the virtual life*. London: Routledge.

Sacks, D. (2003) *The Alphabet*. London: Hutchinson.

Sampson, G. (1985) *Writing Systems: a linguistic introduction*. London: Hutchinson.

Shortis, T. (2001) *The Language of ICT*. London: Routledge.

Tyner, K. (2003) 'Beyond Boxes and Wires: Literacy in Transition', *Television and New Media*, 4 (4): 371–88.

Vygotsky, L.S. (1980) Mind in Society: Development of Higher Psychological Processes. Cambridge, MA: Harvard University Press.

Werry, C. (1996) 'Linguistic and Interactional Features of Internet Relay Chat', in S. Herring (ed.) *Computer Mediated Communication: Linguistic and Social Perspectives*. Amsterdam: Benjamins.

Wilson, F.R. (1998) *The Hand: how its use shapes the brain, language and human culture*. New York: Pantheon.

Part II

Youth and adolescence

No single divide: literacies, new technologies and school-defined versus self-selected purposes in curriculum and pedagogy

Colin Lankshear

INTRODUCTION

This chapter presents a variation on two themes that are quite familiar to educationists interested in literacy education. These are, respectively, the idea of a digital divide and of differences and tensions between learners' in-school and out-of-school language and literacy practices. Since the mid-1990s a growing corpus of work in literacy studies and allied fields has begun to focus on divides between home and community-based social practices involving digital technologies in which young people participate, and those they are recruited to within formal educational learning contexts (e.g. Chandler-Olcott and Mahar, 2003; Jacobs, 2004; Leander and McKim, 2003; Leander and Aplin, 2004). Unlike much of the work done on the digital divide – which measured differences between categories of people (e.g. by age, income, location, employment status, etc.) with respect to their physical access to, use of, and facility with computing technologies and the Internet – this emerging corpus is more qualitative than quantitative in emphasis. It is especially relevant to two high-profile themes within current educational research: namely, student (dis)engagement in learning and the degree of 'authenticity' inherent in learning activities.

With respect to *disengagement*, and particularly in reference to boys, it is widely remarked that the kinds of pursuits involving the use of new technologies that young people participate in enthusiastically outside of school often differ markedly from what they get to do with computers in school. They find their out-of-school pursuits 'engaging', and undertake them freely and enthusiastically. By contrast, school-based uses of new technologies are often experienced as boring (along with literacy *per se* in the case, especially of boys, we are told), if not insulting. Consequently, they turn off.

In terms of *authenticity* a key argument involves the claim that classroom learning activities are often 'pretend' rather than 'real' versions of social practices. For example, learners 'play at' doing Internet searches by merely selecting among the limited range of sites that teachers have pre-selected and saved on the school server. By contrast, it is argued, within their own times and spaces young people have opportunities to lead 'authentic' online lives: to communicate freely with peers, buy and sell on line, build and participate in virtual worlds, join discussion groups in areas of personal interest, move in and out of affinity groups and the practices organic to them (Gee, 2003, 2004), and so on.

There is much to reckon with in such lines of argument. It is important, however, not to overstate the case. To date relatively few studies have investigated *the same learners* across their in-school and non-school practices involving new technologies. We know what *many* learners do in classrooms, and what *many* learners do out of school, but much less about how the practices across sites of specific learners compare and contrast. Hence we do not know what kinds of 'divide' – or *divides* – might exist and be educationally significant, There are strong grounds for believing that, *overall*, the inherent 'qualities' of learners' experiences of and practices with new technologies differ significantly, and that some of these differences should be taken into educational account. But which ones, how much, and why are much less clear. Moreover, it may be as important and useful to identify and discuss points of commonality that range over different users, different purposes and different sites.

Some recent work (Leander, 2003; Leander and McKim, 2003; Leander and Aplin, 2004) suggests that emphasizing a distinction between physical sites – in school/non-school – may be misleading. Rather, what seems more important is what might be called the locus of *selection of purposes* mediated by new technologies, e.g. 'school-selected' and 'self-selected' purposes. This position, discussed below, underpins the focus on 'school-defined' versus 'self-selected' purposes I am adopting here.

Moreover, it is important to ask what follows so far as curriculum and pedagogy are concerned from the (mere) fact that variation and tension – even *significant* variation and tension – may exist between in-school and out-of-school practices, or 'school-defined' versus 'self-selected' purposes involving the use of new technologies (or books and other technologies, for that matter).

These points will guide subsequent discussion.

DIVIDES AND PURPOSES/GAPS AND CONTINUITIES

In this section I will briefly overview some typical examples of research about young people's information and communication practices and purposes involving new technologies within classroom and non-school settings.

1. A very clear example of a sharp 'division', provided by Steve Thorne (2003), actually involves a post-school classroom from an undergraduate French course. Wanting to integrate a range of CMC tools and activities into the course, the teachers included an assessment component requiring students to engage in email communication with key pals in France. Emailing proved very unpopular with some of the students, a number of whom forsook the assessment component and accepted lower grades rather than engage in emailing. When asked why they did this, two nineteen-year-old female students spoke disdainfully of email as a friendship communication medium, explaining how they associated it with 'communication between power levels and generations', not between age peers and friends (Thorne, 2003: 7).

Grace:	= ...we communicate with a lot of people now through AOL [instant messenger]. That's...how I talk to all my friends at different colleges=
Stef:	= and here=
Grace:	= We don't send e-mails back and forth to each other to like catch up. Like we just talk [using IM].

. . .

Researcher:	So you don't use e-mail that much normally?
Stef:	I almost never do. I just use it for teachers and stuff=
Grace:	= teachers, yeah. Or my Mom [laughs].

(Thorne, 2003: 5)

These power and cross-generational associations connoted the inappropriateness of email as a medium for 'age-peer relationship building and social interaction'. Yet these were the teachers' main purposes for the intercultural exchanges. For Grace and Stef there were 'right' (appropriate) and 'wrong' (inappropriate) cultural tools for the kinds of exchanges occurring between them and their key pal, François. The meaning of cultural tools, and their perceived acceptability or appropriateness as media for teaching and learning activities are often closely linked to how individuals see themselves – their affinities, identities, etc. – and these associations may run deep. Grace, particularly, saw email as an unacceptable medium for social age-peer exchange, *even within the context of artificial social interactions that had been induced for curricular purposes.* Part of the way Grace saw herself was as a person who does *not* communicate socially in close and friendly ways by means of email. She would, however, have been prepared to use IM for the curriculum activities, had it been available as an option.

2. Presentation software such as PowerPoint is a perennial favourite application within classrooms, where it is widely used in primary school

as a medium for story-telling and within secondary school as a prop for presenting student work or for formal speech-making, and so on. Some of my research with other colleagues (Knobel and Lankshear, 1997; Lankshear and Snyder, 2000) has involved comparative studies of students' experiences with using presentation software in classroom activities and in personal interest ways at home. Two cases from a single sequence of studies are indicative of the range of experiences we found across school and non-school sites.

In one school site, a team of Year 8–10 students were collaborating on the rapid production of a slide show to accompany and augment the principal's end-of-year speech to the school community. The presentation was to comprise static and video-recorded images of the school year in a form that could be integrated into the principal's address. Pressure on time and on the availability of technical resources required the production process to be broken into specific tasks. These were delegated to individual students, or pairs of students, who undertook, explicitly, a responsibility to perform them – during class-time and lunch breaks. Tasks included using a digital camera to photograph tuckshop staff and specialist teachers (physical education, music), grab image stills from video and convert them to digital images, interview staff and students, use text art software to create headings for slides, etc. From time to time during the week available for production, the teacher met with the team as a group, and in between they reported to her with completed components. With time short, the teacher simply told and showed the students how to use the equipment and explained as economically as possible the steps needed to complete their respective tasks. Part way into the task, most of the participants began to lose interest and get distracted.

The result was a particular kind of slide show presentation. It was a prop that contained text, photos and video snippets as illustrations of what the principal was communicating, rather than a *production* in its own right. While it was well received by the community on speech night, the presentation was largely a heteronymous engagement for most of the participants. This was apparent in the hierarchies involved in different aspects of the production process, the extrinsic forms of motivation employed as the teacher struggled to keep the students interested and involved, the division of the job into so many tasks, and the fragmented involvement of participants as a result. For student participants, choice about content was shaped by the contours of the principal's speech. The format for gathering and collecting data was pre-given, in the form of a chart of components (headings) and elements of components (sub-headings) presented to the students, who worked to a predetermined formula – although they had some autonomy over detail (what pose they would photograph a teacher in; where the sports field would be photographed from, etc.).

In a contrasting example studied at the same time, Jack (fifteen years) sat at the family computer, opened PowerPoint and selected a file from the directory. The screen filled with a limitless sky flecked with clouds before bursting into a bright cacophony of sound, colour and movement as the familiar title from an animated television series, *The Simpsons*, dropped onto the screen to the opening lines of the show's theme song. This was followed in quick succession by a selection of images of the Simpson family going about their everyday lives. The title page gave way to a parade of slides, one for each family member and major character in the show. In order of appearance these slides depicted Homer, Marge, Bart, Lisa, Maggie, Itchy and Scratchy, Mr Burns, Ned Flanders, Krusty, Apu, Moe and Barney, as well as providing a credits page. Each slide showed a full-colour image of the character, accompanied by a few pertinent statistics (e.g. age, occupation) and followed by a short text headed: 'little known facts'. Images and lines or phrases of text appeared in synchronization with the melody of the song selected to accompany the particular character depicted on each slide. The show ran for around six minutes.

The first time Jack had seen a PowerPoint presentation had been at his school's Sports Awards night a few months earlier. 'It was all right, but it was just headings for the topics for the night. The backgrounds were cool, though'. There were few images in the school presentation, but Jack had been impressed by the idea. Spending at least an hour and a half each day over two weeks, Jack searched official and unofficial Simpsons websites on the Internet, downloading graphics, scanning in images, and gathering information for the biodata to accompany each character. He supplemented this with information from his Simpsons collector cards. Jack also began experimenting with the palette of functions built into the software and found he was able to attach sounds and music to each slide. This sent him on another search of the Internet, where he found hundreds of sound files. Some were compatible with the PowerPoint software. Others had to be converted to the right format using software that he and his father had spent considerable time locating and downloading from the Internet. Further ideas and hints for using PowerPoint effectively were gleaned from friends at school.

Jack's 'ways' with PowerPoint contrast sharply with the previous example. His project was open-ended, intrinsically motivated and 'liberal', in the sense of existing for its own sake – emerging from a popular youth culture space rather than from 'other-directed' purposes, directives and routines. Indeed, Jack explicitly contrasted his presentation with the one he encountered within the formal school context. He had multiple intended audiences: himself (primarily), his mates at school, and people at large who are interested in *The Simpsons*. The presentation evolved over several months on the basis of experimentation (techniques and effects), exploration (hunting down new resources), and the personal/self-directed pursuit of expertise.

3. Often the tensions and complexities that exist across spaces and purposes are expressed most elegantly by young people themselves. The following transcript was logged by Angela Thomas (Anya) on the Palace (Percirion, electronic interview, November 2004; see reference to the Palace in the transcript below). She posed some general questions about new technologies and school. The following excerpt focuses on a response from President (or, occasionally, Emperor) Percirion, a 14-year-old Australian male student who attends a private school (see Thomas, forthcoming: Ch. 4).

Anya: Do you think schools are adequately preparing you for the future, especially in regards to technology?

President Percirion (UFP): my school is most certainly teaching us about Technology.

President Percirion (UFP): We have a 'Computer lab' which has enough electricity flowing through it to power a small African country

Anya: So what computer skills/knowledge are you getting at your school, Perc?

President Percirion (UFP): Typing...

President Percirion (UFP): I'm a 42-words-per-min typer

President Percirion (UFP): How to Use the Internet

President Percirion (UFP): How Not To Use the Internet...

. . .

President Percirion (UFP): We usually... have free rein on the Internet

President Percirion (UFP): But there's a boundary

Anya: Yes?

President Percirion (UFP): This is where the powerful Imagination kicks in.

Anya: tell, tell

President Percirion (UFP): 'Inappropriate material', so to speak

President Percirion (UFP): And we're also learning how to use various computer systems

President Percirion (UFP): Which I am sure will be out of date by the time we leave.

Anya: What various computer systems?

President Percirion (UFP): Excel, Word, More Excel, Office.

President Percirion (UFP): PowerPoint

. . .

Anya: ... Are there any kinds of things you do with new technologies in your life outside

	of school that are missing INSIDE school (in your school learning)?
President Percirion (UFP):	Yeah
President Percirion (UFP):	No Sim Games in school
President Percirion (UFP):	and certainly no Electronic Romance of the Three Kingdoms
Anya:	Should they be in school?
President Percirion (UFP):	No ...

. . .

President Percirion (UFP):	Our computers are stocked to the gills with edu-programs
President Percirion (UFP):	They even have Stories of Democracy, Stories of Dictatorship, Stories of < Insert government here >
Anya:	And do those programs teach you what you think it's important to know?
President Percirion (UFP):	Not all of them
President Percirion (UFP):	But then again
President Percirion (UFP):	no computer program
President Percirion (UFP):	or internet screen
President Percirion (UFP):	Can teach me virtue, honour and piety
President Percirion (UFP):	They teach me some things
President Percirion (UFP):	the rest
President Percirion (UFP):	are only achieved
President Percirion (UFP):	by social interaction.

. . .

President Percirion (UFP):	E.g., Palace [A graphical chat site. See www.thePalace.com].
Anya:	So do you think schools should let you come online and get involved in social interaction?
President Percirion (UFP):	No.
President Percirion (UFP):	School is for learning maths
President Percirion (UFP):	and english.

Percirion esteems the *social* nature of online worlds, has learned many social values through his role-playing SIM game and through interacting with friends on the palace. On one occasion he told Anya that what he had learned about relationships online has helped him greatly off line – notably, learning a sense of tolerance because:

> online, people come, go ... there's a whole world of people to talk to, you need to learn tolerance. It's the community and the people that

kids can interact with that's really teaching them a lot about the social world. But maybe this is just my irritation with what schools do coming through – I mean schools claim to be teaching ICT (a term I hate) but they only do the 'I' (information) bit and always seem to neglect the 'C' (communication).

4. Kevin Leander and colleagues have recently undertaken research across online and offline contexts, tracing how the participants use a range of new information and communication technologies, including instant messaging, chat, email, searching the Internet and building websites, and gaming. This research was designed to help enhance understanding of the use of literacy practices for identity and social networks and to further illuminate the 'situatedness' of literacy. The work involved developing reflexively new methodologies that 'follow the moving, traveling practices' of participants on line and off line to clarify relations between practice, context and identity (Leander and McKim, 2003), and has explored how 'digital literacies' are taught and used within school settings and how students engaged in digital literacy practice in their homes. Data were obtained by surveys and interviews, and a small number of students (seven), for whom permission was obtained, were observed bi-weekly in their home settings and their Internet use was tracked for several hours weekly.

Some preliminary and provisional findings about relationships and differences between practices at home and at school are emerging from the study, which suggest much more complex and interesting patterns than the idea of a simple home–school digital divide might imply. As mentioned above, Leander and Aplin prefer to distinguish between 'school-selected' and 'self-selected' practices than between 'home' and 'school', since the boundaries between these sites are fluid – and especially so when new technologies are implicated. They note, however, that their distinction should be read as suggesting that students' different forms of engagement are not distinctively shaped by physical settings, and not as implying that students choose not to engage in school. (The same rider applies to the distinction between 'school-defined' and 'self-selected' practices used here).

Three of the seven cases observed at home as at well as school attended a private girls' school that made extensive use of mobile computing within a wireless environment. The other four attended a co-ed public middle school. Among even this small group of seven cases there was considerable variation in terms of purposes and practices, in class, as well as at home. We can get a good sense of the nature and extent of this variation by considering some early study findings under four broad headings, focusing mainly on the students from the girls' school whose 'digital literacy lives' were the richest and most diverse.

Pursuing school-defined purposes at home

Observations in the home revealed marked variation among the three female case study participants with respect to the time spent and kind of approach taken to pursuing school-defined purposes using computing and communications technologies at home. One student was *never* observed doing any school-defined work at home. A second student accessed the school intranet for assignment purposes and on multiple occasions used the family computer to get information for a school task the evening before it was due. The third student had a strongly academic orientation to almost all of her computing and Internet activity at home and worked systematically on school-defined purposes at home – moving through orderly sequences of information gathering, drafting, and revising processes.

Pursuing self-selected purposes at home

Overall, for most of the total population surveyed, interviewed and observed, home uses of new technologies were dominated by social and recreational purposes: following popular/youth cultural interests, gathering information on subjects of personal interest, using email and IM to communicate with friends and family members, playing games, downloading music and pictures, maintaining web pages and weblogs, shopping, etc. Within this overall prevalence of self-selected pursuits, however, the detailed observation of case study participants again revealed considerable variation. For example, the female participant, who was never observed doing school-related work at home, spent most of her time on line getting music files and gathering information about the entertainment world, with a lesser emphasis on playing games, locating 'cheats' and IMing close friends. By contrast, the other female participant, who did a lot of social and recreational 'work' on line at home, devoted most time to various forms of social networking: weblogging (her own and interacting with friends' blogs) and IMing in particular. A distinctive feature of her digital literacy practices at home was the intensity of her multitasking among blogging, IMing, phone conversations, emailing, *and* school-defined purposes.

Pursuing school-defined purposes at school

While the kinds of purposes pursued in class using computers off and on line are more or less the kinds of things we would expect to see in general terms – essay-writing, project work, maintaining journals, doing tests, creative writing, etc. – the fact that one of the study sites involved a wireless laptop environment meant that some highly distinctive features of classroom digital literacies were apparent by comparison with most of the classrooms for which published research findings are available to date. For example, the start of lessons coincided with the spontaneous emergence of 'walls' of laptops, accompanied by the tap-tapping of note-taking and online searching. Some teachers remarked on the radical changes they perceived in classroom dynamics and, notably, reduced levels of discussion. Laptops became 'academic organizers'. Seeking and obtaining feedback on work in progress from teachers and peers became organic and practically immediate, as students fired off drafts and received responses by email. The sheer *amount* of writing that was done, and done *rapidly*, stood out as a feature – across note-taking, drafting, responding, etc. Furthermore, much of this writing seemed to take on characteristics of 'non-academic' text production, such as IMing: rapid, unproofed or rapidly proofed, little emphasis on evaluating information obtained, 'just in time' and 'on the fly', etc. The ease of producing wordage quickly seemed to support a high level of last-minute production of assignments. A further notable feature – which teachers seemed to be aware of – was the amount of 'flexing' that went on around school tasks, as when students would work on tasks for one subject (e.g. French) during a class in another subject (e.g. English). High levels of such 'flexing' and 'multitasking' were apparent in these classrooms.

Pursuing self-selected purposes at school

Not surprisingly, many students spent much time in class engaging in self-selected purposes. This extended to gaming, shopping, and down-loading music, as well as including the 'more to be expected' activities like emailing, private chatting and IMing. Leander (Lankshear and Leander, 2004: 328) notes:

> [one] participant ('Angie') was continually involved in playing some sort of online game, and was likely involved in other online interactions during the school day, using her laptop in a wireless environment. While we continually observed her participating in this activity (during classroom observations), and 'mode-switching' between gaming and coursework, she would not discuss this with us.... Angie seemed set on presenting more of a student persona about her work in school.

Interestingly, some of the students who engaged most in pursuing self-selected purposes during class time did not believe they were thereby learning less than they otherwise would, and, even when they were 'drifting' on their screens, demonstrably participated as much as or more in class discussion than their 'on-task' peers. Two of these students claimed that being able to go to other places during time in class when they already knew about the matters under discussion alleviated boredom. Their capacity for multitasking seemingly allowed them to maintain one eye on task while going about other business. Notwithstanding such self-appraisals, before the research was over some teachers were already limiting the time laptops could be used to points in lessons they deem appropriate. Notably, the researchers found high levels of safety-consciousness among the study participants, who avoided communication with unknowns and were very careful about what information they gave out about themselves across both sites of practice.

NO SINGLE DIVIDE

To date, there has been very little systematic research comparing home and school digital literacy purposes and practices. We know especially little about home computing practices in low SES communities. Even where systematic research has been undertaken on a small scale – and, given the resource intensity and intrusiveness of home-based observations it is unlikely that such research can be other than small-scale, although there can and should be many such projects – the very provisional findings available to date caution against blanket statements about *the* relationship between 'out-of-school digital literacies' and digital literacies within school curriculum and pedagogy. Relationships will be many and varied from context to context, case to case. In short, there is no single divide and, as the work of Leander and colleagues suggests, there will be a lot of fluidity between home and school across 'school-selected' and 'self-selected' purposes.

At the same time, as Leander's work suggests in common with the other examples presented above, in general, and overall, the varying things young people in societies like our own freely choose to do most of with computing and communications technologies, and the ways they do them, tend to differ considerably from what they do in school and how these things – including the 'same' things, like using presentation software and weblogging – get done in classrooms. So far as curriculum and pedagogy are concerned, however, the question that arises here is 'so what?'

IMPLICATIONS OF ACTUAL AND POSSIBLE DIVIDES

As President Percirion implies above, it does not follow that, because particular digital literacy practices are engaged in widely outside of school, or are done in particular ways out of school, they should be addressed in certain ways, or even taken account of, within school. Steve Thorne's (2003) account of the IM–email conflict involving Grace and Stef provides a useful starting point for considering some of the issues that might be at stake here.

Nothing obvious follows for curriculum and pedagogy from the mere fact that learners like Grace and Stef might prefer to use one communication application rather than another, any more than it follows that, just because some new application or hardware comes onto the electronics market, it needs to be adopted in schools. Certainly, curriculum and pedagogy must not be driven by technological change at the level of artefacts. Yet, as Thorne's work shows, the pedagogical and curriculum issues surrounding the relationship between in-school and non-school 'cultures of practice and use' run deep and cannot simply be ignored. When the gap between school and non-school/popular cultures of use gets too wide, even 'good' (in school terms) students start to refuse to participate in teacher-designed activities. The Graces and Stefs of the world are the very kinds of people we identify as mainstream 'made-for-school' students. They are not 'marginal' students; they are not 'misbehavers'. But they have their limits. Grace opted out of a required part of the course, and one that carried assessment weight to boot. She constitutes a seminal example of the kind of things schools can increasingly expect to encounter if the gap between the scholastic and the everyday gets too wide.

The point, however, is not simply to import everyday cultures of use into the classroom holus-bolus. This is one of the many object lessons to be drawn from Jim Gee's book, *What Video Games Have to Teach us about Learning and Literacy* (2003). In each chapter, Gee derives particular *principles* of effective learning from the aspects of video gaming addressed in that chapter. The chapters collectively build a stock of thirty-six principles of effective learning as exemplified by successful video games, most of which are conspicuous by their absence in school-based learning. Gee begins his discussion from the premise that to be successful in the market a game must be capable of being learned effectively by all kinds of players. Clearly, however, Gee is not arguing that classrooms should simply be turned over to games-playing on the grounds that they embody excellent learning principles. Rather, the question is how to incorporate such principles into school learning. This *may* involve importing certain tools and components of gaming cultures of practice and use into classrooms. But, if so, the extent to which this occurs, and how it occurs, will be matters decided on the basis of principles, values, purposes, and the like appropriate to *education* as a social practice rather than *gaming*.

HOW THINGS MIGHT LOOK: A CURRICULUM 'THOUGHT EXPERIMENT'

Clearly, an important challenge exists in regard to how best to integrate young people's 'savvy' about, and interest in, contemporary media into educationally worthwhile work. Elsewhere (Lankshear and Knobel, 2004)

I have identified principles and criteria on the basis of which we can address the 'so what?' question that arises for curriculum and pedagogy from the kinds of differences we have encountered. Space precludes revisiting them here. What we find, however, is that when we appeal to such principles and criteria (or other sets, such as Gee's) it is not difficult to identify diverse ways in which to make productive integrations of this 'savvy' and interest into sound classroom-based teaching and learning. Variations will occur in relation to the particular students, their prior experiences and circumstances, and the wherewithal that a given school and its community has available to support teaching and learning. In the following imaginary example I attempt to think through the broad contours of a learning activity that might take the kinds of students involved in the various studies mentioned above from where they are to 'places' they might usefully go in their school-based learning.

Two teachers and a small team of students in Years 10–12 are working with two academics from the local university who have expertise in life-history and oral narrative. A municipal council has commissioned a project to develop an oral history of the two longest-established migrant groups in the city. This involves conducting life-history interviews with elderly residents from the groups in question, focusing on their experiences of settling in their adopted land.

The teachers and students have been invited to participate in the project as part of a collaboration between the university and the school. The partners have established clear lines for roles, resources and responsibilities. The academics are primarily responsible for taking the teachers and students through the process of producing credible life histories: how to prepare appropriate interview schedules; use prompts and probes to elicit further information on aspects of life history that arise in the course of the interviews; obtain informed consent, organize and analyze interview material; pursue follow-up interviews on relevant points; and how to write up the life histories.

The school is providing students to assist with data collection and assuming responsibility for infrastructure; for collecting and storing data – space on the school server and audio, and video and photo recording equipment. The students and teachers are also to schedule interviews and maintain up-to-date records of completed work.

The school participants establish a project website for archiving the digital sound and image files and electronic copy of notes made during interviews. It will also be used to organize and store other electronic material providing contextual information for the project. The researchers envisage presenting the 'project' via an array of media, including a dedicated website, and official CD-ROMs/DVD, journal and newspaper articles, a photographic and poster display, and selected image and sound 'bites' that will feature in digital touch-screen, information 'kiosks' established by the city's tourist information bureau.

The teachers and students also set up a weblog for the project for maintaining a record of all completed work. Participants make short posts to the weblog whenever an interview has been completed, new material is uploaded to the website after meetings, and so on to ensure a permanent sequential record of how the project unfolded, of gaps to be filled, and of roles played by participants.

In a typical 'snapshot', two students who are preparing for an interview with an elderly migrant couple are not sure about the appropriateness of one of their questions. They email the life-history specialist they are working with, who sends them back some advice and also arranges to meet later with all the student interviewers to suggest ways of sensing when ground is becoming tricky. Importantly, she suggests that the students might like to 'clear' their questions with participants before doing the interviews, since this would also help the interviewees to prepare themselves for the interview itself.

One student team member has accepted responsibility for generally overseeing both the archival website and the weblog for the project. The website is a password-protected database containing all digital archival material generated in the project. It can be accessed by all team members for the various research purposes from any location with Internet access. These purposes include uploading new data; keeping tabs on what has already been collected (and not); preparing data for analysis and printing out data to be analyzed; and generally maintaining a record of progress to date. It is the main digital database for the project, and also a potential future source of secondary data for subsequent projects. The student in question maintains this website, in collaboration with her counterpart in the university and her English teacher.

The same student follows up on comments and organizes the structure of the blog. She also checks spelling, maintains the URL lists, and generally performs the kinds of tasks undertaken by webmasters. The blog serves as an audit trail for the project and as a repository of the team's thinking over time. As the project unfolds, team members blog ideas about patterns they are starting to see in the data post links to online resources relevant to an aspect of the study, and list brief summaries, citations and location details of relevant offline resources (books, newspaper articles, artefacts in people's homes) etc. The blog also accommodates ideas, information and suggestions (e.g. things to follow up on, other people to interview, locations of documents and artefacts) relevant to the study posted by members of the public at large.

In a second typical 'snapshot', a pair of students who have just interviewed a couple are ready to enter the data. One of the students connects the small digital recorder (with inbuilt camera) to a computer with the necessary software in the classroom (or at home, or in the school computer lab, or at the Internet café or library) and uploads the digital audio and image files. When the upload is complete, she logs on and FTPs (i.e. uses a rapid transfer software application) the file to the project website for archiving. Her partner meanwhile logs on to the Internet and posts a short message to the project weblog, notifying that the interview has been completed and the relevant files sent to the website.

When students have completed and archived their interviews, they transcribe them verbatim, and send copies to the interviewees for comments, clarifications and amendments. While listening to the recordings, they are looking for 'themes' – recurring motifs, ideas, matters of distinctiveness, emphases, etc. – that will provide an interpretative structure and point of view (or perspective) for subsequently representing the life history in the narrative 'write-up'. Students make preliminary decisions about the kinds of themes they think are most important. They discuss with one another and their teacher(s) how the transcripts support their interpretations and how they might be used – e.g. as succinct quotations – to help 'carry' the interpretative line. After identifying some preliminary themes, the students arrange to discuss their ideas with the academic partners. Over several weeks, students, teachers and academics decide on themes and lines of interpretation (making 'sense' of the 'lives' entrusted to them) and negotiate appropriate arrangements for including the interviewees in 'checking' lines of interpretation.

Decisions have to be made about reporting the project outcomes. Some life histories may lend themselves to extended written presentation in print text (e.g. in oral history journals, newspaper stories, etc.) and/or as files that can be read online. Others may lend themselves best to vivid video presentations assembled as short segments of 'footage' (e.g. of artefacts, relevant scenes, images of people or events) with 'voice-overs' spliced from the original interviews. Others again may (also) lend themselves to still photographic or poster displays, and so on. Complementary or contrasting life histories might be combined as 'moments' in larger and more complex representations of group life in the community. In a series of meetings and working sessions, the teachers and students discuss with academics, and other persons from the community (or, electronically, at distance – thereby building up a network of 'critical friends') with relevant expertise, aspects of design for web presentation, video editing and presentation, photographic collage, etc., in order to achieve an optimal (re)presentation of the life histories.

CONCLUSION

Variations and tensions between school-defined and self-selected uses of computing and communications technologies that straddle school and non-school sites of practice are complex. Notwithstanding this complexity and our strictly limited knowledge to date about the extent to which variations are patterned relative to social/cultural/economic variables, it is clear that the issues posed for curriculum and pedagogy are deep and subtle, and demand informed, principled and imaginative responses.

NOTE

This chapter owes much to the generosity of Angela Thomas and Kevin Leander, who have made available to me material from previously unpublished work. I am very grateful to them for their generosity and for their exemplary collegial ways.

REFERENCES

Chandler-Olcott, K. and Mahar, D. (2003). 'Tech-savviness' meets multiliteracies: Exploring adolescent girls' technology-mediated literacy practices. *Reading Research Quarterly*, **38** (3): 356–85.

Gee, J. (2003). *What Video Games Have to Teach Us about Learning and Literacy*. New York: Palgrave.

Gee, J. (2004). *Situated Language and Learning: A Critique of Traditional Schooling*. New York: Routledge.

Jacobs, G. (2004). Complicating contexts: Issues of methodology in researching the language and literacies of instant messaging. *Reading Research Quarterly*, **39** (4): 394–407.

Knobel, M. and Lankshear, C. (1997). 'Ways with Windows: What different people do with the same equipment'. Invited keynote address. First Joint National Conference of the Australian Association for the Teaching of English, the Australian Literacy Educators' Assocation, and the Australian School Library Association, Darwin, 8–11 July. (Published in Conference Proceedings.)

Lankshear, C. and Knobel, M. (2004). Planning pedagogy for i-mode: From flogging to blogging via wi-fi. Published jointly in *English in Australia*, **139** (February) / *Literacy Learning in the Middle Years*, **12** (1): 78–102. (Special issue of the International Federation for the Teaching of English).

Lankshear, C. and Leander, K. (2004). Social science research in virtual realities. In Somekh, B. and Lewin, C. (eds) (2004). *Research Methods in the Social Sciences*. London: Sage, pp. 326–334.

Lankshear, C. and Snyder, I. with Green, B. (2000). *Teachers and Technoliteracy*. Sydney: Allen and Unwin.

Leander, K. (2003). Writing travellers' tales on new literacyscapes. *Reading Research Quarterly*, **38** (1): 392–97.

Leander, K. and Aplin, B. (2004). Report to Ridgeview Academy. Nashville: Vanderbilt University, Peabody College, Department of Teaching and Learning. Mimeo.

Leander, K. and McKim, K. (2003). Tracing the everyday 'sitings' of adolescents on the internet. *Education, Communication and Information*, **3** (2): 211–40.

Thomas, A. (forthcoming). *e-selves: Identities and Literacies in Virtual Communities*. New York: Peter Lang.

Thorne, S. (2003). Artifacts and Cultures-of-Use in Intercultural Communication. *Language Learning & Technology* 7/2: 38–67. Available online: http://llt.msu.edu/vol7num2/pdf/thorne.pdf

Chapter 7

Informal literacies and pedagogic discourse[1]

Gemma Moss

This chapter examines the relationship between the social organization of literacy in the informal domain and the social organization of schooled literacy, using as its focus media texts and their place inside and outside school. Drawing on data documenting children's consumption of a range of media texts that circulate outside of official school contexts, I argue that, while middle-class and working-class children acquire broadly similar competences around such texts in the informal domain, they demonstrate a markedly different attitude towards the organization of schooled knowledge.

The data stem from a series of interlinked research projects which tracked the same children over a four-year period between 1989 and 1993[2] and were therefore able to show how media tastes are formed and change in particular localities over an extended period of time. The media encompassed TV and video, as well as print media such as comics, magazines and books. The children were aged between seven and eleven when recruited to the initial research project, and between eleven and fifteen when the final project finished. They came from four London schools: an inner-city secondary school with a predominantly working-class catchment area and one of its feeder primary schools, and a suburban, selective secondary school with a predominantly middle-class catchment and one of its feeder primary schools. The data consist of interviews and questionnaires which were conducted at regular intervals over the four-year period.

INFORMAL LITERACIES

One of the defining characteristics of the readership for the range of media texts considered in this chapter is that it is established outside of school in non-pedagogic contexts. Take television texts as an example. These are not regarded by adults as requiring tuition: the television is on and children watch. Of course, adults may proscribe certain kinds of texts as 'unsuitable', but their future suitability does not depend on younger viewers satisfying selective competency criteria. No one will test them on what they already know to establish their readiness to go on somewhere else. In this sense, these texts and their readers belong to the domain of informal literacies. By contrast, literacy in school is fundamentally part of a pedagogic process. Legitimate access to it depends on being taught a necessary set of skills in a necessary order. Arguments may and do rage over how those skills can be defined, their relevant sequence, and the style of teaching they require. Nevertheless, teaching there will be, organized in a sequential pattern. Without it, the assumption is that there will be no literacy. Official literacies and schooling go hand in hand.

In the case of informal literacies, analysis of the data undertaken by the author elsewhere (Moss, 1996a) has shown how understanding of texts is built as a social activity between people in particular contexts over time. This happens predominantly through talk. Talk about texts is one of the key ways in which readership networks are established. It is through talk about texts that what it means to read and to be a reader are jointly negotiated (see Maybin and Moss, 1993). And this kind of talk about texts often precedes rather than follows much direct knowledge of the texts themselves. In respect of the data drawn on here, this was particularly evident in relation to horror videos, which were of considerable interest to most of the sample during the period of data collection. While the horror genre was very popular as a subject for talk, close analysis of the data showed that very few of the children had actually seen much of it (Moss, 1993a). As the material the children were interested in – including slasher movies such as *Nightmare on Elm Street* – was mainly certified for viewers over 18 years of age, this was perhaps not surprising. What was of more interest was how the children made use of (i) the few fragments they had actually seen (trailers or snatched moments glimpsed before an adult intervened) and (ii) the secondary sources they had encountered (general media coverage; advertising; others' conversations) to claim the necessary expertise. All these resources were called upon to produce a version of the horror text and a view of its readership (Moss, 1993a). Indeed, once a topic such as this achieves currency among a large enough group, it becomes self-sustaining as whatever is known gets pooled and further circulated through the talk. The data provide clear evidence that the social competences to 'read' particular texts are therefore established primarily between people, rather than in relation to the text alone (Moss, 1996a).

Literacy in school and literacy in the informal domain are both bound by the contexts in which they are produced. Both are inherently social processes. In one sense, the kinds of arguments made above about the importance of the role of talk about text in constructing literacies in the informal domain could as easily be made about the role of talk about text in constructing literacy in school (see Baker, 1990; Dombey, 1988; Mills, 1988 for varying accounts which all attest to the importance of social talk in becoming literate). However, the contexts themselves differ radically. The different social settings in which official and informal literacies are formed produce markedly different structures of knowledge, and should be treated as different objects of study within a sociology of knowledge (Bernstein, 1996). They are not interchangeable. In this chapter, it is this contrast in knowledge structures in informal and official domains that I wish to explore, using Bernstein's concepts of horizontal and vertical discourses.

HORIZONTAL AND VERTICAL DISCOURSE – CONTRASTING FORMS OF KNOWLEDGE

Bernstein (1996) describes the difference between forms of knowledge in the informal and official domains as follows:

> The form of knowledge usually typified as everyday, oral or common-sense knowledge has a group of features: local, segmental, context dependent, tacit, multi-layered, often contradictory across contexts but not within contexts. Today the objects of such knowledge are likely to be volatile and substitutable for each other. I want to call such a discourse a horizontal discourse. I shall distinguish a horizontal discourse from a vertical discourse. A vertical discourse takes the form of a coherent, explicit, systematically principled structure, hierarchically organized, or it takes the form of a series of specialized languages...
> (Bernstein, 1996: 170–1)

> School contexts created by vertical discourse are directed to the production of classified competences or performances of a non-segmental type. These procedures are not consumed by their context and are linked not to context but to other procedures organized temporally. The initial context takes its significance from the future and not from the present. It is not that these contexts are unembedded, but that they are differently embedded from the segmental contexts of horizontal discourses.
> (Bernstein, 1996: 179)

The quotations above come from *Pedagogy, symbolic control and identity*, in which Bernstein paints a sharp contrast between horizontal forms of knowledge which evolve outside of the setting of formal schooling; and vertical forms of knowledge which are specific to it.

For Bernstein, part of what sets schooling apart from other, more informal contexts in which knowledge is formed and retailed, are the strong developmental trajectories which go hand in hand with the codifying of knowledge in institutionalized settings. The school curriculum is always vertically sequenced: in the context of the current national curriculum in the UK, knowledge is divided into what is appropriate for particular age groups or particular ability groups and set out progressively. The curriculum defines both the sequence of knowledge and how it will be accessed. For Bernstein, such sequencing is vertical in so far as it makes clear what must already be known before the next layer of knowledge can be added. Competence at one level determines access to another. In this sense, knowledge is hierarchically structured. Such vertical sequencing ensures an orientation to the future. What learners know now must always stand in relation to what might come next, as well as what has gone before. In some senses, therefore, schools discursively construct the development they subsequently monitor and check.

Bernstein is quite clear that within schooling the sequence of knowledge can be built in different ways. Indeed, he suggests that at the moment we are witnessing a fundamental shift from competence-based to performance-based conceptions of pedagogic practice (Bernstein, 1996: 54–63). Competence-based models of pedagogic practice are centred on the learner, and the progress they make as they learn. Development is recorded through intense observation and monitoring of the individual. Comparisons are often drawn between the progressive sequence of development established within pedagogic settings and 'natural' processes of maturation occurring outside the context of official pedagogy – the developmental sequence of language acquisition has been one prime object of such enquiry. Such points of comparison legitimate the developmental sequence employed in pedagogic settings. The turn in media studies towards investigating and documenting what children already know and understand about the media has been of precisely this order. Revealing a developmental sequence in naturalistic settings becomes a means of underpinning the hierarchical sequence the subject builds for itself in schooled settings, and helps secure a footing for the subject, establishing its bona fide credentials, within the school curriculum (see Bazalgette, 1989; Buckingham, 1993).

By contrast, performance-based models of pedagogic practice focus on what is to be learnt – the subject knowledge – and judge development less in terms of inner control than in terms of the standard of output produced at the end of the pedagogic cycle. These perspectives produce different kinds of developmental trajectories, different kinds of pedagogic relations between students and teachers, yet each is part of pedagogic practice as a whole (see Bourne, 2000). While competence-based models appeal more for their legitimation to what happens outside schooling, like performance-based models, they are bound by the pedagogic context and the role they play within it. Both construct a vertical discourse (Bernstein, 1966). The reference to media studies and its motivation for exploring children's knowledge in informal settings is important to this discussion, as it highlights how inextricably the pedagogic imperative is linked to notions of development, and the principles of vertical structuring which Bernstein describes. Pedagogic discourse seeks to replicate itself elsewhere. It looks outside the confines of schooling, only to find confirmation of what it already is. By contrast, Bernstein insists on a radical difference between the forms of knowledge constructed in school settings and those produced in non-pedagogic settings. Bernstein's concept of horizontal discourse provides a different set of expectations about what knowledge in the informal domain might look like and how it can be described. It is precisely in his terms that I will explore my data to identify the very different formation of informal literacies.

INFORMAL LITERACIES AS HORIZONTAL DISCOURSE

For Bernstein, vertical discourse is oriented to the future, and what the competence will become by the end of the pedagogic process. By contrast, horizontal discourse is oriented to the present:

> A segmental competence or literacy usually has a specific, limited realization. Its function is, so to speak, consumed in its realization. The temporal modality of segmental competences or literacies is the present tense. Segmental competences or literacies are then culturally localized and evoked by contexts whose reading is unproblematic. Such competences or literacies, although localized, are likely to develop a range of realization strategies depending upon the exigencies of the context of their enactment.
>
> (Bernstein, 1996: 179)

In speaking of 'segmental competence' Bernstein is referring to specialization within the informal domain. One informal literacy may look quite different from another, while its general principles of production are the same. In following the ways in which children's interest in and use of different media evolved and changed over a four-year period, it is possible to see precisely this kind of 'segmental competence' forming and dissolving over time. At particular moments, particular texts or genres become the object of intense social interest and activity for particular groups of readers. Readership networks form and re-form around them. In the sites the research documented, this happened consecutively for different lengths of time, and involving different, often shifting, portions of the potential audience. As part of this process, the competences required of the texts' readers become established and (temporarily) maintained. Informal literacies therefore arise precisely where there is a social necessity for display of expertise or familiarity. With the demise of the context for such a display, the competences go too.

Some of these shifting allegiances can be seen by briefly reviewing the data as a whole. The beginning of the period of data collection in 1989 could partly be characterized as the moment of *Home and Away*, a daily Australian soap opera. In relation to the children in the four London schools where data were collected, there was already intense interest and commitment to another Australian soap, *Neighbours*. (Its youth audience in the UK has actually ensured its continuing production in Australia. It has little following on home ground). In 1989, the *Neighbours* audience, who then included most of the sample children, were beginning to build a new segmental competence in relation to *Home and Away*. This had little to do with transferring the kind of conceptual knowledge about soaps which media studies privileges from one text to another; much more to do with adopting a stance in relation to the new text which established the grounds of readers' familiarity with it. This was the social arena in which their competence as fans could be weighed and acknowledged. This pre-occupation with shifting allegiances to particular soaps was to remain during the length of the study. (Anecdotal evidence suggests that, more than ten years after the original data were collected, soaps have now lost ground to a more varied set of interests among the current child audience). At the same time, over the period of data collection the horror genre came and went as an interest among a large section of the sample, lasting longest at the two suburban schools. Other segmental competences were of shorter duration, and involved a more localized section of the sample: during 1992, WWF (World Wrestling Federation) became a key focus among the boys in the suburban primary school. *Sweet Valley High* books seemed to have had a similar period of popularity with girls at the suburban secondary school but rapidly lost ground during their first year there in 1989 (Moss, 1993b). These texts did not gain equivalent attention across the rest of the sample during the research period.

Bernstein speaks of such segmental competences as having 'a specific, limited realization. Its function is, so to speak, consumed in its realization' (Bernstein, 1996: 179). By this he means that the competence is tied to the (social) context in which it is enacted. It does not set out to travel beyond that particular setting and will not be conceived of as having currency beyond that. Indeed he goes so far as to argue that the activation of a particular competence 'requires the local context, practices and relation-ships. Where such contexts practices and relationships are absent, or cannot be read unproblematically, the competence/literacy may not be demon-strated' (ibid.: 179).

The different segmental competences the sample formed around different kinds of media texts were closely tied to the contexts of their consumption. For the middle-class teenage girls in the sample, for instance, horror videos were primarily viewed in the context of sleepovers. During the year that sleepovers featured as the main means of socializing outside school for this group, talk about who had been at whose sleepover and who had seen which horror film provided a key context in which claims to be part of the horror genre's readership were most strongly voiced. When sleepovers were replaced by eating out as the mark of sophisticated teen relationships, interest in horror went too, leaving no apparent trace. The competences acquired around horror videos were not built on in subsequent media interests, but remained distinct, tied to the original context for consumption. Such competences are segmental, in Bernstein's terms, because they evolve in relation to the particular. Multiple, and in some senses, conflicting competences may be built simultaneously precisely because they are strongly boundary-marked by different eliciting contexts. Nine-year-olds who could voice a putative sense of themselves as (adult) horror viewers, able to withstand gruesome sights, could also voice an intimately childish view of their relationship to Edd the Duck, a popular puppet then fronting Children's BBC (Moss, 1993a).

This account runs contrary to the attempt by media studies to treat such informal competences as 'conceptual understandings', potentially portable property which can be abstracted from the current context (informal social interactions) and applied anywhere (including formal schooled settings), becoming in the process decontextualized and abstracted concepts. I will develop this distinction further through analysis of the WWF data collected during the research period.

WWF *WRESTLING* – HORIZONTAL DISCOURSE OVER TIME

WWF videos, magazines and associated merchandising were a major pre-occupation for many of the boys in the suburban primary school classroom in 1992. Using questionnaire returns on their media consumption to identify their media interests, I interviewed a group of four nine-year-old boys who seemed most committed to WWF. During the interview I used copies of the WWF *Wrestling* magazine, which they were then collecting, in an attempt to reduplicate the kind of conversations I saw happening among groups of boys in informal settings as they pored over the material together. Whether I quite achieved that aim or not (Moss, 1996b), what is clear is that the interview provided my interviewees with the chance to display their expertise to me, an expertise which they presented in terms of knowing the rules of wrestling; knowing the characters involved; their narrative histories and the settings of the action. Part of the conversation revolved around the question of how believable the action was, whether people really got hurt, or whether key events – the burning of wrestler Hulk Hogan's face with a blow torch, for instance – were fake. From the point of view of media studies, this would be characterized as talk about modality judgements, and would therefore qualify as being conceptually important (Buckingham, 1993). But from the point of view of the participants, talk about faking had a very different function. On the one hand the fact that much of the action could be considered 'fake' actually ensured that the boys had access to what otherwise purported to be scenes of violent, physical conflict, in which terrible punishment was meted out between wrestlers, and the bad guys played dirty, inflicting appalling injuries on their foes in moments of unbridled passion. Its potential 'fake' status (encoded within the texts themselves) is one way in which wrestling is presented to the audience, child and adult alike, distancing everyone from the moments of burlesque violence, talked up to be what in fact they are not. In this context, the violent action becomes a kind of exaggerated play, with no real consequences for the actors involved. (Contrast this with boxing's treatment of the same theme). In the context of these nine-year-olds, 'fake' becomes their passport to view, legitimating their access to what, if it were real, they would almost certainly not be watching.

On the other hand, for the boys themselves, doubts remained about the status of much of the material they were familiar with. At some point during the course of their interview, all of the participants asserted both sides of the argument: that fights and acts of violence were faked; and that they were not:

Akim: There's actually a match in here when Sergeant
         Slaughter . . . burnt Hulk Hogan's face.
Neal: Yeah, I know, I saw it where his face is all burnt.
Gemma: That's disgusting!
Ralph: No look, it's in this one, {finding the picture} (. . .) they came
         in his dressing room, but it's, it's fake, it doesn't show Hulk
         Hogan's face 'cos it didn't touch him.

'Fake' renders their position legitimate and morally permissible, as well as smart, able to suss out what is really going on; while the 'reality' of what they see heightens their macho status. They are well able to view what others would be too scared or wimpish to endure. Witness the following exchange which took place right at the end of the 1992 interview. Two of the boys were still looking through the magazines when two girls wandered into the room where we were, just as I had asked the boys why they thought no girls in their class were interested in WWF:

Akim: Maybe some girls are soft, and you know, they don't like
         fighting, they think (. . .)
Gemma: But I mean, a lot of this isn't really nasty fighting from what,
         well it's nasty, but it's also fake though.

> *Neal*:   Well it is, get lots of blood in cage fights, there's blood all over people's face.
>
> *Gemma*:   So you think it's just 'cos this is gory.
>
> *Akim*:   Yeah, probably.
>
> *Neal*:   I don't think girls like to watch people having their faces smashed up like what happens with Virgil, he whacks his nose and broke it.
>
> *Claudia*: Errgh! [expression of disgust]

Neal, perhaps with the girls in mind, categorically talks up the violence involved in wrestling in terms which had been the subject of considerable dispute among the group of boys just moments earlier. In this instance, the girls react with the anticipated disgust to the boys' representation of what wrestling is about: 'it's tough, it's nasty, people get hurt'. Meanwhile, Neal's insistence on the real violence he has witnessed allows him to claim status for himself and simultaneously gender the audience. He is with the macho boys; against the softy girls. This was a particularly live issue in this classroom context, where WWF was enormously popular with the boys alone, indeed, they actively excluded girls from taking part. (Several of the girls had already complained to me that the boys would never let them look at their magazines).

This is one example of the way in which the boys police the boundaries to their own competence. For them the potentially fake status of the wrestling texts remains insider knowledge. Indeed, the terms in which I construct the contrast 'fake'/'really nasty' in the comments I made above are very different from theirs – and in this context look totally out of place. The worthy adult's view! (Note also the difference between their take on the text and mine in the previous quote: for me, it's OK if it's fake, it's not if it isn't; my distinction, not theirs).

One year later and the WWF craze had come to an end. In questionnaire returns about their current media interests only two of the original group even logged that they had once been interested in WWF. For the others WWF simply seemed to have dropped out of view altogether. I decided to re-interview the same group of boys about WWF, using some of the same materials along with current issues of the magazine. This elicited a very different response to the texts. As they flicked through the pages of the magazines, the boys mainly used the opportunity to demonstrate why they'd gone off wrestling and distance themselves from the texts. Here 'the fact' that they had discovered it was fake was cited as a key factor:

> *Geoff*:   If I never found out it was fake I would probably still be on it, probably.
>
> *Several*: Yeah.

Labelling wrestling as 'fake' now operates in a different way. In 1992 it left open the ambiguous nature of the material. It was apparently violent and yet nobody really got hurt. It encouraged a particular kind of play with the text. But in 1993 'fake' becomes the means of disengaging themselves from wrestling. Back then they were duped, now they can spot the con:

Ralph: Yeah, look at that kick.
Akim: Exactly, look.
Geoff: Yeah, they probably, they probably, the glass would probably smash because they would put it on the floor to ma.., he just stood there like that.
Neal: Yeah, the thing is I can't really believe we didn't realize it was fake.

Of course, Neal is precisely right here. The claims that they were turned off wrestling after they realized it was fake is in fact rewriting history. What 'fake' serves to disguise now is the extent of their involvement with something which from the perspective of 1993 looks vaguely foolish.

Geoff: There's this teddy bear that my sister had when she was young and like it's about as big, it's a bunny rabbit and I used to punch it, slam kind of thing (laughter).
Akim: Yeah, that's what I used to do.
Neal: I used to pile drive my panda.
Gemma: So what was, what was, was that part of the fun, what was fun at the time?
Several: Yeah.
Ralph: It's entertainment.
Neal: I wouldn't have liked it if I didn't do the wrestling with my brother, probably and that teddy.

The practice they remember having engaged in when WWF wrestling was current has little to do with displaying expertise – indeed they almost compete to show how completely they've forgotten what they once knew. Instead they remember WWF as being about having likes and dislikes among the wrestlers, and about enjoying the rough and tumble of the physical play that accompanied acting out wrestling. In this account, the fact that when they were fans they didn't recognize the texts as 'fakes' places the responsibility for their erstwhile level of engagement firmly with the producers of the material – they were innocent dupes of some duplicitous process which palmed off phoney goods as the real thing. This lets them off the hook in relation to all they can now recall of what they used to do.

WRAPPING UP WWF *WRESTLING* IN BERNSTEIN'S TERMS

The point that Bernstein makes about horizontal discourse is that it serves a function in the immediate present. It emerges in relation to a particular set of circumstances and will travel no further. Trying to detach what the boys have to say about faking the action in wrestling in these two particular contexts and turn it into a kind of free-standing modality judgement on the nature of media texts would be to transform it from the exigencies of the present into something more akin to pedagogic discourse. Pedagogic and institutionalized settings might well set out to do this, but they would have effectively recontextualized the original discourse, in the process turning it into something else.

Bernstein suggests that informal literacies will be 'contradictory across contexts, but not within contexts. Today the objects of such knowledge are likely to be volatile and substitutable for each other' (Bernstein, 1996: 170). How the boys enact what it means to read and be a reader of WWF *Wrestling* in 1992 differs from how they enact what it means to be a reader in 1993. In 1993, they display a different set of competences. But this is not a story of conceptual development in which progressive study of the texts reveals how they are constructed. Rather, their take on the constructed nature of the texts serves a different purpose as they move from engagement to disengagement. Indeed, over this same period the key focus of interest for this group had changed to other media texts, mainly computer magazines, which had become the most sought-after items to circulate. One object had been substituted for another – bringing with it a different set of competences.

In the data overall, these shifts and changes in allegiances can be mapped out for the sample as a whole over time. Such allegiances are rarely singular. An interest in WWF evolved for this group of boys in this classroom alongside a more widely shared interest in horror videos and/or soaps, and in distinction to more specialist (and shorter-lived) interests in, for instance, *Fighting Fantasy* books (books modelled on computer games which the reader can steer their own way through). Informal literacies in my data look like temporary conjunctions of texts, contexts and readers which coalesce at particular moments in time. When the particular conjunction breaks up it leaves little apparent trace of what has gone before. If readership networks and the texts they relate to are in flux, so too are the competences they command.

INFORMAL LITERACIES FROM THE OFFICIAL PERSPECTIVE

Media studies, by and large, seeks to take out of this rapidly shifting scene some more enduring characteristics which can become the object of academic analysis. Some of the difficulties in doing this are encapsulated by the British Film Institute (BFI) study pack on the pop duo, Wham. Now chiefly remembered for its lead singer, George Michael, the study pack was published shortly after the group had already very publicly broken up. The BFI presented it as a case study on the music industry's approach to record promotion (Ferrari and James, 1989). By packaging it in this way it hoped to outstay the demise of popular interest in the actual object of study. Yet, in the classroom, this kind of attempt at recycling old material, which has in some cases long since lost its immediate currency with the audience, often provokes considerable difficulties for the students. Detached from the context which made it live, what are they supposed to make of it? (See Buckingham, *et al.*, 1990). Under these circumstances, such material can only make sense if submitted to another kind of (vertical) discourse.

So far, I have been outlining ways in which informal literacies differ from schooled literacies, in terms of the forms of knowledge they generate. Yet media studies makes it its business to transfer texts from one domain to another. I have been arguing that in a pedagogic setting such texts become subject to a very different discourse and are effectively transformed as objects of knowledge. The confusion which can arise for both students and teachers as texts make their way from one discursive setting to another has been the subject of some comment in media studies (Buckingham and Sefton-Green, 1994). Much of this has focused on clarifying the role of the teacher and reasserting their discursive primacy. But there is also a sense in which teachers reach out to the informal domain in the belief that this will enable students to make the most of what they already know. Knowledge in the informal domain is treated as potentially useful cultural capital for those who in other circumstances have very little to draw on in school settings (Dyson, 1997). What of the students? How do they react to the presence of informal texts in the formal domain? How far are they aware of the different principles at work in each setting?

INFORMAL VERSUS SCHOOLED LITERACIES – THE STUDENTS' VIEW

Towards the close of the period of data collection, I conducted a round of interviews with the children in the sample which focused on their use of texts in both domains: formal schooled settings and the informal settings in which they circulated texts among themselves. The interviews were structured so as to encourage participants to reflect on the kinds of texts they'd already encountered in school, and what had been done with them. Students were given a sample text of a kind that might be used in English, in this case a children's book, and asked to consider if and how it could be used in the classroom context they were familiar with. They were then given another sample text, in this instance a media text associated with more informal contexts, and asked to consider if and how it could be used in school. Finally, they were asked to choose a media interest of their own and talk about whether or not it had a place in school. This round of interviews generated some interesting responses.

All of the interviewees gave clear accounts of the pedagogic routines in which texts in official contexts were embedded. None of them, either working-class or middle-class students, thought that the media texts (those I chose for them, or those they chose for themselves) would transfer across into official settings, except possibly into art. This was so even for the interviewees in one school who were all then doing media studies. For students, the bar to the transfer of material from one domain to another seemed to hinge around notions of what was 'ours' (their own) and what was 'not ours' (the school's); what was 'play' and what was 'work' (see also Solsken, 1993); what was private and what was public. Here are some examples of the kinds of things they said:

On X-Men Comics:

> *Nigel*: I think comics should stay as a hobby and not, they shouldn't bring it in school because not everyone will want to do it and/it, it's really up to the person who, it's their prerogative what they want to do. I don't think they should bring it into school.
>
> (Middle-class boy aged 15)

On computer games:

> *Sudan*: People have like arguments about them, like some people say 'I'm brilliant at my game', and like, if someone wants to play their game they're going to say 'No, you can't play, it's my game' and then the teacher's going to turn it off.
>
> (Working-class boy aged ten)

On the *Sweet Valley High* series:

> *Lucy*: Also, it, when it's really embarrassing, you're not going to want to go and read something like this to Mrs E are you? It's really, it's difficult, isn't it// If you're in the middle of one of these books where it says they go to a shop and she tries on bras, you're not going to want to read that to Mrs E, are you?
> *Mia*: Yeah, when everyone is listening around you.
>
> (Middle-class girls aged 11)

It is as if they cannot imagine another way of negotiating the presence of these texts on the school curriculum which doesn't involve them being run over by school routines and school ways of doing things, and in the process being transformed beyond recognition. Resources which confer status and prestige outside of official school contexts become problematic in the context of the classroom.

SCHOOLED LITERACIES – A CONTRAST IN SOCIAL CLASS PERSPECTIVES

The children who were recruited to the sample came from both middle- and working-class backgrounds – indeed the schools were deliberately chosen to reflect such contrasts in social composition, two drawing from mainly working-class, two from mainly middle-class catchment areas. The kinds of informal literacies I documented in my data showed little variation between middle-class and working-class children, except in terms of the quantity of resources available. Middle-class children had access to more media resources, and more time to invest in their use, perhaps because they were also less likely to be allowed to 'play out', simply hanging round with their friends on the street. In the older middle-class age group, there tended to be more specialization, with boys in particular priding themselves on their collections of scarce resources, but this seemed incidental to the way in which competences were formed around particular texts. However, in relation to their respective take on the school curriculum, much greater contrasts emerged between the two groups. Although both working-class and middle-class children frequently found school boring:

> Celia: Usually English books, books that you do in English you just assume are immediately empty and they're going to be boring.
> (Middle-class girl aged 15)

middle-class children consistently represented both the nature of the curriculum and their relationship to it in ways which differed from their working-class counterparts.

Middle-class children saw the school curriculum as defining literacy in terms which are hierarchical and progressive. They represented themselves as at particular point on this ladder of expertise.

> Dean: Would this book be suitable for use in English lessons?
> Celia: Yeah, I think it would, [...]
> Maria: Yes, it would because it looks/it looks very kind of childish and young.
> Dean: Let me see.
> Debbie: Crap.

Maria: It looks like a sort of kiddie's book, It looks very um ...
Dean: (Reading the title) *Run to the Ark* (He goes on to read out the blurb) [...]
Dean: Umm. This is a Puffin book which suggests to me that it is a children's book.
Debbie: Yeah, and the cover looks like it's for ten-year-olds
Celia: Think it would be better for the first year [of secondary school]
Maria: Yes.
Debbie: I'd probably read it in the first year but I wouldn't read it now.

(Middle-class 15-year-olds)

Through their talk, this group fix the text's appropriate place in a sequence of school knowledge, and their own place in relation to that order. The vertical structure of schooling is apparent in what they say. In measuring themselves against the school curriculum the middle-class children measure themselves against a hierarchical sequence. Some of them may be more or less far up the ladder, but there is a pathway mapped out for them through the work they undertake. The literacy curriculum for them is a means which serves an end. Whether they like what they do or not, is largely irrelevant to accomplishing that purpose:

Celia: When you have an assignment it just goes on for ever, it's really awful when your English teacher misses the home-work and about three weeks later says 'Oh, you missed the homework about three weeks ago so you're going to have to do it tonight' even though you've got three projects to do.
Maria: Right, and then that's not the only problem, you've just finished an assignment that you just did last weekend, you've handed it in and then on the Monday morning ... she gives out another assignment.

(Middle-class 15-year-olds)

This is schooling as work, work which you aim to get through, its reward lying at some point in the future.

By contrast, none of the working-class children focused on the hier-archical sequencing of school literacy in this way. In making judgements about particular texts, they were much more likely to react simply in terms of their own immediate preferences:

Hayley: It sounds, it sounds good, Miss. I should like to read that book.

(Working-class 11-year-old)

They talked about what they were currently doing in school in terms of what they liked or disliked. Where they tolerated or engaged with school procedures they showed no signs of appropriating its sequential structures for their own purposes. Where they underlined their resistance to schooling, they indicated that for them school work does not provide a meaningful alternative to play; it simply imposes its own authority:

> *Int*:   If Mr L say was to bring this (tabloid newspaper) into an English lesson, what do you think he would do with it?
> *Annie*:   Probably pick out something like this (laughter) I don't know, (flicking through the pages) where is it?
> *Natalie*: Pick out something really detailed.
> *Annie*:   Yeah, the politics or something like that.
> *Carla*:   Yeah! (laughter, as they choose the most boring looking article they can find)
>
>   (Working-class girls, aged 15)

In the one case in the data when three working-class girls get close to identifying a kind of educational pathway, vertically and hierarchically sequenced, they do so with reference to two middle-class girls in their class whom they depict as clearly orienting themselves differently to school work. In this section of the interview, they've been talking about how boring Shakespeare is, now a compulsory part of their English lessons:

> *Int*:   Do you think anybody gets anything out of the old stuff?
> *Annie*:   It depends really.
> *Carla*:   The old people (laughter)
> *Annie*:   Depends who's=^{3}
> *Natalie*: =teaching us
> *Annie*:   No, it depends who's interested in it [...]
> *Natalie*: I think, I think, yeah, if you've got an interest in it and you can understand it properly, then yeah [they suggest who might understand]
> *Annie*:   Maybe J and D would understand that, I mean if you're interested in, then you'd do it because you want to go to college and do English again, that's probably all you would get, that's what Sir said anyway.

By contrast, they represent themselves as excluded from this pathway:

> *Annie*:   There's all these words like 'Thy shall' and all this rubbish and words you've never even heard of before (laughter)
> *Carla*:   There is, and you don't understand three quarters of it anyway.

Int:	What, are you having to write about it as well?
Annie:	Yeah, then we watched the film of it and I didn't understand and (laughs) I was laughing.
Natalie:	Really true, and that [...] the face of that woman (laughter) Every time she said something me and Annie started laughing.
Annie:	Yeah, sir kept on shouting 'Be quiet you silly girl' (in posh voice) (laughter)

(15-year-old working-class girls)

Schooling is about surviving this kind of social regulation, not buying into a process which is leading somewhere else. This group of 15-year-old girls were nearing the end of their compulsory schooling. One was a persistent truant at the time of the interview, one had been so during a substantial part of her earlier school career. My argument is not that they are lacking the cultural capital to connect with the literacy experience which is on offer in their English classroom, but that they have made a realistic appraisal of their own futures and schooling in this context offers them nowhere to go. They show no signs of having appropriated schooling's sequential and hierarchical knowledge structures because such structures are quite literally taking them nowhere.

LITERACIES IN AND OUT OF SCHOOL

Informal literacies create different kinds of knowledge structures from schooled literacies, tied as they are to the exigencies of the present moment. Competences which form as part of informal literacies depend upon the specifics of the eliciting context. While the eliciting context endures, so will the competence. Remove the contexts which sustain such literacies and the literacies themselves pass without trace. They cannot be reconstituted in their original form, as the boys' talk about WWF one year after the craze had passed shows. Informal literacies are regulated quite differently from official literacies and the institutionalized trappings of schooling which the latter inevitably bring with them. Precisely because of the differences such modes of regulation engender, informal literacies do not automatically act as a powerful resource within schooled settings. The children in my data recognize this. When informal literacies are transferred over to pedagogic settings, they and the texts they are associated with are themselves transformed, and recontextualized. None of the children interviewed wished this for the texts they had themselves invested in.

The children in my data experience both forms of literacy: the informal and the official. They all travel between them, as they travel between home and school. Differences emerge in terms of what they make of this. For middle-class children the hierarchical and sequential structuring of school knowledge seems both more visible and more inclusive. Working-class children do not represent school knowledge structures, nor their own relationship to them, in the same way. I see this not as evidence for conceptually different understandings, but as evidence of a clear difference in their own sense of their socially constructed futures: schooling tells them different outcomes to their place in the world.

CONSTRUCTING A NEW LITERACY CURRICULUM: THE POSSIBILITIES FOR FUSION

More than a decade away from the point in time when these data were collected, what does this argument mean for how we think about curriculum content, both what the content of the literacy curriculum is now and what it could be? In the discussion above I have highlighted the instability of informal literacies, and their capacity to shift-shape according to context and over time. In Bernsteinian terms, the ways in which they do this are characteristic of their horizontal construction. I have argued that this very instability and the plurality of their potential reference points make the transfer of informal literacies into the vertical structures of schooled knowledge problematic.

But, of course, schooled literacy changes over time too. It can itself be predicated on more or less rapprochement between literacy practices that happen inside and outside its own domain (Moss, 2002). I have argued elsewhere that right now governments and their agencies are increasingly hastening the move towards performance pedagogies (Bernstein, 1996) and in the process strengthening the boundaries between home and school practices while tightening control over what should be taught and how (Moss, 2001a; 2002). Yet, almost in parallel, a large weight of professional opinion is revoicing the proposition that schools make too little of what children already know. This time round, and from a variety of quarters, comes a sense that the literacy curriculum is profoundly out of step with the times, unable to accommodate to the flow of new media or respond to the new possibilities for the increased combination and integration of verbal, visual and aural resources which digital technologies herald (Kress, 2003). From this point of view, children's out-of-school knowledge begins to stand for knowledge of the media forms which schools overlook, dominated as the latter institutions are by a paper-based view of literacy, coterminous with the media technologies of an earlier age. Appealing to children's knowledge of contemporary media then highlights how far school knowledge is predicated on a historically specific and static view of what literacy is (Lankshear, chapter 6, this volume). But if this helps identify a problem, does this kind of appeal solve the question of what the school literacy curriculum should become? Lankshear, for instance, identifies a number of dilemmas which both schools and pupils face as technologies which are already in use out of school begin to enter into the school's regulatory ambit. How does the argument I have made above contribute to such discussion?

It seems to me entirely possible to accept the proposition that the school curriculum, particularly in the secondary sector, looks increasingly tied to the priorities of another age, while remaining much more cautious about whether or in what ways the knowledge that children themselves already have can act as a remedy for this. I think there are a number of issues which require further consideration before the best ways of co-opting resources familiar from non-pedagogic contexts into literacy classrooms can finally be settled. This is not to rule such an objective out altogether or absolve schools from the job of connecting with what their pupils know. But I would argue that any such strategy needs to take account of the following:

1. It is possible to overestimate how expert or knowledgeable children are about out-of-school texts and new technologies (Moss, 1993a). Many such resources are not equally shared either between individuals or within communities (Moss, 2001b). Moreover, in the context of informal peer talk, where knowledge claims play a highly charged role in establishing a social hierarchy between peers, children need few objective reference points for the claims they make about their expertise. So those who know very little about current topics of peer interest, such as horror, football or warfare, can sound as if they do among the right audience (Moss, 2003). However, schools use very different criteria to adjudicate between claims about depth of knowledge. This can create problems for both teachers and pupils, especially if it is uncertain whose criteria for judging expertise are really in play at any given time.

2. The co-option of what children know outside of school into school will always entail transformation. How such transformations can best be effected will probably remain a matter for ongoing negotiation in particular local settings. In arguing for 'a transformative pedagogy of literacy fusion' which could merge children's cultural interests with school requirements, Elaine Millard rightly suggests that 'Effective fusion relies heavily on ... teachers' attentiveness to the interests and skills brought into the classroom and their skill in helping children to transform what they already know into stuff that will give them agency in a wider world' (Millard,

2003: 7). If transformation, rather than seamless incorporation, is the goal, then teachers need to be very clear about what they are hoping to transform into what and how that process will be accomplished. They may also want to consider what is best left outside schooled settings. Children themselves may well have strong views on what falls which side of this line. Such views should be respected.

3. Deciding what needs to change about the literacy curriculum within schools and what needs to stay the same is a long-term process. Teachers will not solve the predicament new media pose by simply following where children lead. Indeed, it may well be that the return to a centrally defined and prescriptive literacy curriculum, focused on traditional understandings of what literacy can do, in fact provides a necessary breathing space in which to digest what is really significant about the new technologies, as well as what is not (Noss and Pachler, 1999). Bernstein makes an important analytic distinction between the instructional and the regulative in pedagogic discourse. To date most of the contributions to reform of the literacy curriculum have concentrated on reforming its instructional content, bringing that content more into line with the proliferation of the new media. Maybe we need to turn much more directly to the regulative aspects of the curriculum and imagine much more precisely what new forms such regulation could take.

Middle-class and working-class children demonstrated different kinds of orientation to schooling and the social futures it represents in the research data presented above. This reminds us that questions about education and pedagogic discourse are also questions about the unequal distribution of social power. Such inequalities cannot be wished away. Bernstein's insistence on the differences between informal and official literacies delineates a clearer basis on which to think through what knowledge is, for whom, and what it might become, as well as what we wish it would be.

NOTES

1 A version of this chapter was first published in *Linguistics and Education* 11 (1): 47–64 (2000). This was a special issue on Knowledge, Identity and Pedagogy: Themes from the Work of Basil Bernstein.
2 Two of these projects, at the beginning and end of the cycle, were funded by the Economic and Social Research Council, UK; the other was funded by the Institute of Education, University of London. The Television Literacy Research Project 1989–91, was staffed by David Buckingham, Valerie Hey and Gemma Moss; Gemma Moss was director and principal researcher on the Informal Literacies Project, 1991–92, and the Negotiated Literacies Project 1993–95.
3 The convention = has been used to signal when one speaker follows another without pause.

REFERENCES

Baker, C.D. (1990). Literacy practices and social relations in classroom reading events. In A. Luke and C.D. Baker (eds) *Towards a critical sociology of reading: Papers of the 12th world congress of reading*. Amsterdam: John Benjamins.

Bazalgette, C. (ed.) (1989). *Primary media education: A curriculum statement*. London: British Film Institute.

Bernstein, B. (1996). *Pedagogy, symbolic control and identity*. London: Taylor and Francis.

Bourne, J. (2000). New imaginings of reading for a new moral order: A review of the production, transmission and acquisition of a new pedagogic culture in the UK. *Linguistics and Education*, 11 (1): 31–45.

Buckingham, D. (1993). *Children talking television: The making of television literacy*. London: Falmer Press.

Buckingham, D., Fraser, P. and Mayman, N. (1990). Stepping into the void: Beginning classroom research in media education. In D. Buckingham (ed.) *Watching media learning*. London: Falmer Press.

Buckingham, D. and Sefton-Green, J. (1994). *Cultural studies goes to school*. London: Falmer Press.

Dombey, H. (1988). Partners in the telling. In M. Meek and C. Mills (eds) *Language and literacy in the primary school*. London: Falmer Press.

Dyson, A.H. (1997). *Writing Superheroes: Contemporary Childhood, Popular Culture and Classroom Literacy*. New York: Teachers College Press.

Ferrari, L. and James, C. (1989). *Wham! wrapping*. London: British Film Institute.

Kress, G. (2003) *Literacy in the New Media Age*. London: Routledge.

Maybin, J. and Moss, G. (1993). Talk about texts: Reading as a social event. *Journal of Research in Reading*, 16 (12): 138–47.

Millard, E. (2003). Towards a literacy of fusion: new times, new teaching and learning? *Reading, literacy and language*, 37 (1): 3–8.

Mills, C. (1988). Making sense of reading: key words or Grandma Swagg. In M. Meek and C. Mills (eds) *Language and literacy in the primary school*. London: Falmer Press.

Moss, G. (1993a). Children talk horror videos: Reading as a social performance. *Australian Journal of Education*, 37 (2): 169–81.

Moss, G. (1993b). Girls tell the teen romance: Four reading histories. In D. Buckingham (ed) *Reading audiences: Young people and the media*. Manchester: Manchester University Press.

Moss, G. (1996a). Negotiated Literacies: How children enact what counts as reading in different social settings. Unpublished PhD Thesis. Open University.

Moss, G. (1996b). How boys handle WWF Wrestling. In B. Bachmair and G. Kress (eds) *Hollen-Inszenierung 'Wrestling'*. Munich: Leske Budrich.

Moss, G. (2001a). On literacy and the social organization of knowledge inside and outside school. *Language and Education*, 15 (2&3): 146–61.

Moss, G. (2001b). Seeing with the camera: Analysing children's photographs of literacy in the home. *Journal of Research in Reading*, 24 (3): 279–92.

Moss, G. (2002). Literacy and Pedagogy in Flux: Constructing the object of study from a Bernsteinian perspective. *British Journal of Sociology of Education*, **23** (4): 549–58.

Moss, G. (2003). Putting the text back into practice: Junior age non-fiction as objects of design. In C. Jewitt and G. Kress (eds) *Multimodal Literacy*. New York: Peter Lang.

Noss, R. and Pachler, N. (1999). The challenge of new technologies: Doing old things in a new way or doing new things? In Mortimore, P. (ed.) *Understanding Pedagogy and its impact on learning*. London: Paul Chapman.

Solsken, J. (1993). *Literacy and gender*. Norwood: Ablex.

Chapter 8

Making it move, making it mean: animation, print literacy and the metafunctions of language

David Parker

In this chapter, I want to outline research findings from an arts and media project, funded by the Arts Council England's New Audiences programme. Most members of the research team had had some previous experience researching media and literacy work in schools; much of their work undertaken jointly with the British Film Institute and King's College, London, under the auspices of the Centre for Research on Literacy and the Media.

The project, which will be described in greater detail below, teamed a poet and an animator-in-residence with a school-based researcher and revolved around the adaptation of a fictional narrative, first into an episodic poem and then into an animated film. The research element constituted an exploration of the relationships between the adaptation process and literacy. We wanted to unpick how traversing genres and media with a single core text as a touchstone might enhance the learning experiences of the young people involved. We were particularly interested in the movement between print and moving-image media and were looking to explore through this a series of hypotheses that arose from previous work (Parker, 1999; Oldham, 1999).

Before we move on to discuss the work in more detail, I will offer a brief overview of some recent research that focuses on the relationship between moving-image and literacy, including our own earlier work. I do this primarily in order to contextualize the project within a broader field, but additionally because it is necessary to provide some of the findings from separate studies across disparate fields that, in combination, seem to aggregate into a set of similar and significant conclusions.

The relationship between media and literacy has a relatively long and fiercely contested history. This is unsurprising, given that it acts as a conduit for aspects of broader educational debate – primarily notions of standards, and a perception of those standards falling in relation to previous rates of literacy attainment. The long-held popular theory that a correlation exists between a decline in literacy standards and a concomitant rise in the consumption of media by young people has been endorsed by the press for many years, despite there being little or no hard evidence to support the claim. Brooks (1997) has shown, through a rigorous comparative study, that, despite public perceptions to the contrary, in real terms, there has been no significant decline in literacy attainment in the UK since 1945. While Brooks found a fall in average performance among eight-year-olds in the late 1980s, which could have been attributed to large numbers of experienced teachers taking early retirement, he also found that reading standards in Britain had remained almost static throughout the past half-century. This is despite the rise and fall of radically different teaching methods throughout that time. Neither traditional phonics teaching nor the 'newer' techniques have significantly improved or worsened average performance.

Nevertheless, simplistic correlations continue to be made between many social problems and the popular media, especially film and television. In reality, within schools a somewhat different story emerges. For many years a body of research has built up from within university education departments, especially within the Anglophone countries, which suggests powerful links may exist between the kinds of narratives children and young people enjoy as consumers and the kinds of learning expectations schools and parents hold as desirable in relation to literacy. Marsh and Millard (2000) compellingly show how 'top–down' models of literacy can fail to connect with what is popular in terms of valued texts among young people and thereby exclude rather than engage. They also illustrate how uses of media can unlock a renewed motivation within learners and create the necessary conditions for re-engagement with literacy and the acquisition of print-based skills.

Similarly, Robinson (1997) has described how a 'social reading practice', one which draws film, TV and video into the ambit of what is 'acceptable' in terms of reading texts, can be enormously empowering for emergent readers. Children, it seems, are able to draw on connections and parallels that are natural to their growing understanding of story and story constructions, moving freely across media and modes, but which the adult world, perhaps through its need to compartmentalize knowledge and experience, seem invisible. Mackey (1999) has also pointed out the multiple levels of reader engagement with film and televisual texts. Her work has shown how it offers a way into structural aspects of narrative – conveyed visually through the medium of the moving-image it can be remade conceptually to fit print-based skills.

At the British Film Institute (BFI), a range of research and development projects, and particularly those that arose out of collaboration with King's College, have examined some of the links that can be exploited by teachers when media is incorporated within literacy teaching. My own work (Parker, 1999) has suggested ways in which structural similarities and differences between films and books can be used to compare moving-image texts and written texts as part of a media *production* process. And (Parker and Sefton-Green, 2000) how, specifically, the process of animation can promote, through a staged interaction with plot, theme and narrative, an incrementally 'framed' engagement with print texts. In an accompanying research project, Oldham (1999) has shown how reading multiple film adaptations of a source print text can raise levels of critical literacy among groups of readers, illuminating both the book and film versions of a single narrative. Her work suggests embedded understandings of narrative structure, along with important skills such as prediction, may be developed through moving-image media, but that they would need teasing out through teacher mediation in order to fully inform understandings of print media. In the USA Van den Broek (2001) illustrates in an online paper[1] the positive relationship between TV viewing and the development of reading comprehension.

Overall, then, there is a growing body of research worldwide that suggests that the simplistic notion of a negative relationship between media and literacy is not substantiated by grounded research studies. The research suggesting other more positive relationships between moving-image culture and print literacy forms the context for the findings of the Animated English project.

THE NEW AUDIENCES 'ANIMATED ENGLISH' PROJECT

The project, funded by the Arts Council England's New Audiences programme, was undertaken at a co-educational, multi-ethnic comprehensive school in West London in 2002. New Audiences was a £20 million initiative which ran from 1998 to 2003. It aimed to encourage as many people as possible to participate in and benefit from the arts.

The Animated English project was devised jointly by the BFI and the School of Education at King's College, London, involved two mixed-ability Year 7 English classes who aimed to create an animated film version of episodes from a comic horror novel, *Groosham Grange*, by Anthony Horowitz. Each class was split into six groups of four or five children, and each group was tasked, while working in conjunction with a poet-in-residence, with adapting a section of the novel into a short narrative poem. The rest of the work, which consisted of ten 50-minute lessons per class, was carried out under the guidance of the BFI's Animation Officer. Each group, after being introduced to some key concepts of film-making and visual design, created a storyboard for their poem, produced the necessary backgrounds, characters and props (using coloured pens and paper), and then filmed their section of the story, shot by shot, refining their approach in relation to the particular affordances of the medium. The finished films were edited using the software package *iMovie*. The pupils were in control of the editing of their material, cutting it, adding sound effects and voice-overs, and employing cross-fades.

Beyond noting changes in language use – wider vocabulary, greater powers of description with regard to space and time – which might occur in children's speaking and writing as a result of storyboarding, filming and editing, this project also aimed to elucidate the narrative links between print and moving-image media. It attempted to demonstrate how an engagement with the different conceptual and technological demands of each medium might lead to enhanced comprehension of storytelling in general. At a more tentative level, it explored how the explicit demands of composition required by the creation of an animated film (ideas of focus, audience, planning, arrangement and editing) might be used as a scaffold for the less evident compositional demands of writing. Finally, it addressed the definition of literacy itself, and asked why the conceptual and compositional skills that can be developed through intelligent use of the new media should not be regarded in themselves as an inherent part of literacy rather than as merely playing a subordinate role. Each of these elements will be outlined and discussed below.

SUMMARY OF MAIN FINDINGS

Our key findings were, in some ways, counter-intuitive. They were based on evidence from a wide range of sources, including our own detailed observation and analysis. These key findings are summarized below in bullet form, and will be discussed in more detail later.

- The Key Stage 3 research project, using animation as a means of promoting writing and a richer understanding of print narrative, reinforces some key aspects of previous research; most importantly, the notion that children are quicker to come to an overall understanding of a complete story when they have an opportunity to engage with it through more than one medium, and this is especially true if moving-image media is used.
- The role of the poet-in-residence, which had been hypothesized as a possible way of structuring the writing of the children, became, at times, too constrictive, in the sense that poetical form overrode the eventual goal of moving-image structure and narrative. A writer-in-residence with a more narrative focus may have offered a smoother transition between each medium.
- The students' compositional skills with regard to structuring a narrative in film were far ahead of their written compositional skills. Those elements that have been identified as key areas of narrative development in children – orientation and coherence – were, through the explicit demands of focalization and sequencing in film-making, significantly

improved. If we add 'content' to these two categories, as a narrative feature that is made explicit through moving image, then we have there terms that correlate to Halliday's (1978, 1985) metafunctions of language the ideational (content), the interpersonal (orientation) and the textual (coherence).

- There is strong evidence from this project to suggest that mediating literature through structured teaching of the moving image creates a cultural bridge that can foster new communities of practice by drawing from childen's existing funds of knowledge of these texts (Moll *et al.*, 1992). Reluctant or emergent readers may become more positive about books when they are enabled to talk about and conceptualize one medium in terms of another.

Yet the development of these key concepts is predicated on long-term planning and recursive opportunity. Using moving-image media production as a catalyst for introducing and reinforcing the general principles or metafunctions in such a way that they may 'cross over' and be of use in strengthening reading and writing print texts can only occur if sessions using media can be regularly timetabled. This leads to a central paradox. In an already overloaded curriculum we need to carve out the space and time necessary to achieve a greater, more inclusive impact on literacy attainment. Animation can be a time-consuming process and so we need to make the time, either by conflating mutually achievable learning aims (ICT and Art and Design are both curriculum 'spaces' that could logically 'dovetail' with this approach to literacy), or reduce the time by looking at moving-image alternatives to animation – i.e. live action filming and editing or the use of archive material through editing work. Some of these pressing problems may be addressed by potential changes to the curriculum in the face of increased awareness of personalized learning and multiple intelligence theory (Gardner, 1999).

THEORIZING THE FINDINGS

So far I have outlined some relevant literature, a description of the Animated English project and a summary of our key findings. Here I want to explore in a little more detail some of the theoretical interpretations that may account for the relationships between moving-image media and literacy that appear to emerge from the project. It has been useful for the research team to look at possible connections between M.A.K. Halliday's (1978) metafunctions of language and research into the development of literacy in children. Halliday's three metafunctions, present in any communicational act, are the *ideational*, the *interpersonal* and the *textual*. These are further refined in relation to visual grammar by Kress and Van Leeuwen (1996).

However, research and exploration into children's literacy begins, almost inevitably, with Piaget. The areas in which he identified a more limited development in younger children – order, causality and orientation – have been refined but not challenged by subsequent research. Clearly, order and causality correspond to Halliday's textual function and the need for coherence within a text; orientation corresponds to Halliday's interpersonal function and the clear establishment of relations between participants in any communicative act. The content of children's narratives – corresponding to Halliday's ideational function – has received less attention. Recent research highlights the influence of personal and situational context on content (Burn and Parker, 2003), but at a simpler level one is looking, in literacy, for imaginative and expressive development; that is, advances in breadth of reference, depth of detail and use of figurative language. The definition of literacy is under much debate, but perhaps it can be agreed, with reference to studies of children's narrative development, that three main criteria by which literacy attainment can be measured are: depth/breadth of content and expression; understanding and use of perspective/orientation/audience awareness; and improved coherence. These three, it is possible to suggest, correspond to Halliday's metafunctions of language: the ideational, interpersonal and textual. It should be no surprise that developments in literacy equate to a more developed understanding and use of the three essential functions common to all communicative acts.

In further support for this contention, it can be shown that many of the requirements for Writing, Reading, Speaking and Listening in the National Curriculum can be sorted under the same three categories. Furthermore, specific differences between attainment levels correspond to development within these three categories, concentrating on varied vocabulary, the extent to which the reader has been borne in mind, and clarity and complexity of expression.

If these three areas constitute literacy, and their development constitutes a valid and important part of the English curriculum, it is necessary to discover the best ways in which such development can be taught and learned. Reference is now made to Gunther Kress and multimodality (Kress, 1993). Following his adaptation, or extrapolation, of Halliday's metafunctions for all meaning-making modes (such as gesture, visual aids, speech, materiality, printed words), it is here not presumed that language is alone the best way to communicate/explore ideas and information. This is true even – or especially – when language itself is the subject of study. There may, indeed, be many ways to foster knowledge, skills and understanding with regard to content, orientation and coherence, but the particular focus of this study is the controversial and relatively new mode of moving image. (This is a mode unexplored and untheorized by Kress). The research question, therefore, is: in what ways can work with moving-image media help to develop the content, orientation and coherence of children's writing (and their comprehension of these elements with regard to their reading)?

Two things must now be established. First: are there elements of the grammar of film, as identified by theorists in that field, which correspond to content, orientation and coherence (that is, which correspond with the areas identified as central to the development of literacy)? Second: what, in Kress's terms, are the specific functional affordances of moving-image media? In other words, can we distinguish the ideational, interpersonal and textual affordances of moving-image media and then demonstrate how these can be used to convey/explore the elements of literacy (content, orientation and coherence)?

It turns out that, not only are there clear correspondences between literacy criteria and the grammar of moving-image media, but that a single – very interesting and potentially useful – quality characterizes the affordance of moving-image media: explicitness. Theoretical accounts of narrative and film, though they differ in emphasis and interpretation, agree upon certain elements that distinguish all film narratives. There is the representation of states of affairs in the world (the representation of character and setting). This is ideational. There is the matter of perspective, point of view, focalization (the relation between the events/characters shown and the audience). This is interpersonal. And there is the question of time (sequence, causality, continuity, coherence). This is textual. Working with moving-image media it is impossible not to deal with these elements. But where, in writing, the ideational, interpersonal and textual demands of narrative can go unnoticed, receiving relatively little critical attention from writers and readers, the explicit nature of film makes it all but impossible for any film-maker or spectator to ignore anomalies, faults and gaps in composition. It is through this quality of explicitness that moving-image media might prove to be most useful in supporting various schemes of work for literacy development. (It will not be argued that explicitness is always a virtue; but it remains true that even where it fails – in nuance, say, or in conveying abstractions, ideas, affections – it fails explicitly and is therefore still valuable as a learning tool).

In the school-based research carried out for this project, it can be shown that the work produced using moving-image media consistently exhibited higher levels of correspondent literacy than that shown in the same children's writing. In other words, areas identified as central to the development of conventional print literacy are confronted and understood much more easily using moving-image media. There is, of course, no direct transfer of these skills straight from one mode to another. Much depends on an appropriate pedagogy. But such clear contrasts in attainment with regard to the same basic elements of literacy point the way towards much future research. With the ideational function, specificity and concreteness of representation were far higher in the films than in the poems. With regard to orientation, awareness of audience was evident in every shot, and there was much discussion and revision as a consequence of the camera acting as 'reader manqué' for the film texts. Point of view was more consistent and precise compared with written work, and imaginative alterations of perspective were used for dramatic effect. With regard to coherence, the storyboarding and filming ensured that causality was a priority in the structuring of these narratives. There were clear representations of action within a consistent time frame, and no – or at least no unacknowledged – disruptive jumps, loose ends, divisions or confusion. All the films were economical in their telling, unlike much of the written work.

These are achievements that in themselves constitute literacy attainment, if we take the broad view of literacy. But the central aim of research in this area must be to find ways in which the skills and levels of understanding in one mode can be used to support and complement those of another. How can the explicitness of moving-image media be used to improve conventional print literacy? Can explicitness be used to reveal some of the seemingly hidden elements of literacy? And can moving-image media demonstrate, through their own shortcomings, some of the qualities peculiar to the art of writing? Vygotsky's suggested Zone of Proximal Development could be brought into play here (Vygotsky, 1980). Just as there is a progression, for Vygotsky, from the interpersonal to the intrapersonal, one might posit that a child could be led from the explicit discovery of certain concepts of narrative and literacy to the internalization of those concepts.

Aside from the metafunctional relations suggested by this research project, there are other, more 'obvious', benefits to literacy from the use of moving-image media in the English classroom. Put simply, there are many elements of the film-making process that correspond to specific requirements of the National Curriculum. The group work on devising narrative poems, creating storyboards and making films clearly involved group discussion and interaction; the need to follow detailed instructions in all these areas required work on listening skills. The need to scan a narrative for plot summary and for details of action, character and setting in order to create a storyboard, incorporated reading skills and encouraged greater familiarity with the text. The listing of events and the narrative poems involved writing skills, and the choice of words used within each film involved suiting writing to a particular medium. Moreover, there were 'obvious' benefits in terms of composition. The careful preparation of materials for the storyboards and filming demanded development of planning skills. And the refinement of work, through the filming process and when editing the filmed material, encouraged revision and criticism of work in process. All these elements can be simply itemized and backed up with evidence from written and spoken data, along with observational notes. But the complicated, expensive and time-consuming nature of film-making means that these benefits alone, though they rebut claims that moving-image work is mindless play and detrimental to literacy, would not be enough on their own to make a claim for the importance of using this technology widely in the English classroom. The focus, therefore, should be on correspondence at a more fundamental level.

The key element in the transference of skills from one area to another resides in pedagogy. As it stands, research into the relations between moving-image media and print literacy can verify certain accidental or coincidental benefits, and can posit analogues between the two modes with regard to narrative and communicational development. What cannot be demonstrated is that simply using the new technology will systematically benefit print literacy across the board. This is because there is no such thing as 'simply using'. The desired learning outcomes, preferred methodology and inherent (or cultivated) ideology of any teacher and teaching system will determine the way in which the established relations develop.

At the far end of this research, one can bear in mind the theorizing that is currently going on in academies with regard to humanities and computing. Scholars such as Richard Lanham (1993) and W.J. Mitchell (1986) have considered how hypertext, the electronic word and imagetext are altering the very notion or essence of literacy.

More immediately, however, there are many potential research projects using moving-image media that spring to mind, based upon more conventional definitions of literacy and its development; projects that focus upon similarities and differences between moving-image and print with regard to content, orientation and coherence; projects, indeed, that focus on the processes of composition (ranging from draft to edit) without necessarily demanding a finished (film) product. What is essential to this, however, is a deep understanding of the relationship between signs, meanings and media, an understanding that moves beyond semiotics and begins to embrace grounded accounts of pedagogy, too.

NOTE

1 http://www.ciera.org/library/archive/2001-02/04OCT99-58-MSarchive.html

REFERENCES

Buckingham, D. (2001) *New Media Literacies: Informal learning, digital technologies and education*. London: Institute for Public Policy Research.

Burn, A. and Parker, D. (2003) *Analysing media texts*. London: Continuum.

Halliday, M.A.K. (1978) *Language as Social Semiotic*. London: Edward Arnold.

Halliday, M.A.K. (1985) *An Introduction to Functional Grammar*. London: Edward Arnold.

Kress, G. (1993), 'Representational Resources and the production of subjectivity: questions for the theoretical development of Critical Discourse Analysis in a multicultural society', London University Institute of Education, unpublished paper.

Kress, G. and Van Leeuwen, T. (2001) *Multimodal Discourse*. London: Edward Arnold.

Lanham, R. (1993) *The Electronic Word: Democracy, Technology, and the Arts*. Chicago and London: University of Chicago Press.

Lynch, J.S. and van den Broek, P., *Fostering comprehension skills in preschool children: Using TV and other media to encourage inference-making*. Paper presented at the Georgia Reading Excellence Act Best Practices Institutes, Savannah and Atlanta, Georgia, December, 2001.

Mackey (1999). Playing in the phase space: Contemporary forms of narrative pleasure. *Signal*. 88, 16–33.

Marsh, J. and Millard, E. (2000). *Literacy and Popular Culture: Using Children's Culture in the Classroom*. London: Paul Chapman.

Mitchell, W.J. (1986) *Iconology: image, text, ideology*. Chicago and London: University of Chicago Press.

Oldham, J. (1999) 'The book of the film: enhancing print literacy at key stage 3', *English in Education*, 33 (1).

Parker, D. (1999) '"You've read the book, now make the film": moving-image media, print literacy and narrative', *English in Education*.

Parker, D. and Sefton-Green, J. (2000) *Edit-Play*. London: bfi.

Robinson, M. (1997) *Children Reading Print and Television*. London: Falmer.

Van Leeuwen, T. (1985) 'Rhythmic Structure of the Film Text', in van Dijk (ed.), *Discourse and Communication*. Berlin: de Gruyter

Vygotsky, L.S. (1980) Mind in Society: Development of Higher Psychological Processes. Cambridge, MA: Harvard University Press.

Chapter 9

Nomads and tribes: online meaning-making and the development of new literacies

Julia Davies

INTRODUCTION: DIGITAL PRACTICES AND ACADEMIC SPACES

For about a decade, I have been responsible at my institution for introducing student teachers to ways of teaching English using information and communications technology (ICT). As in many educational institutions in the UK, the ICT teaching space is a dedicated room, devoid of anything 'non-ICT' where all computers are bolted to fixed narrow desks. It is a well-invigilated, specialist area, almost sterile in comparison with other classrooms, and the reading material in the room comprises solely instructions for accessing particular programs and sites. Even now, so many years into the 'technical revolution', a strange 'othering' of technology persists. Yet this situation in educational institutions seems almost anticipated by the student teachers – bizarrely irrespective of their comfortable and embedded use of technologies elsewhere in their lives. (One might guess that their own experiences as students have shaped their expectations). That is, this 'othering' is upheld within the academy even by those who embrace it fully in their everyday lives elsewhere.

   This situation tends to be replicated in schools, so that when student teachers undertake their school practice, they need to book dedicated ICT rooms for their teaching and need to plan work so that specific tasks are set for working in this specific environment. In ICT rooms there is rarely room to even use paper and pen, for example, or to use a 'blended' approach, where one could choose to use technology or not as appropriate. The uneasiness with which the hardware of ICT lies within academic space not only has implications for literacy practices that take place there, but also signifies a dislocation of ideologies between traditional academic literacy and new literacy practices. This means that, as Gee argues:

> Children are having more and more learning experiences outside of school that are more important for their futures than is much of the learning they do in school.
>
> (Gee, 2004: 5)

Invariably, when I arrive to begin teaching in the university ICT area, students have already switched on their machines and begun to write or to read. They are usually immersed in activities, such as replying to email, using MSN, looking up train times, reading articles, checking out education sites, or of course just surfing. It usually takes some time to lead the students into a group away from their own textual activities, so that I can begin our work. Similarly, in my most recent school visits (in the North of England), the lessons began in this familiar way: pupils had arrived early, logged on and begun to work with onscreen texts. I also witnessed student teachers expressing profound frustration at pupils' unwillingness to disengage from their individual activities, to listen promptly and to begin 'proper' school work, yet it is very rare to see pupils so resistant when requested to stop reading books. Additional rules which are applied to educational ICT spaces provide further tension where teacher vigilance is increased to protect precious items and to ensure student safety. This makes the space less 'everyday' and there is a sense in which creativity and experimentation are perilous. I have visited schools which deny access to search engines for fear of viruses, for example. Everything becomes 'uptight'. In school, it seems, students' motivation to learn independently or collaboratively through engagement with digital texts often seems to be eerily and ironically in defiance of restrictions applied within the school's ICT spaces.

Whilst this chapter mainly focuses on the out-of-school practices of teenagers, I have begun the discussion by describing their use in educational (academic or institutional) spaces, in order to delineate the very different spatial contexts of home and school digital literacy practices. The specific nuances (conditions) of the educational ICT context not only alter the practices in superficial ways, but are also indicative of a range of deeply inscribed impediments to the embedding of new literacy practices in schools (Gee, 2004; Lankshear, Chapter 6, this volume; Lankshear and Knobel, 2003, 2004). I believe that, even when ICT equipment permeates our class-rooms, unless underlying and incumbent mistrusts, misgivings and mis-information are addressed, we will still remain unable to incorporate ICT, or 'digital literacies' seamlessly into official academic teaching and learning practices. I believe we need to learn from, and take full account of, the way digital literacies are used elsewhere, in order to make a meaningful transition and understand the place of education in school in relation to out-of-school practices. We could certainly learn from the way that motivated on line youth learn with and from each other in groups of mixed age, ability and gender.

Today's world is highly textual: we surround ourselves with artefacts such as the television screen, the portable DVD player, digital music players, the games console, the pc, hand-held gameboys, mobile phones, books, post its, newspapers, etc. We immerse ourselves in narrative, reports, role plays and so on, responding in different ways to the range of texts on offer. Developments of new literacies are fast paced and are impacting on how we live our lives, how we conceive of social space and time, and how we interact with each other. We continually move through and between texts; our lives are already intertextual, and the texts are increasingly of the digital variety.

Lankshear and Bigum (1999) have described 'outsider' and 'insider' mentalities, where those who are 'at home' with new technologies and familiar with digital texts are 'insiders'. They describe 'outsiders' as adopting an

> old wine in new bottles' syndrome. The teachers seemed often to be looking for technological applications that resonated with their pedagogical styles and, generally, with fitting new technologies into classroom business as usual – encouraged, of course, by syllabus guidelines which lend themselves precisely to this kind of thing.
>
> (Lankshear and Bigum, 1999: 456)

I interpret those 'on the inside' as understanding not just operational functionalities of new technology, but as those who use it to 'get on with' their lives. Conversely, 'outsiders' are unable to see beyond the gadgetry, and negotiate the mechanics with difficulty, as well as seeing it as peripheral to the 'real' stuff of life. Outsiders see paper-based texts as more credible and authentic, while digital texts are of less value. I believe that schools as institutions (not the individual teachers) are generally made up of 'outsiders' and therefore at the moment lacking credibility and proficiency in leading the young forward into meaningful technical practices that will help them learn. Luke and Luke (2001) refer to 'babyboomer teachers and academics' who have 'little sense of "lack"' in regard to new technology practices (ibid.: 102). They talk about a 'generational disjunction' (ibid.: 105) where adults have become 'outsiders' to kids' 'insider know-how' (ibid.: 103). I would concur with this, but would add that younger teachers find it hard to challenge such attitudes when the curriculum and spatial arrangements for ICT practices do not allow them to incorporate ideologically different practices.

In this chapter, I will show a little of how some young people have come to learn in online 'communities of practice' (Lave and Wenger, 1991) or within 'affinity spaces' (Gee, 2004). I want to show how online group learning is both enthusiastic and informal as well as well-organized and accommodating of heterogeneity.

The theoretical underpinning to my work is found within the New Literacy Studies (Barton and Hamilton, 1998; Street, 1995), social anthropology (Ito and Okabe, 2004), social geography (Matthews *et al.*, 2001), learning theories, (Lave and Wenger, 1991; Gee 2004) and multimodal text analysis (Kress and van Leeuwen, 2001). As Barton and Hamilton comment, 'Literacy studies is essentially an interdisciplinary endeavour' (1998: 18) where researchers seek to

> redefine the relationship between the individual and the social, developing new concepts to express the links between the micro interactions which make up experience of everyday life and the large scale formations which shape and are shaped by this local realm.
>
> (ibid.)

THE NEW LITERACY STUDIES

I have argued that ICT education usually ties technology to particular spaces, governed by strict rules, set in isolated areas, and decontextualized from other school subject spaces. This distance is further still from home digital practices of 'screenagers' (Rushkoff, 1996) or those who are digitally 'at home' (Lankshear and Knobel, 2004). Lankshear and Knobel have argued that the 'taxonomy of educational objectives' in schools ties literacy education to constructs which pay little regard to other types of legitimate literacies. They say that in current practice:

> Learners' funds of knowledge very often have no place in the classroom and cannot have – since this would jeopardize professional expertise and challenge sectional interests that are served by schools.
>
> (Lankshear and Knobel, 2004: 4)

Barton and Hamilton (1998) have provided useful frameworks for developing notions of literacy, or literacy practices, which should be regarded, like language itself, as social and as rooted in specific contexts. They argue:

> Literacy is primarily something people do; it is an activity, located in the space between thought and text. Literacy does not just reside in people's heads as a set of skills to be learned, and it does not just reside on paper, captured as texts to be analysed. Like all human activity, literacy is essentially social, and it is located in the interaction between people.
>
> (Barton and Hamilton, 1998: 3)

My research shows how their motivation to act as social agents involves teenagers in the development of new literacy practices and I reflect on how the stimuli of popular cultural interests and new technology motivate the young to work collaboratively in creative, organized ways.

TEENAGE TRIBES – INHABITING BORDERLANDS

The everyday, almost perpetual use of certain digital technologies, most pertinently mobile phones by the young, challenges conventional senses of space. As Ito and Okabe (2004) argue, youthful use of technologies collapses current understandings of space through new social practices and new technologies. They suggest that technology enables the same social patterns that have been in existence for some time to evolve in small but socially significant ways. Their work shows how mobile phones enable the young to keep in perpetual contact and allow them to monitor their own life rhythms against others' without bringing disharmony to their current social presence. It is clear here, as well as in my data from teenagers' online activities, that social motivation drives their practices, whereby they can inhabit family space as well as sharing 'affinity spaces' (Gee, 2004) with like-minded others.

Matthews *et al.* describe teenage street society:

> These are places where young people can piece together their own identities, celebrate an emotional sense of togetherness and stand apart, if only temporarily, from the adult world that surrounds them. 'Streets' are places betwixt and between cultures, neither entirely owned by young people nor fixed adult domains. As such they comprise 'contradictory cultural landscapes' from which signs of autonomy and separateness are both created and inevitably blurred.
>
> (Matthews *et al.*, 2000: 77)

The home is not always a good place for teenagers to meet their friends, 'The space of the home…dominated by parents, accommodates their identity as a child, but not as friend', notes Rheingold, and he continues, explaining that new communication allows a freedom to 'construct a… place of intimacy, an open channel of contact' (Rheingold, 2003: 4) even within the home, either by talking on mobile phones or through the Internet. To communicate in a space where it is possible to move beyond the surveillance of the adult world, while still remaining within the domestic domain, is to exist in a space with permeable borders. The space allows movement beyond boundaries while staying within them, giving access to a world and to discourses beyond the home. Websites, then, are places where the young can interact beyond the gaze of their parents;

like street corners, these spaces can develop into places with a micro culture of their own, residing bizarrely within and outside other spaces. It is through imaginative and determined uses of technology that many 'screenagers' have managed, to collaborate in creative play and investigations.

NOMADS AND TRIBES: LEARNING TOGETHER

Online spaces are an exciting, attractive arena where social skills are at a premium, tested and developed in many ways, ideal locations for teenagers to try out voices, to wander nomad-like from home, enjoying being in a group or 'tribe'. The medium through which this social work gets done is textual; and these texts are rich, varied and very exciting for they indicate a gear change which has social, political and educational ramifications. Their gravitation towards each other on line allows them to express group solidarity.

Lave and Wenger (1991) have described 'communities of practice' where individuals are, through a process of enculturation, 'apprenticed' to a group and come gradually to learn and take on the values of that group. Rheingold (1998) has written about the way in which emotional support can be gleaned from such communities, especially by those who may otherwise feel alone, such as through illness or disability. Practical as well as emotional help is offered in such groups, yet he emphasizes that 'virtual communities are not the norm...[they] must be nurtured'. He continues that, 'In order to succeed a virtual community has to have an affinity' (Rheingold, 1998: 173).

The 'social glue' of online communities is often generated by clearly articulated, shared popular culture interests such as Barbie dolls, Bratz, Britney Spears or Harry Potter, and so on. But more subtle, tacitly signalled allegiances can bind the groups, such as shared linguistic and literacy markers, multimodal affordances, demonstrations of group knowledge and acceptance of specific value systems. Thus knowledge about associated popular culture texts, events, artefacts such as books, films, CDs, gigs, posters and even clothing all have high social and cultural capital in such groups and lend members credibility.

Gee's (2004) development of the notion of affinity refines aspects of Lave and Wenger's work (1999) and describes how 'affinity spaces' are collectively constructed through the sharing of common interests and knowledge exchange. In Gee's account, aspects of 'communities of practice' are critiqued, where he reflects that the ideas of 'membership' and 'belongingness', implicit in the notion of 'community', are problematic. In using the terms 'nomad' and 'tribe' I emphasize the propensity to move about according to what place seems most lucrative or able to sustain a particular culture. In moving from place to place, nomads share knowledge and acquire new knowledge, often returning to a 'base' in order to benefit communities or to trade expertise or goods. Within the idea of 'tribe' there is also a sense of shared history, with nomads moving through spaces sometimes independently, sometimes joining others in their spaces. In my account below I draw on Gee's notion of affinity spaces as this links well with my way of thinking about teenagers' movements through the web, collaboratively making meanings and learning together. But first I briefly explain my approach to the data.

MULTIMODAL DISCOURSE ANALYSIS

This chapter draws evidence from one such tribe, sharing an affinity space on the Internet; it is a group of mainly teenagers focusing on 'Babyz' (Mindscape, 1995). This was a software package which several years ago was extremely popular, predominantly among girls and young women, yet continues to attract a following. I consider the intertextual devices used to link the sites together which help them cohere as an affinity space, taking a semiotic approach, partly derivative of Williamson's work (1978), which exemplifies written words and visuals combining as signs in advertising. Williamson deconstructs individual advertisements, considering how advertisements interrelate, collectively inducting readers into understanding the codes and grammar of advertising, where meanings become culturally embedded. This kind of learning happens through the community rather than through school, and I report on how this also works on the Internet. I show how groups of sites cohere in similar ways, linking as affinity spaces where values and meanings are jointly expressed and at how this helps define particular 'tribes'. Kress and Van Leeuwen (2001), like Williamson, emphasize the need for semiotic as well as linguistic analysis, demonstrating how multiple modes such as music, colour and movement contribute to textual meanings. My multimodal analysis concentrates on features that demonstrate how specific expressed interests within online spaces help teens move into tribes and learn. Thus I look at how specific social practices bind groups together in beneficial ways.

JOINING A TRIBE

The so-called online 'Babyz Community' refers to itself as 'The BC', self-consciously defining itself as a discrete group. The game is a development of cyber pets, where players are invited to adopt 'Babyz' from a choice offered at the start of the game and the players/'mothers' then help them grow and learn, by feeding them, interacting with them through play and even reading them stories. (As I have described previously (Davies, 2004), the language of the game positions its audience as traditionally maternal). The group's 'core generator', as Gee describes it, is the software game 'Babyz' (Mindscape, 2004) although ownership of the game is not an entry requirement to the space.

Mindscape's official site[1] advertises and endorses the product showcasing the game, providing free 'downloadz' and activities where, for example, players can display their Babyz in 'pageantz'. Such promotional sites are now commonplace, not just for software like *The Sims*,[2] but also for merchandise such as *Barbie*,[3] or *Bratz*,[4] for example. These include community pages or clubs to join, facilitating online interaction. This makes good business sense, but payoffs exist for imaginative consumers, and sites usually allow play without product purchase. Satellite sites abound in all of these examples, for this is one of the processes by which affinity spaces evolve, many of which (but not all) link back to the official site. Babyz.net, then, was a major portal into the 'BC' affinity space but, due to its inactivity, the site is no longer as important as those that have arisen around it. Thus it is users themselves who are the dynamic force and impetus for its sustenance. They now provide the portal to the game, instrumental of others' entry to the space.

Babyz sites proliferated at an incremental rate during the 1990s and many of these remain on Google, with some now defunct, while some users have changed tack or diversified, concentrating also on more recent popular culture phenomena such as *The Sims*.[5] Yet ten years since the software was produced, the BC continues to flourish and the space is now furnished with texts and discourses which reflect a social history. More experienced players support others by providing online advice on how to manipulate the programmes to produce new clothes, or Babyz.[6] Newbies tend at first to perform in different ways, taking part in role-play activities, enjoying being within the space as well as defining it through their discourses and perpetuating its survival through their presence. Thus the players contribute in different ways, taking on roles according to their ability and experience levels. There is a sense of common endeavour despite this variance.

Some players accrue high status through their specialist knowledge; the status is detectable in their ubiquity across the affinity space. Carloyn remains one such, a longstanding, active participant, who shares her knowledge in her site,[7] but who also responds to requests for help from individuals. She exemplifies what Gee refers to as a 'strong generator' (Gee, 2004: 85), inventive in her work and influential on others. In the example below a number of helpers are thanked by this 12-year-old:

> I also want to tank Sandi from Forever Babyz 'cause she changed my babyz bubble colours, eye colours and little walkers to. She did

that for a lot of my Babez. Just like Kelly!!! I also want to tank Carolyns Creations, Costume Shop, Forever Babyz (Sandi u da most and u da bomb!!!)

(http://www.freewebs.com/thebabyzgarden/)

Technical help is sometimes given through message boards or via forums. Below, technical support is given to someone who says their Babyz seems 'ill' and despondent. The first respondent explained that the player should send the Babyz to grandma's house and if that does not work to download orange juice from the official site. This was apparently to no avail as the player could not then locate the orange juice in her game:

Hi I'm sue and I've been playing babies for about a year. The same thing happend to me but it turned out it wasent in the correct folder so perhaps yuo should check that it is not in a zipped folder as this will not work and that it is in the TOYZ folder. To find this folder then you should go into windows explorer go into C drive then into program files then you should find a folder called mindscape, open it go into babyz, then resources, then toyz, save it in there the file should look like the rest if this still dosent work then you have probaly got a duffed up file so you should delete it quick incase it has a bug in it. If it still dosent work send me an email and I'll send you a copy of mine with detailed instructions on how to put it in. I hope your babyz get better as i am a thougher player of it and i have grown guite attached to my babies and I'm sure you have to yours.

(http://www.voy.com/28923/176.html)

Here we see a number of players supporting one another, pooling knowledge and working together. The problem is taken seriously and the language shows markers of friendship and understanding. For example, the respondent begins with an informal greeting 'Hi'; she introduces herself (pseudonym used here) and then seeks to reassure – 'the same thing happend to me'. This is the second tactic used to display experience, the former being shown in 'I've been playing babies for about a year.' The inclusion of these markers reflects the perceived need to gain trust and display credentials prior to advising. The information given is clear, despite the lapses in spelling and grammar, reflecting expertise in the program's organization. The young players are acquiring transferable skills – ones likely to serve them well in the future – looking for virus files, for example. Further, the adviser offers additional help by way of email, recognizing the different possibilities for a range of communication modes. She sees that the forum has already had lengthy correspondence with this problem and is tactfully moving the discussion away from the message board. Interestingly, there is no text-message speak in the whole message; within the parameters of the Babyz space these seem *not* to be significant cultural motifs and are rare. Home pages tend to adopt pastel colours, resembling traditional, middle-class nursery wallpaper. The affinity space is defined through these hues as well as through the familiar faces of the 'Babyz' that populate the sites. Players recognize the code of the affinity space and actively use them.[8]

These visuals unify the sites, although each one is individualized with its unique welcome or home page; players keep to conventions, thus managing creativity within them, such as using customized pictures of their Babyz, importing pictures of flowers and toys, or even designing their own, using Microsoft paint, for example. Links are ubiquitous and high profile; the convention of reciprocity ('you link to me: I link to you' mentality) assures cohesion within the affinity space. There is a sense of team work and collaboration to maintain the consistent approach. Players are vigilant in watching over each other's work, updating their own space within the larger space in order to 'keep in step' with the whole. Some sites use background music, usually of the kind heard from musical cot-mobiles; others have moving features such as butterflies or bubbles. They inform each other where to acquire these and how to apply them.

Participants design items which they share, allowing copying but usually requesting acknowledgement and a link. For example, in one site visitors are offered the chance to piece together their own Babyz and then use them elsewhere:

> You are allowed to use the pictures you make on your homepage but please do not use any of the basic elements they did take me a very long time to make. Thanks from www.d-r-n.com
>
> (http://www.d-r-n.com/utils/babymaker.html)

This babymaker site is up to date and highly technical, borrowing knowledge from the newly fashionable 'dollmaker' sites[9] where characters are put together from kits and fixed together on a palette before being moved as a whole elsewhere. This web author (working bilingually, therefore maximizing his audience and presence across the space) has, nomad-like, gained expertise elsewhere, and adapted it for the BC use. He has made use of 'dispersed knowledge' (Gee, 2004), which in turn gives the Babyz affinity space a stronger presence and up-to-date currency. His work enables newbies to build their own sites without game purchase, thus allowing a further portal to the game for such players. While this site is relatively new, it is already a ubiquitous link across the Babyz space, making this player a strong generator.

Other players are more interested in making their presence felt through role play. Responses and readiness to comply in role-play is essential to such players. Invitations to interact follow this kind of style:

> Got a sick baby? Too busy to give your baby the care they need? Need a vacation?
> Whatever the reason, If you need a babysitter or doctor...
> ...If you need a Doctor:
> Email me at...
>
> (http://www.freewebs.com/seasonalbayz/)

This is the language of advertising and the player uses a series of direct questions to attract respondents. The words position other players as busy, caring, tired parents who find it hard to cope. Invitations to reply are always clear, and some sites request the completion of online forms such as adoption certificates, school applications and so on. This allows extensive role play and some forums show the results of these, with players describing who was a successful applicant for a teaching post at a new school, for example.

In this extract, we see evidence of a piece of play from over a long period:

> Hey Katy,
> I have some good news!!!! I dont think Tanner was abused! He came to me sick but very happy! After a couple hours rest he was roaring and ready to go, but it dosent matter, I still would like to adopt him. Were did you get him, what did the person say, and what was the persons email adress. I would like any other babyz that were abused. He is a four crawler and says a couple words. Thanks for letting me adopt him and email me back PS: I cant send email right now but Ill send you a pic in a day or so
>
> (http://members.boardhost.com/y2kb2000/)

It is clear from the message that a great deal of previous correspondence has taken place, with the exchange of a Baby involving at least three people. There is a narrative here about adoption of abused Babyz and two leads are sought for email correspondence. The player's story requires corroboration from others and in this she is being quite coercive in shaping Katy's response. This is a transferral of playground play into the affinity space of the Internet and the player uses the different affordances well, requesting email response.

The theme of abusing Babyz is an important one in this space. As I have discussed elsewhere (Davies, 2004), a number of sites once arose where authors, as part of their play, claimed to be 'abusing' Babyz.[10] While the 'abuse' existed only as online discourse, the shock expressed was profane since the play broke the rules of the culture. While the abusing sites have gone from the web, anti-abuse sites and pages still remain.[11] These anti-abuse sites maintain the cultural values of the group, defining the parameters of the discourses, leaving abusers as clear outsiders. Knowledge of this background remains and works as a kind of social history backdrop, displayed knowledge of which acts as a kind of portal. Engaging in online chat allows newbies to become acquainted with such narratives and thus able to participate in the discourses that define the tribe and set out territorial values.

As Kenway and Bullen argue:

> The Internet is not only a source of information and games for students. It offers children and youth a means to 'distribute' their voices and views in ways that they enjoy. It also offers them the opportunity to blend the playful and earnest.
>
> (Kenway and Bullen, 2001: 181)

As the examples above show, practices beyond the school, which often develop around popular culture stimuli, allow players to deconstruct and reconstruct what is offered to them and are supported in this endeavour by working with equally motivated, genuinely interested others – some of whom are highly supportive adults. Age seems unimportant in the interactions, however; it is experience and involvement that are paramount. Babyz enthusiasts gather information from a range of places and reorganize what they find in creative ways. The Babyz group I have described here is not unique in the way it has proliferated and in the way in which it accommodates all kinds of players within its space. There is a great number of online spaces which youngsters can and do access, such as rap zones where, among other things, poetry is written. In online spaces, all kinds of knowledge are valued and there are many ways in which participants can gain respect, do well and offer support. Possibilities for success are broad.

CONCLUSION

Gee's theorizing of the affinity space (Gee, 2004) usefully describes how individuals carve out roles for themselves in such spaces and how they learn in cooperative ways. He uses this as a model of learning, critiquing school approaches which lack the multiple routes to participation modelled by online spaces. The evidence I have offered above is presented to substantiate the view that there is much that we, as teachers and teacher educators, can learn from the way in which individuals operate in online spaces. Second, I wish to argue that we should regard new literacy practices in positive ways. These new practices lend weight to the view that literacy is essentially a social practice and this in turn indicates that schooling needs to take on pedagogical approaches which recognize this. As I have shown, there are many benefits for learners working together on joint projects, each having a role, able to take responsibility for different things and to learn from each other in a cooperative way.

Further, schools do not seem to value, celebrate or invest in the skills students bring with them to school. Their online practices tend to be 'othered' rather than embedded in everyday events. It is crucial that we look for ways of embedding technological practices into mainstream curricular and pedagogical experiences, since mainstream usage in schools is currently antithetical to practices elsewhere and does not sufficiently invest in society's increasing seduction to engage with new texts and new practices on line.

Moreover, there are discourses of disapproval that pervade many homes, schools, and in the media. Not all youngsters are able to access the kinds of spaces I have described above. Phrases expressing adult disapproval abound, with reference to 'mindless' activities, of 'hours wasted' and the need to divert children's attention to more 'worthwhile' pursuits. These emotionally charged worries and arguments are clearly based on desires to raise children in ways that will help them lead worthwhile lives. However, they are re-runs of age-old scripts which have similarly denounced television, film and pop music, with discourses often mourning notions of better-spent childhood pasts, and/or relating to the subversion of traditional values and moral codes. Concerns over spellings used in text messages, of elliptical constructions and of whimsical emoticons, are perhaps worries that partially derive from associations between dangerous digital landscapes and technological developments. It is only through situating online learning in schools that youngsters can be taught to conduct themselves in safe ways. Multimodal representations of digital activities (emoticons, text message spellings etc.) seem socially threatening and undermining of the status quo. Although the young do seem to be using these judiciously, there remains an important role for teachers in advising on issues of appropriateness and context. These multimodal developments evolve from new social practices created by the existence of a new social space which occupies an intangible, but highly significant, position in the digitally developed world; they therefore need a place on the curriculum quite urgently.

My vexation with these views derives from my concern that parents and teachers veto their own opportunities for educating teenagers about the rules for engagement on line. While I am aware of the riches of the Internet and of the skills that many young people are already developing apace in their interactions with each other, I am anxious that access to these for all is increased, rather than denied on the basis of uninformed assumptions. There needs to be a curriculum in place that ensures equity.

I see the Internet as providing a place for play, for staging teenage drama, for experimenting with voices and identities, for asking questions of themselves, of each other and the world. I have used the example of the Babyz community to illustrate how such opportunities are provided. These kinds of opportunities, however, need to be made available to all, and the models for learning applied creatively in a range of subject areas.

How the new literacies are operating socially needs to be understood by educators and their pupils alike; literacy practices are social and thus it is not just skills which need to be taught. I began this chapter with a discussion of the place of ICT in schools and, as I have shown, an environment which emphasizes skills and isolates technology from social practice is inappropriate.

NOTES

1 (http://www.babyz.net/)
2 (http://thesims.ea.com/us/)
3 (http://www.barbie.everythinggir.com/)
4 (http://www.bratzpack.com/index2.asp)
5 (http://katierox.freewebspace.com/).
6 (http://www.geocities.com/babyz49/)
7 (http://carolyn.thepetzwarehouse.com/)
8 See for example, http://mysite.wanadoo-members.co.uk/babyz_world; http://hometown.aol.com/elizadez/myhomepage/; http://www.dmwright.com/babyz/.
9 (http://www.over-the moon.org/dollz/dollmaker/make.html)
10 (www.geocities.com/abusingbabyzisfun/sad.htm)
11 http://www.expage.com/Babyzabuseiswrong; http://babyzrule2.tripod.com/Babyz/id5.html)

REFERENCES

Barton, D. and Hamilton, M. (1998) Local Literacies: *Reading and Writing in One Community*. London: Routledge.

Davies, J. (2004) 'Negotiating Femininities on-line,' *Gender and Education*, **16** (1): 35–50.

Gee, J.P. (2000) 'The New Literacy Studies,' in D. Barton, M. Hamilton and R. Ivanic (eds) *Situated Literacies: Reading and Writing in Context*. London: Routledge, pp. 180–96.

Gee, J.P. (2004) *Situated Language and Learning: A Critique of traditional Schooling*. London: Routledge.

Ito, M. and Okabe, D. (2004) 'Intimate Connections: Contextualising Japanese Youth and Mobile Messaging', forthcoming in R. Harper, L. Palen and A. Taylor (eds) *Inside the text: Social Perspectives on SMS in the Mobile Age.* http://www.itofisher.com/mito/archives/itookabe.texting.pdf accessed November 2004.

Kenway, J. and Bullen, E. (2001) *Consuming Children: Education – Entertainment – Advertising.* Buckingham: Open University Press.

Kress, G. and Van Leeuwen, T. (2001) *Multimodal Discourse: The modes and media of contemporary communication.* London: Edward Arnold, co-published in the USA by Oxford University Press, New York.

Lave, J. and Wenger, E. (1991) *Situated Learning.* Cambridge: Cambridge University Press.

Lankshear, C. and Bigum, C. (1999) 'Literacies and New Technologies in School Settings', *Curriculum Studies*, 7 (3): 445–64.

Lankshear, C. and Knobel, M. (2003) *New Literacies: Changing Knowledge and Classroom Learning.* Buckingham: Open University Press.

Lankshear, C. and Knobel, M. (2004) *Text Related Roles of the digitally 'at home'.* Paper presented at the American Research Association Annual Meeting, San Diego. http://www.geocities.com/c.lankshear/roles.html accessed November 2004.

Luke, A. and Luke, C. (2001) 'Adolescence lost, Childhood regained: On early intervention and the emergence of the techno subject', *Journal of Early Childhood Literacy*, 1: 91–120.

Matthews, H., Limb, M. and Taylor, M. (2000) 'The Street as Third Space', in S. Holloway and G. Valentine, *Children's Geographies: Playing, Living, Learning.* London: Routledge, pp. 63–79.

Mindscape (1995) Virtual Babyzsoftware. USA: PF Magic/Mindscape.

Rheingold, R. (1998) 'Community development in the Cybersociety of the Future', in D. Gauntlett (ed.) *Web Studies.* London: Edward Arnold.

Rheingold, H. (2003) *Smartmobs: The next social revolution.* Cambridge, MA: Perseus.

Rushkoff, D. (1996) *Playing the future: How kids culture can teach us how to thrive in an age of chaos.* New York: HarperCollins.

Street, B. (1995) *Social Literacies: Critical approaches to literacy in development, ethnography and education.* London: Longman.

Williamson, J. (1978) *Decoding Advertisements: Ideology and Meaning in Advertisements.* London: Marion Boyers.

Web addresses (all pages accessed November 2004)

http://www.babyz.net/
http://babyzrule2.tripod.com/Babyz/id5.html
http://www.barbie.everythinggir.com/
http://www.bratzpack.com/index2.asp
http://carolyn.thepetzwarehouse.com/
http://www.dmwright.com/babyz/
http://www.d-r-n.com/utils/babymaker.html
http://www.expage.com/Babyzabuseiswrong;
http://www.freewebs.com/seasonalbayz/
http://www.freewebs.com/thebabyzgarden/

http://www.geocities.com/babyz49/).
http://hometown.aol.com/elizadez/myhomepage/
http://katierox.freewebspace.com/).
http://members.boardhost.com/y2kb2000
http://mysite.wanadoo-members.co.uk/babyz_world
http://www.voy.com/28923/176.html

Part III

Teachers and schooling

Chapter 10

Tightropes, tactics and taboos: pre-service teachers' beliefs and practices in relation to popular culture and literacy

Jackie Marsh

The aim of the study reported in this chapter was to determine the attitudes, beliefs and experiences of pre-service teachers in relation to the use of popular culture in the primary literacy curriculum. The study, conducted over a period of four years, focused on the student teachers' construction of the literacy curriculum and explored how far the students' attitudes and practices correlated with those of teachers in other studies who have expressed negative views towards the use of popular culture (Lambirth, 2003; Makin *et al.*, 1999; Suss *et al.*, 2001). This chapter discusses the ways in which student teachers' curricula and pedagogy, already constrained by external factors, were further limited because of perceived, rather than actual, restrictions. To begin with, however, teachers' views towards popular cultural material in classrooms will be reviewed.

TEACHERS' ATTITUDES TO POPULAR CULTURE AND LITERACY

Research that has explored teachers' beliefs and practices with regard to popular culture and literacy has identified the concerns that many educators have with such material. Dyson (1997) reports on discussions of ten primary school teachers from San Francisco, in which they reflected on their experiences of and attitudes towards the use of popular culture in their classrooms. Examples of such uses were videos, popular food chains in socio-dramatic play areas and magazines. Dyson suggests that 'The genres associated with commercial media (e.g. videos, advertisements, and television shows) did not, in and of themselves, cause any ideological uneasiness. But the *content* of media forms could' (Dyson, 1997: 174). Thus, some teachers expressed concern over representations of women in magazines, or the violence which permeated some of the media stories. One teacher, Kristin, encouraged children to reflect on the ideological tensions in the media material they reworked in their stories, developing their critical literacy skills. In this way, the responsibility for challenging racist, sexist and exclusive discourses was not just the teacher's, but also the children's. This pedagogical approach which embraces the use of such texts remains unusual in the reported studies on teacher beliefs, however. Green *et al.* (1998) interviewed twenty-eight teacher graduate students in Australia. They asked the teachers to compare the amount of time the children they taught engaged with electronic media with their use of print media. In their feedback, the teachers complained about the individualistic nature of the computer games that the children used, the gender imbalance in the use of the games and the way in which reading was a less favoured pursuit of the children. Green *et al.* suggest that a number of this new generation of teachers

> ... seem to be thinking and talking about Nintendo in ways that are more like their parents than their little brothers and sisters. They are concerned to make a link between computer game play and antisocial, aggressive, 'non-literate' behaviour. On this basis, it would seem that teacher education has a long way to go ...
>
> (Green *et al.*, 1998: 35)

This negative attitude towards popular computer games is not confined to Australian teachers. A study by Sanger *et al.* (1997) in the UK demonstrated that most of the teachers who took part in their survey disapproved of the kinds of games likely to be used by many children. In addition, Lambirth (2003) reports on the results of a survey of sixty-five primary teachers who took part in a writing research project. The teachers were asked to rate the extent of their use of popular culture in the writing curriculum on a scale of five (very extensively) to one (not used at all). The majority of teachers did not rate the use of popular culture more highly than two. During interviews, Lambirth suggests that the teachers demonstrated a rather ambivalent stance towards popular culture, on the one hand speaking with warmth and affection of their own childhood encounters with popular texts, and on the other indicating revulsion for contemporary popular culture. This is, perhaps, indicative of 'an unquenchable desire among (a particular generation of) educators, and particularly among early childhood educators, for a return and restoration of childhood before the Fall' (Luke and Luke, 2001: 95).

Seiter (1999) also suggests that beliefs and practices with regard to the use of popular culture reflect epistemological stances towards childhood itself. In a study of twenty-four pre-school teachers and child-care workers in the USA, Seiter found that the teachers displayed a diverse range of opinions on the subject and illustrates some of the themes which emerged from her case studies of two very different settings. In one setting, a Montessori school, the teacher, Sarah, banned videos and Disney films from the classroom. Sarah held very negative attitudes towards the media, felt that it encouraged children to be passive and worried that they were being introduced to inappropriate material. In contrast, Seiter (1999) provides a description of the practice of Gloria, who taught in a private nursery. Gloria was enthusiastic about television for children and encouraged its use in the nursery. Children were allowed to watch videos and engage in fantasy play related to the programmes. Seiter suggests that these two contrasting views are located in two very different paradigms, in which children are viewed either as active constructors of meaning in their world, in the case of Gloria, or as passive victims, who need to be protected from the ravages of media, as Sarah imagines to be the case.

Overall, it would appear that the limited work available on this subject indicates that many teachers express negative attitudes and beliefs towards the use of popular culture and the media, and there is little evidence of its extensive use in elementary and primary classrooms. Of those teachers who do acknowledge its value, many are concerned about the oppressive discourses which are located within the texts. It is only occasionally, as in the cases of Kristin and Gloria, that we find teachers who are aware of the attraction that the media holds for young children and who are committed to developing children's abilities to engage critically with the material at the same time as allowing them to explore the pleasures they receive from it. If this approach to the material is to be developed, then pre-service teachers need to be aware of the possibilities and limitations. One of the aims of the study reported in this chapter was to explore pre-service teachers' beliefs and practices with regard to the use of popular culture in the literacy curriculum and to determine the influences on these beliefs and practices in order to inform future work in initial teacher education.

THE STUDY

The study was undertaken in a number of stages over a period of four years and centred on students who attended a university in the north of England (Marsh, 2003). The university offers a wide programme of initial and continuing teacher education courses at undergraduate and postgraduate level. This study focused on students undertaking a three-year under-graduate course, the BA (Hons) Primary Education with Qualified Teacher Status (QTS).

In Stage One, all 119 first-year students, who were registered on the course and attended classes in the first weeks, completed a questionnaire which explored their attitudes, beliefs and experiences with regard to the use of popular culture in the primary literacy curriculum. Of the 119 students who took part, 97 per cent self-identified as white, 83 per cent were female and 43 per cent were aged 25 years or older. This student profile was typical of initial teacher education courses across England at that time. Measures were taken to increase the internal validity of the questionnaires used, including using sets of questions rather than single opinion items, repeating questions using slightly different wording and incorporating both positively and negatively worded statements dealing with the same issue (Oppenheim, 2000). Eighteen students took part in follow-up group and individual semi-structured interviews at various stages throughout the course over the next three years in order to explore these aspects in further detail. They also completed concept-maps which outlined the influences on their construction of the literacy curriculum. In the last weeks of the course 43 students who attended a lecture completed a final questionnaire. This chapter reports on the data arising from both questionnaires and interviews.

RESTRICTED BELIEFS AND PRACTICES

Throughout the four-year study, data from the questionnaires and interviews indicated that the student teachers expressed favourable attitudes towards the inclusion of popular culture in the primary literacy curriculum. For example, Figure 10.1 indicates the responses to a question which asked students to state how far they agreed with a particular attitudinal statement. The lower the number, the higher that particular statement was ranked by the overall cohort of students.

The statements have been shortened for ease of presentation in Figure 10.1. Table 10.1 indicates how these relate to the original wording in the questionnaire.

From an analysis of Figure 10.1, it can be seen that those statements which demonstrated a positive attitude towards popular culture were the ones that attracted most agreement from students. The statements which were disagreed with most strongly were the statements that demonstrated a negative attitude towards popular culture. This picture was also reflected in the comments made on the open sections of the questionnaire:

> I believe anything may be used 'within reason' to keep a child's interest in a subject matter.

> In moderation most aspects that children are interested in can naturally be incorporated and used as a motivational tool.

> I believe that although popular interests should not be the base of teaching, it is important to get children involved in teaching/ learning by relating some work to these interests.

What is notable in these extracts is the use of hedging statements which suggest that there should be limitations on the use of popular texts ('within reason', 'in moderation') and that they should not be the base of teaching. This was obviously perceived by some of the students as an area

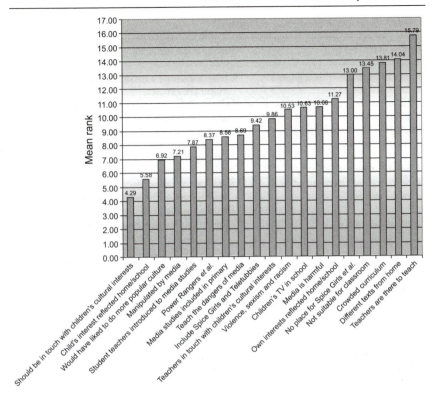

Figure 10.1 Mean ranking of attitudinal statements (1 = high ranking, 16 = low ranking).

which could get out of control if not contained. What was also clear from these data is that the generally positive attitudes related to the way in which popular cultural texts could be used to enhance motivation and orientate children towards schooled literacy practices; none of the students indicated that the study of popular culture was a useful literacy practice in its own right, as a means of enhancing critical literacy skills (Alvermann *et al.*, 1999) or developing skills in relation to the production and analysis of media texts.

Despite the broadly positive attitudes and beliefs expressed throughout this study, the use of popular culture in the literacy curriculum during the pre-service teachers' placements was minimal. This disjuncture between reported beliefs and practices was shaped by a number of discourses. Perhaps the most important consideration in any analysis of the student teachers' experiences should be the nature of the prescribed curriculum itself, for this inevitably shapes practice. This will be discussed in the next section, before I move on to look at some of the other factors which impacted on students' decision-making processes.

Table 10.1 Explanation of wording in Figure 10.1

Wording in Figure 10.1	Wording in questionnaire
Should be in touch with children's cultural interests	Teachers should be in touch with children's cultural interests
Children's interests reflected home	I feel that it is important that children's interests at home are reflected in the school curriculum
Would have liked to do more popular culture	I would have liked to have done more work on popular culture and the media throughout my own school experience
Manipulated by media	Children are manipulated by the media
Student teachers introduced to media studies	I think that student teachers should be introduced to the teaching of media studies in the primary school
Power Rangers et al.	Programmes such as *Power Rangers* and *Ninja Turtles* should not be included in the school curriculum because of the violence in them
Media studies included in primary	I would like media studies to be included in the primary English curriculum
Teach the dangers of media	Children should be taught about the dangers of the media in school
Include Spice Girls and Teletubbies	Things such as the Spice Girls and Teletubbies are of interest to children, therefore they should be included in the curriculum
Teachers in touch with children's cultural interests	Teachers are in touch with children's cultural interests
Violence, sexism and racism	Children's popular culture is problematic because much of it contains violence, sexist and racist elements
Children's TV in school	Children's TV programmes should not be material for work in school unless they have some educational value, e.g. teach reading skills directly or provide factual information about things
Media is harmful	Much of the media is harmful to children
Own interests reflected home/school	I felt that my own interests at home were reflected in the school curriculum
No place for Spice Girls, et al.	Schools are a place for education, not trivialities such as Spice Girls and Teletubbies
Not suitable for classroom	Books children read at home are very often not suitable to use in the classroom
Crowded curriculum	The English curriculum is already crowded enough, there is simply not time for things that are not essential, such as work on popular culture
Different texts from home	Schools should introduce children to literature they will not meet at home and not waste time on texts they may already know from home
Teachers are there to teach	Teachers are there to teach, not worry about children's cultural interests

CLASSIFICATION AND FRAMING OF THE CURRICULUM

The students' teaching placements took place in the first few years of the operation of the National Literacy Strategy (NLS) in England (DfEE, 1998), a strategy that introduced the use of a curriculum framework which outlines the content that should be covered in each term of a child's primary experience. Using Bernstein's concepts of 'classification' and 'frame' (Bernstein, 1974), a picture emerges of the way in which this framework militated against students' use of popular cultural texts. Classification was the term Bernstein used to describe the degree of boundary maintenance between subject matters, with strong classification suggesting clear boundaries. Frame, on the other hand, refers to the pedagogical context in which knowledge is transmitted. Strong framing means that the content, organization and delivery of what is to be transmitted is not in the control of the teacher or pupil (Bernstein, 1974: 205–6). The National Literacy Strategy demonstrates strong framing and classification, as there is a curriculum structure for each year, from Reception to Year 6. Throughout the study, the pre-service students indicated that the framing of the curriculum in this way had prevented the use of popular culture:

> *Hannah:* I think possibly as well because the literacy is so new into schools, that they're probably a bit, not running scared of it a bit, because it is so structured, you know, you open your file up and you've got exactly, even down to what words they should know at every age and teachers are probably, you know, more concerned with sticking to this than and as Rachel says, big book scenario, you know, this is what we've got to do because this is the literacy hour and in itself it's probably making itself quite restrictive unless teachers go on INSET days where things like this are promoted and their horizons are broadened a bit.

The 'big book scenario' to which Hannah refers here is the use of enlarged text for whole-class reading sessions. Space metaphors were often used by students to indicate that there had been no 'room' for the use of popular culture:

> *Jackie:* Did you use popular culture on your own teaching practice?
> *Louise:* No. Not, not really at all.
> *Jackie:* Right. And what were your reasons for that?
> *Louise:* Because I think it was so tightly scheduled most of the time anyway that it didn't leave room for anything else that you wanted to do. Not that I'd really thought about it too much

anyway because I knew how tightly the curriculum had been planned before I went in ...

The lack of space offered by a curriculum that has strong classification and framing was a key inhibiting factor for the students throughout the study. Bernstein would classify this as a 'performance model' of education in which 'Space and specific pedagogic practices are clearly marked and explicitly regulated' (Bernstein, 1996: 59) and in which learners are expected to produce specific outputs and acquire specialist skills in relation to this output (in this case, output would be related to NLS objectives). In addition to the constrictions on curriculum space, when the NLS was first introduced, it was suggested that all of the activities scheduled should take place within a 'literacy hour', an hour which has a number of constituent parts that are timed, e.g. 20-minute whole-class session, 20-minute group and individual work, 20-minute whole-class plenary session. As Merchant (2002) notes, this invites a Foucauldian analysis of the way in which power is related to time (Foucault, 1977) and, in the pedagogical practices of the NLS in its first years of operation:

> We can also see the creation of 'disciplinary time' in which levels and stages are drawn up with an accompanying 'seriation' of activities against which progress can be measured and acts of detailed control and regular intervention made possible.
>
> (Merchant, 2002: 1)

The quadrant in Figure 10.2 indicates how time and space constrained the students' curriculum planning. Along the horizontal axis, the allocation of time within the curriculum is represented along a 'constrained' and 'non-constrained' continuum. The vertical axis represents the use of space in the curriculum and the continuum moves from 'constricted' to 'non-constricted' use of space. The data at all stages of this study suggested that the majority of students participating had felt that their construction of the curriculum was represented by Quadrant 1, and this is where the NLS certainly fitted in terms of its use of time and space. As students experienced conditions which moved towards Quadrant 4, they were more likely to be able to use popular cultural texts in the literacy curriculum.

Whilst the strong classification and framing played a part in restricting the students' practice, there was evidence from the study that a wide range of other factors influenced the choices they made. These included: lack of confidence; their own school experiences; perceived suitability of texts and lack of guidance. Each of these factors will be considered in turn.

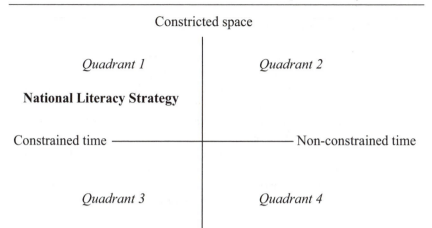

Figure 10.2 Time/space continua.

LACK OF CONFIDENCE

As is to be expected, beginning teachers are less confident than those with more experience (Farrell *et al.*, 2000). Certainly, 'confidence' was a key marker which appeared throughout the interview transcripts. In particular, 'confidence' was associated with a familiarity with school routines and resources. Students suggested that they would not have the confidence to work with popular cultural and media texts because they represented the unknown:

> *Ruth*: I think having the confidence to actually do it – having the confidence. I might feel unconfident because it's very ... it's not something you observe other teachers doing. So, actually doing it off your own bat is quite a big step.
>
> *Mary*: I think probably as I become more confident in my own abilities, I will do my own individual things – confidence in what you're doing really, isn't it?

In these statements, both of the students indicate that they would prefer to follow established practices rather than introduce novel ones that were untried and untested. Rachel agreed with these views, suggesting that, for her, big books provided safe ground:

> *Rachel*:   I think, another thing for me is that I probably wouldn't have had the confidence and the skill to . . . when I'd got the big book, I was safe, you know, I could talk about content, I could talk about indexes, I could talk about glossaries . . . the layout and things like that. It was a safe area for me because it was all there, I could see it, you know, whereas to go away and maybe bring a newspaper article in or something like that, or a report . . . especially for children so young, I probably wouldn't have had the skills to be as successful with a resource such as that in comparison to the big book resources.

Rachel uses the term 'safe' twice in this extract. She obviously feels that she needs to be secure in her knowledge about the teaching material she uses and is not willing to take risks. This sense of popular culture as presenting risky material surfaced in many of the other interviews. The need for security may also, of course, be located in traditional discourses of teacher–learner relationships, where teachers are the experts and need to transmit this knowledge to pupils. With regard to popular culture, the children are very likely to have greater knowledge than the teacher, and this can lead to insecurity. In addition, Rachel's dependence on the construction of knowledge as discrete items which can be ticked off a list ('I could talk about content, I could talk about indexes, I could talk about glossaries, . . . the layout and things like that') could be seen symptomatic of the way in which the NLS has framed the teaching of literacy.

'Confidence' was also related to the need to ensure that one felt comfortable with the material to hand:

> *Gemma*:   You have to be careful as well that you don't sort of like try to get on their level too much with it 'cause I can always think of particular teachers that, comprehensive, not so much primary teachers, but trying to get in with you with it, sort of like, pretending they know. I don't know whether it was just me being an adolescent, you know. But, in sort of thinking, 'Well, the teacher – they don't really understand it'. Do you know what I mean? They didn't seem to know what era it came from. Do you know what I mean? And I think it's important to be comfortable with what you're actually trying to get across. That's like with any text that you're using, isn't it really?

The concern that pupils might think that teachers were trying to be 'trendy' in their use of popular culture is one that has been discussed elsewhere (Marsh and Millard, 2000), but there seemed to be a real concern among the students that they needed to be familiar with popular cultural texts in order to be in control of the material. The lack of confidence to use popular culture, therefore, can be seen to be inextricably linked to the general levels of confidence felt by beginning student teachers (which can be low when first undertaking school placements (McIntyre *et al.*, 1996) and the level of subject knowledge they felt they held in this field.

The concept of self-efficacy, rather than confidence, was felt to be more salient in relation to an analysis of the students' experiences. Bandura (1997) suggests that, 'Perceived self-efficacy refers to the beliefs in one's capabilities to organize and execute the courses of action required to produce given attainments' (Bandura, 1997: 3). There are, according to Bandura, four sources of influence on self-efficacy. These are 'enactive mastery experiences' (previous experiences of a given task/ behaviour), vicarious experience (observing others' experiences of a given task/behaviour), verbal persuasion and physiological and affective states (ibid.: 79). From the interview data, it can be seen that students' lack of enactive or vicarious experiences with regard to the use of popular culture in the literacy curriculum led to feelings of low self-efficacy and thus lack of action in this regard. Bandura argues that 'Beliefs of personal efficacy constitute the key factor of human agency' (ibid.: 3) and the data certainly reflect this with regard to the use of popular culture. However, self-efficacy can be represented as an individualized, psychological construct when, in fact, it is related to a lack of power/agency in certain situations. So, although students used the term 'confidence' quite a lot in relation to their lack of attention to the use of popular culture, and this can be seen to link to Bandura's concept of self-efficacy, an alternative analysis could be that their level of confidence was related to the lack of power they had as a student in the school system. This, indeed, is often a major constraining factor for students (McIntyre *et al.*, 1996) and this lack of power underpins the experiences related in the interview data.

OWN SCHOOL EXPERIENCES

Students' own experiences, either as an observer or student in school, had been instrumental in shaping their conceptions of the literacy curriculum. This was further supported by data from the group interviews.

> *Jackie*:   Are you sympathetic towards (the use of popular culture) or not?

Sue: I was and also I put that I didn't have that opportunity when I was at school and I think it was missed really. Because it was very formal, my education really.

Jackie: You've never experienced popular culture at all then?

Sue: I can't remember doing, I mean, I might have done, but...I can't really remember. You'd think you would wouldn't you? Doing something like, you know, that were more interesting, I think.

Jenny: But I never had it at school.

Sue and Jenny's own learning experiences, prior to taking up teaching, were typical of the students interviewed. Hannah made clear the link between this lack of experience and her reluctance to use popular cultural and media texts:

Hannah: I would have not been prompted to think, 'Oh I could use a comic' or...I'd have thought it was maybe a taboo thing in school.

Jackie: Now, where did you get that message from?

Hannah: I don't know...I think just...phew...probably because it didn't happen to me in school, I ...you know, I didn't do any popular culture...I don't know and I just think because it's all the big books and everything else, I haven't seen teachers using it, so I presume that it's not a done thing in school.

Many of the students appeared to assume that the use of popular culture was 'not a done thing in school'. The pervasiveness of the use of big books in schools that Hannah's comments highlights, a staple ingredient of the NLS, was a thread which appeared throughout the interviews. The majority of students reported that they had not observed the use of popular culture in school, either as an observer or as a pupil.

The lack of experience in relation to the use of popular culture and the literacy curriculum was to be a key thread throughout the study. This confirms other work which stresses that prior life experiences provide the cornerstone of teachers' beliefs and attitudes (Lortie, 1975; Shuell, 1992; Powell, 1992, 1996) and that the experiences that students have as pre-service teachers in classrooms shape their own classroom practice (Lortie, 1975; Powell, 1992; Raymond *et al.*, 1992). Tang Yee-Fan (1998) argues that this is a rather deterministic view which discounts individual teacher's agency and their resistance to aspects of their own histories. It is clear that life history is only one element of the complex tapestry into which are woven teachers' beliefs and practices; however, it does play a key role, as Hannah's experience indicates.

PERCEIVED SUITABILITY OF TEXTS

A number of students expressed concerns about the suitability of the substantive content of popular cultural texts, as was the case in Dyson's (1997) and Seiter's (1999) studies.

> *Rachel*: You see, I'm torn with the popular culture thing. I really do think it has got a place in school but there are certain elements of it, I feel, that may not be suitable such as violence and with song lyrics and things like that that there's probably things in it that, you know, aren't suitable for certain children, you know . . . there's a level of the language and you know obviously the Spice Girls is possibly quite clean, can we say, whereas you wouldn't take . . . I don't know... a Nirvana tape in and say 'listen to this' because there's a lot of things, negativity and a lot of swearing and things. I don't know whether I'd feel comfortable teaching that.

The notion of the level of comfort or discomfort with regard to the use of popular cultural texts was a recurring feature of the data. Discomfort with the nature and language of texts obviously did not appear in general to extend to more canonical texts, yet a number of traditional texts routinely used in the literacy curriculum contain similar language and themes (Marsh and Millard, 2000). Rachel did, in fact, recognize this herself:

> *Jackie*: Where would you draw the line then?
> *Rachel*: I think it's difficult because then you go into school and somebody says . . . we were changing sentences round the other day in English and we were looking at a 'bloody hatchet', meaning it had been used to kill someone and the kids just went, 'Oh you're swearing', you know. So it's difficult isn't it because we do have a reaction to words like that and, you know, whether they would focus in on the fact that there were swear words in there rather than your actual objective for teaching.

Rachel's response here was unusual, however. In the main, students appeared to feel that popular culture had a monopoly on contentious issues. Violence was another area of discomfort and Rachel was typical of the student group in voicing her concerns:

> *Rachel*: Well, you mentioned here things like Ninja Turtles and things like that which are quite violent and you do think of kids

reconstructing that in the playground...I don't know, it's something I would probably want to get away from.

This is a stance which has been strongly supported by a range of work which suggests that violence in the media is responsible for all kinds of atrocities, from the killing of Jamie Bulger to nuclear war (Brooky, 1998; Stutz, 1996). However, it has been pointed out numerous times that there is little conclusive evidence to suggest that there is a direct effect between the watching of screen violence and children's use of violence in everyday life (Barker and Petley, 1997; Gunter and McAleer, 1997). This alludes to the way in which childhood is constructed by many as a site which should exclude all potentially controversial subjects (Marsh and Millard, 2000), rather than developing the children's skills as critical decoders of texts (Comber and Simpson, 2001). Teacher education courses need to introduce students to a wide range of popular material in order to allow them to identify the many positive ways in which it can be used in the classroom. For example, Meacham (2004) illustrates how young people's interest in rap music can motivate them to engage in the literacy curriculum and can encourage them to become skilled rap artists themselves.

LACK OF KNOWLEDGE/GUIDANCE

Another theme that flowed through the interviews was that of a lack of knowledge about children's popular culture. Many students did not feel comfortable with their level of knowledge about children's popular culture:

Mary: The popular poems or raps wouldn't have got the same, the same objectives.

Amy: ...Well they weren't available. I suppose I could have probably created my own had I got more knowledge at the time but...

Level of subject knowledge is linked to practice (Medwell et al., 1998) and students did attribute their lack of use of popular cultural themes to their lack of knowledge of the area. A number of students suggested that having more guidance in university sessions with regard to content and theory would have helped them to feel more confident about using popular cultural texts:

Rachel: Yeah, because I, I feel I've become confident with the big book because we've looked at it in class and sort of been given ideas about how to use it in the classroom, so if the

Liz: same had happened with newspapers or ... you know, whatever, I probably would have felt confident to give it a go.
And also I think possibly, having an academic background,
you should be able to justify why you were doing things
better. So if you did have any opposition, even though, say
your boss came in or something, you can justify it. It makes it
a bit easier. Do you know what I mean?

Liz's request for a stronger theoretical background for her practice was
notable, given that much of the literature tends to suggest that student
teachers eschew theory, introduced to them at university, in favour of
what they consider to be the 'real' practice of schools (McIntyre *et al.*,
1996). This did not appear to be the case with many of the students, who
often expressed an interest in developing theoretical knowledge through
reading. Rachel suggested that the fact that there was little published
material on the topic was a hindrance for her:

Rachel: And also, there's not a lot of literature on it. I mean, we're big
ones for going out and saying, 'Oh, I've bought this book,
it's really good, it's got all these things in it, you know, you
must look at it, or read it or buy it or whatever...' ... there
doesn't seem to be hardly anything written because I would
go to that, I would think 'Yeah, that's great', because I'd
like my teaching to be quite individual and I want it to be
remembered, you know. I don't want to go in and reel out
these lessons and they're all sitting and saying, 'Oh God,
we're doing this again' and you know. I would like it to be,
you know, interesting. But, obviously, because we're so
inexperienced, we have to go to somewhere to look for these
ideas that we might find useful or we could adapt, maybe.
There seems very little literature ... you know, written about
what's good, what's bad or what's a good idea and what's
probably a bad idea to use for, you know, popular culture.

On the one hand, this thirst for reading to develop underpinning knowledge
can be seen in a positive light. However, a poststructuralist reading of such
data might indicate that Rachel's concern for finding instructional texts can
be seen as an indication of a foundational stance towards teacher knowledge
which

> ... appears to communicate that the knowledge for teaching exists
> somewhere outside the teacher, derived from research and other
> authoritative sources, and is then applied to the challenges of teaching.
> (Grossman and Shulman, 1994: 9)

Such a stance needs to be challenged through initial teacher education courses which focus upon more constructivist notions of teacher knowledge (Grossman and Shulman, 1994) in which pre-service teachers identify ways in which they themselves can construct a theoretical framework for teaching which takes account of their own tacit knowledge (Polanyi, 1967). This is not to deny, of course, that pre-service teachers do need to draw from a range of sources in the development of their own practice and, indeed, such sources can provide valuable support in the shaping of theory, ideology and practice. In the above extracts from the interviews, what can be seen is students' lack of 'pedagogical content knowledge' (Shulman, 1987), that is knowledge of ways of teaching with popular culture, a situation which can be helped through the judicious use of support materials.

There is no space here to discuss the other limitations on pre-service teachers' practices identified in the study, although there were numerous others (see Marsh, in press, for further analysis). However, whilst these restrictions on practice were a dominant theme throughout the data, it was clear that the students themselves also imposed restrictions on their practice at times. This issue will be considered in the following section.

THE PANOPTICON

An English philosopher of the nineteenth century, Jeremy Bentham, designed an architectural structure which was intended to serve as a prison, which he classified as a Panopticon. Foucault adopted the design to analyze the way in which power operates and positions the subject in this process. Foucault, in *Discipline and Punish*, describes Bentham's Panopticon thus:

> We know the principle on which it was based: at the periphery, an annular building; at the centre, a tower; this tower is pierced with wide windows that open onto the inner side of the ring; the peripheric building is divided into cells, each of which extends the whole width of the building; they have two windows, one on the inside, corresponding to the windows of the tower; the other, on the outside, allows the light to cross the cell from one end to the other. All that is needed, then, is to place a supervisor in a central tower... The panoptic mechanism arranges spatial unities that make it possible to see constantly and to recognize immediately...
>
> (Foucault, 1977: 200)

The effect of the Panopticon, Foucault argues, is that it induces in the inmates a permanent sense of being observed and controlled; there is no escape from the regulatory gaze. What happens, therefore, is that the subjugated become self-regulatory and perpetuate the discursive construction of power through their own actions. It becomes no longer necessary for an external body to regulate the subjects; they become expert at controlling themselves and limiting their own behaviour. In the interviews above, these pre-service teachers indicated that they were not overtly instructed to avoid the use of popular cultural texts, but avoided them anyway, which resulted in a lack of thought about alternatives.

Foucault also suggests that the normalization process (Foucault, 1977: 183) embedded within any assessment procedure serves to extinguish individual practice. Certainly, the need to perform well in placement and pass the teaching practice was an overriding concern of students, which limited the extent to which they were innovative:

Hannah: I think we felt as though we went in our teaching...not that we are criticizing our teaching practice, we went in on teaching practice and it was so new and we were all so desperate to get it right...

Rachel: You just followed everything by the book, didn't you?

Hannah: Yes, and we were planning and we were...

Rachel: Although you had your own ideas on things, it wasn't anything WOW, it was like following a model of what had already been done.

Hannah: Because we knew we'd got to sort of meet these standards for the portfolio and one thing and another, hadn't we?

Rachel: And we were more worried about that than thinking about how diverse you could be.

Hannah: ...being original.

This normalization process impacted on the pre-service teachers' practices in a number of ways. As Hannah and Rachel indicate, the need to meet externally imposed standards often led to a lack of creativity in approaches to classroom planning. In Louise's case, it led to a retreat from any contestation of the status quo through overt sanctioning of the use of popular culture when she realized, belatedly, that she had used material that had been banned in school:

Louise: The last teaching practice I was in if I tried anything remotely exciting that was dangerous because they couldn't take it if it was too exciting so you had to keep it safe so I can understand why students don't... The last teaching practice that I did I did some maths sheets and there were some Pokémon pictures on the top, 'Agh, they've got Pokémon

	on the top, we're not allowed these!' So straight away you are in the wrong really.
Jackie:	Oh, the children were censoring you?
Louise:	Yes, so you know, – 'We've been banned Pokémon – are we allowed to use these worksheets?'
Jackie:	What did you do?
Louise:	I said I didn't know they were Pokémon, you know, I just passed it off. You've got to be careful when you are on teaching practice.

The self-sanctioning behaviour of these pre-service teachers was exacerbated by the fact that they were in a relatively powerless position as students on placement. This is, inevitably, a period when students are subjugated to a number of discursive practices which serve to ensure that they are located in specific ways as apprentices in these particular communities of practice (Lave and Wenger, 1991). However, whilst being restrained by the pressures of schools, the students erected their own boundaries and thus reinforced the 'dividing practice' (Foucault, 1982) in which they were constructed as subjects. These self-imposed restrictions on practice, combined with the barriers to curriculum innovation outlined previously, meant that the use of popular culture in these pre-service teachers' school placements was severely limited throughout their course.

CONCLUSION

The findings from this study have a number of implications for initial and continuing teacher education. Teacher education programmes need to address issues relating to the potential role of popular culture in the literacy curriculum if they are to address adequately notions of curriculum and ideology. In particular, students should have opportunities to explore the matches and mismatches between pupils' out-of-school literacy practices and those they encounter in the school curriculum (Brooker, 2002; Gregory and Williams, 2000). The work of Xu (2001a, 2001b) has indicated that introducing pre-service teachers to the potential use of popular culture in the literacy curriculum can change practice and develop understanding of the way in which out-of-school literacy practices can inform the curriculum. In addition, teacher education needs to provide both pre- and in-service teachers with the opportunity to deconstruct the factors which impact upon the construction of the curriculum and help them to find strategies that can enable them to be more assertive in their dealings with schools. These measures may increase their autonomy over the construction of the literacy curriculum through the isolation and enhancement of factors which develop independence in curriculum construction. Without these developments, pre-service teachers may be limited in their ability to construct a literacy curriculum which challenges established practices and offers children an appropriate education diet for the twenty-first century.

REFERENCES

Alvermann, D., Moon, J.S. and Hagood, M.C. (1999) *Popular Culture in the Classroom: Teaching and Researching Critical Media Literacy*, Newark, DE: IRA/NRC.

Bandura, A. (1997) *Self-efficacy: the Exercise of Control*, New York: Freeman.

Barker, M. and Petley, J. (eds) (1997) *Ill Effects: The Media-Violence Debate*, London: Routledge.

Bernstein, B. (1974) *Class, Codes and Control*, Vol. 1, 2nd edn, London: Routledge and Kegan Paul.

Bernstein, B. (1996) *Pedagogy, Symbolic Control and Identity: Theory, Research, Critique*, London: Taylor & Francis.

Brooker, L. (2002) *Starting School: Young Children Learning Cultures*, Buckingham: Open University Press.

Brooky, M. (1998) 'Television and Children', *Raphael House Newsletter*, 30 April, pp. 1–4, accessed 4 June 2000 at: http://www.rh.steiner.school.nz/article18.htm.

Comber, B. and Simpson, A. (eds) (2001) *Negotiating Critical Literacies in Classrooms*, Mahwah, NJ: Lawrence Erlbaum.

Department for Education and Employment (DfEE) (1998) *National Literacy Strategy*, London: HMSO.

Dyson, A.H. (1997) *Writing Superheroes: Contemporary Childhood, Popular Culture, and Classroom Literacy*, New York: Teachers College Press.

Farrell, M.A., Walker, S., Bower, A. and Gahan, D. (2000) 'Researching early childhood student teachers: Life histories and course experience', *International Journal of Early Childhood*, 32 (1): 34–40.

Foucault, M. (1977) *Discipline and Punish: The Birth of the Prison*, Harmondsworth: Penguin.

Foucault, M. (1982) 'The Subject and Power', *Critical Inquiry*, 8: 777–95.

Green, B., Reid, J. and Bigum, C. (1998) 'Teaching the Nintendo generation? Children, computer culture and popular technologies', in S. Howard (ed.) *Wired-up: Young People and the Electronic Media*, London: UCL Press.

Gregory, E. and Williams, A. (2000) *City Literacies: Learning to Read Across Generations and Cultures*, London: Routledge.

Grossman, P. and Shulman, L.S. (1994) 'Knowing, believing and the teaching of English', in Shanahan (ed.) *Teachers Thinking, Teachers Knowing: Reflections on Literacy and Language Education*, Illinois: NCRE/NCTE.

Gunter, B. and McAleer, J. (1997) *Children and Television* (2nd edn), London: Routledge.

Lambirth, A. (2003) ' "They get enough of that at home": Understanding aversion to popular culture in schools', *Reading, Language and Literacy*, Vol. 37, 1, pp. 9–14.

Lave, J. and Wenger, E. (1991) *Situated Learning: Legitimate Peripheral Participation*, Cambridge: Cambridge University Press.

Lortie, D. (1975) *Schoolteacher: A Sociological Study*, Chicago: the University of Chicago Press.

Luke, A. and Luke, C. (2001) 'Adolescence Lost/Childhood regained: On Early Intervention and the Emergence of the Techno-Subject', *Journal of Early Childhood Literacy*, **1** (1): 91–120.

Makin, L., Hayden, J., Holland, A., Arthur, L., Beecher, B., Jones Diaz, C. and McNaught, M. (1999) *Mapping Literacy Practices in Early Childhood Services*, Sydney: NSW Department of Education and Training and NSW Department of Community Services.

Marsh, J. (2003) 'Tightropes, tactics and taboos: An enquiry into the attitudes, beliefs and experiences of pre-service and newly qualified teachers with regard to the use of popular culture in the primary literacy curriculum', unpublished PhD thesis, University of Sheffield.

Marsh, J. (in press) 'Pre-service teachers' beliefs and practices in relation to popular culture and literacy: Interactions of habitus, capital and field', *Reading Research Quarterly*, **41** (2).

Marsh, J. and Millard, E. (2000) *Literacy and Popular Culture: Using Children's Culture in the Classroom*, London: Paul Chapman.

McIntyre, D.J., Byrd, D.M. and Foxx, S.M. (1996) 'Field and Laboratory Experiences', in J. Sikula, T.J. Buttery and E. Guyton (eds) *Handbook of Research on Teacher Education*, New York: Simon & Schuster/Macmillan.

Meacham, S. (2004) Literacy and street credibility: Plantations, prisons and American literacy from Frederick Douglass to fifty cent. Paper presented at ERSC Seminar Series, University of Sheffield, March 2004.

Medwell, J., Wray, D., Poulson, L. and Fox, R. (1998) *Effective Teachers of Literacy*, EducationOn-line, http:www. Accessed 26 January 2002.

Merchant, G. (2002) *Adventures in digital literacy: The electronic texts of 7–10 year olds*, Paper presented at the BERA Conference, University of Exeter, September 2002.

Oppenheim A.N. (2000) *Questionnaire Design, Interviewing and Attitude Measurement* (new edn), London: Pinter.

Polyani, M. (1967) *The Tacit Dimension*, New York: Norton.

Powell, R.R. (1992) 'The influence of prior experience on pedagogical constructs of traditional and non-traditional preservice teachers', *Teaching and Teacher Education*, **18**: 225–238.

Powell, R.R. (1996) 'Epistemological antecedents to culturally relevant and constructivist classroom curricula: a longitudinal study of teachers' contrasting world views', *Teaching and Teacher Education*, **12** (4): 365–384.

Raymond, D., Butt, R. and Townsend, D. (1992) 'Contexts for teacher development; Insights from teachers' stories', in A. Hargreaves and M.G. Fullan (eds) *Understanding Teacher Development*, New York: Teachers College Press.

Sanger, J., Willson, J., Davies, B. and Whitaker, R. (1997) *Young Children, Videos and Computer Games*, London: Falmer Press.

Seiter, E. (1999) 'Power Rangers at Preschool: Negotiating Media in Child Care Settings', in M. Kinder (1999) *Kids' Media Culture*, Durham NC: Duke University Press.

Shuell, T.J. (1992) 'The two cultures of teaching and teaching preparation', *Teaching and Teacher Education*, 8 (1): 83–90.

Shulman, L. (1987) Knowledge and Teaching: Foundations of the new reform. *Harvard Educational Review*, Vol. 57, 1, pp. 1–22.

Stutz, E. (1996) 'Is electronic entertainment hindering children's play and social development?', in T. Gill, *Electronic Children: How Children are Responding to the Information Revolution*, London: National Children's Bureau.

Suss, D., Suoninen, A., Garitaonandia, C., Juaristi, P., Koikkalainen, R. and Oleaga, J.A. (2001) 'Media childhood in three European countries', in I. Hutchby and J. Moran-Ellis (eds) *Children, Technology and Culture: The Impacts of Technologies in Children's Everyday Lives*, London: RoutledgeFalmer.

Tang-Yee Fan, S. (1998) *The Impact of Personal History on Student Teachers' Learning to Teach*, Paper presented at the Research Student Conference, BERA Conference, Belfast, August 1998.

Xu, S.H. (2001a) 'Exploring diversity issues in teacher education', *Reading Online*, 5 (1), accessed Dec. 2001 at http://wwww.readingonline/org/newliteracies/lit_index.asp?HREF=action/xu/index.html

Xu, S.H. (2001b) *Preparing Teachers to use Students' Popular Culture in Connecting Students' Home and School Literacy Experiences*, Paper presented at the Annual Meeting of the American Educational Research Association, Seattle, WA.

Assets in the classroom: comfort and competence with media among teachers present and future

Muriel Robinson and Margaret Mackey

MODELS OF LITERACY

The conservative myth

We are all familiar with the deficit model of literacy: *Children rot their minds with television, they destroy their morals with video games, they gratuitously set themselves at risk on the Internet. All these nefarious activities interfere with their ability and their willingness to sit down with an improving book. Schools need to crack down on all the different ways their students waste their time.*

This account is something of a caricature, but variations of such attitudes can be traced in many corners of the literate world, and they certainly flourish in many of the world's newspapers. The deficit model of all the ways that old and new media interfere with the development of good literate citizens is not hard to find.

Kathleen Tyner's suggestion that we should instead think in terms of an asset model is an answer to some of the deep pessimism of the deficit model. 'An asset model for media teaching assumes that mass media and popular culture content can work as a benefit to literacy instead of as a social deficit' (Tyner, 1998: 7). She does not develop this model in great depth, but the idea is a fruitful one for tackling the simplicities of the negative view.

We have discussed elsewhere (Robinson and Mackey, 2003; Mackey, 2002; Robinson and Turnbull, 2005) the changing asset models of young children today with regard to a whole range of media. We have argued that even pre-school children are often confident users of all the technologies – including old technologies such as books – that they find in their homes. We know that they can draw on a wide range of assets to make sense of new situations, as shown by the case study of Verónica, a young Mexican child (Robinson and Turnbull, 2005), making connections across media and between situations to increase her understandings of the world and her ability to interpret new challenges. However, at the same time, there can be dangers inherent in too romantic a version of the asset model.

The progressive myth

The alternative story to the deficit model is very upbeat, and runs along these lines: *The classroom is full of media-literate kids who are savvy in ways far beyond their teachers' comprehension or interest. Teachers need to get used to not being the expert, because they are bound to teach students who are far more knowledgeable than they in the ways of new media. The answer lies in giving kids the chance to showcase their skills and experiences.*

This scenario is perhaps not quite such an extreme caricature as its conservative equivalent, but in its countervailing simplicity it is redolent of different hazards. School children may indeed be more aware of many media forms than at least some of their teachers, but the variation in exposure, experience and sophistication is very wide – among students and among teachers as well. Furthermore, technical skills are not the same thing as critical response, and many children – as in other arenas – simply do not know what they do not know.

In fact, many, if not most, children in the Western world will move through very different classroom situations – with diverse access to, and experience with, new media both at home and at school. If children are to be able to maximize the use of these assets as they encounter literacy practices within formal schooling, it is important either that their teachers be confident users of newer technologies or, at a minimum, that they be able to take an informed and committed interest in those formats that their pupils value.

Their teachers, however, will also have divergent media backgrounds and skill sets. To some extent, the generation gap within the teaching profession itself is significant in this discussion. But is it too simplistic to suggest that older teachers are lacking the media sophistication that younger teachers, like their pupils, take for granted? We actually know very little about the media skills and competencies of teachers present and future.

THE CASE FOR YOUNG PEOPLE AS EARLY ADOPTERS

Young people are more likely than their elders to engage enthusiastically with new media forms and hardware. Rheingold, who demonstrates his case powerfully with examples drawn from a range of countries, observes: 'It is worth noting that adolescents, those aged fourteen to twenty, are often the early adopters of mobile communications and are among the first whose identities, families and communities begin to change' (Rheingold, 2003: 25). Pre-service teachers fall in the upper end of this age range, and it seems reasonable to assume that many of them may also be early adopters, or at least not so technophobic as some of their elders.

In this chapter, we offer a test of this 'reasonable assumption' based on work with small groups of education undergraduates. As colleagues who have worked with pre-service teachers in two different countries, we began an exploration of the media backgrounds and experiences of small sample groups of pre-service teachers in England and in Canada. Our idea was to achieve two snapshots, one in each country, which would enable us to make some more informed comparisons and begin to answer certain important questions. For example, we wondered if there were strong national variations. We considered the hypothesis that younger pre-teachers in both countries might resemble each other rather more than they resembled the older pre-teachers. We wanted to find out if the age variation was more a stereotype than an actuality.

For these reasons, we mounted two pilot studies, one in Lincoln, England, and one in Edmonton, Canada. Both studies involved pre-service teachers in the primary sector. In both cases, students completed a very similar version of a survey of media experiences. This chapter presents the findings of these surveys and explores the implications of the study for teachers and teacher education.

THE SURVEY

A copy of the survey we created is included in the appendix to this chapter. This survey was developed and refined over a period of two years. Different incarnations were piloted in different teaching situations, and comments of students have been fed back into its development. The survey was also vetted and improved by individual colleagues with advanced technological skills and interests.

The survey was designed to be filled in quickly. Participants were asked to circle those media technologies with which they felt themselves to be comfortably familiar, to underline those with which they had a moderate acquaintance, and to leave blank those with which they were not at all familiar.

Inevitably, in a time of rapid technological and social change, despite our substantial piloting exercise, we inadvertently omitted items that would have enhanced the list. For example, we may have missed a trick by failing to ask about bulletin boards – the asynchronous electronic discussion format that provides an entry point into digital conversation for many users. We also discovered that we had not paid enough attention to digital photography as a meaning-making tool when we realized that one of our research assistants uses her camera in a variety of meaning-bearing ways. Clare is a second-year student studying music and education studies who is rarely seen without her digital camera. On a recent visit to France, Clare recorded each day in still images which were then used each night to retell the story of the day and to share with others in her travel group any experiences they had missed. Now a selection of the photos have been combined with music to form a chapter in her DVD-format photo album. Not even the superficial fact of Clare's confidence with the technology is captured by the survey, yet there is a clear relationship to other meaning-making technologies.

Despite these gaps, and others which will have appeared by the time this report appears in print, we are confident that our survey provides a glimpse into the multiple ways that people take on new forms of communication technologies.

ADMINISTERING THE SURVEYS

Methodology for the Edmonton study

The Canadian survey was conducted as follows: pre-service teachers in the elementary (or primary) stream taking a spring session of a compulsory course on teaching language arts were invited to fill out our survey of media experiences. The forms were completed and submitted anonymously.

A total of forty-nine education students, out of three classes, completed the survey from a potential total of sixty-nine, a response rate of 81 per cent. Participants ranged in age from 20 to 44. Twenty-five of these students were aged 24 or under and they were grouped in one category. Twelve students were aged 34 or older, and they were grouped in a second category. The remaining 12 were aged between 25 and 33. Only three participants were male.

Methodology for the Lincoln study

The same survey as was used in Edmonton was distributed to students from four classes of second- and third-year pre-service primary school teachers at a college of higher education in Lincoln in the UK. A few minor modifications were made to reflect the UK situation, largely with regard to potential radio and television experiences; most of the terminology (such as 'movies' rather than 'films') was left unaltered and appeared to pose no problem. Seventy-four out of 80 distributed sheets were returned, a response rate of 92 per cent. As Table 11.1 indicates, 31 of the responding students were 24 or under, 18 were between 25 and 33 and 24 were 34 or over. The Lincoln group included eight males (four aged 24 or under and one over 34) and 65 females. One UK student did not give details of age or gender. It is worth noting that the group of third-year students was made up almost entirely of over 24-year-olds and that the older respondents were therefore also further through their course of study than the younger respondents.

Table II.I Age range of the surveyed population: Edmonton and Lincoln

	24 or younger	25–33	34 or older	Age and gender not given
Edmonton (*n* = 49)	25 (51%)	12 (24.5%)	12 (24.5%)	0
Lincoln (*n* = 74)	31 (42%)	18 (24%)	24 (33%)	1 (1%)

For the purposes of contrast, we compared the responses of the youngest and the oldest groups in each country, in terms of what they chose to identify by circling, thus indicating considerable comfort and familiarity. The raw numbers were converted into percentages in order to facilitate comparison. These data are, as appropriate, set in the context of total response rates and of gender responses, though the very low number of male respondents means that any discussion of gender is inevitably somewhat inconclusive (the low representation of men certainly has its own implications for the primary classroom).

This procedure represents a rough-and-ready scientific method, but the resulting profiles do offer some food for productive thinking about the kinds of new teachers who are making themselves ready to enter the classroom. In future work we will want to go deeper into the experiences of individuals to understand how they acquire and draw on their assets. Now, though, it is time to consider what this first exploration of relatively uncharted waters has shown and how it compares both with the Smartmob generation described by Rheingold and with what we know of contemporary teens.

THE SUCCESS STORIES

In a discussion of an asset model, it seems appropriate to start by discussing the success stories. Some interesting data emerged in relation to those forms of electronic text that must now be included among the success stories. The Canadian study showed that 100 per cent of the younger group and 92 per cent of the older group were happy about writing and reading emails. Ninety-six per cent of the younger group and 92 per cent of the older group were comfortable with searching the Internet for specific information. Finally, and as a result of deliberate efforts on the part of their home department, 88 per cent of the younger group and 100 per cent of the older group claimed comfort with using WebCT.

Broken down into age-specific responses, 80 per cent of the younger UK group were confident with email, as were 88 per cent of the older group, compared to an overall figure from all respondents of 82 per cent. This is an interesting inversion of the Canadian finding. Similarly, 83 per cent of the older group were comfortable searching the Internet for specific information as against 61 per cent of the younger students. Very few had any experience of WebCT, which is not used at the UK college (nor was any other virtual learning environment (VLE) then in regular use). This is where the level of experience of the students may be a factor, since, as identified earlier, the more mature students also tended to be further on in their study, but there may be other issues, and this possibility is explored below.

Interesting gleams of insight into contemporary life are presented by figures that do not exactly qualify as 'success stories' in the demanding percentages outlined above, but still indicate breakthroughs in certain niche markets. Comfort with online banking is remarkably prevalent among the Canadian respondents, expressed by 84 per cent of the younger group and 75 per cent of the older group. And one surprisingly high pair of totals for both Canadian groups was the use of ecards – those online greeting cards that people send to their electronic correspondents. Sixty-eight per cent of the younger group and 41 per cent of the older group claimed comfort with this niche genre. Just as Barton and Hamilton found surprisingly high quotients in particular local and social uses of literacy in their study of reading and writing in a Lancaster community (1998; see pages 123–4 and 150 for interesting discussions concerning the significance of selecting paper greeting cards), so these respondents seem to find that pre-designed online greetings fill a need in their lives.

Online banking and shopping are taking off more slowly in the UK group, with 46 per cent and 53 per cent overall using online banking and shopping respectively. The age-related responses reveal a very particular picture. Seventy-one per cent of the older group use online banking, and 75 per cent use online shopping. Only 26 per cent of the younger group, and only 18.5 per cent of young female respondents, bank on line, and 39 per cent shop on line (41 per cent of young females). Nor have ecards taken off in such a big way in the UK, with completely confident responses from only 19 of the total sample of 74 (26 per cent), and an even lower figure for each of the target groups (21 per cent of the older respondents and 19 per cent of the younger ones, with none of the young men responding positively). Reading around the responses from the perspective of a tutor who has taught pre-service teachers, a story of lifestyle for mature students can be constructed in which the need to maximize available time may drive technology use and asset acquisition in a different way from the lifestyles of those under-24s (Table 11.2).

One familiar electronic text that is not often thought of in such terms is the DVD. Ninety-six per cent of the younger Canadian group, but only 75 per cent of the older group, claimed comfort with movies on DVD (Table 11.3). Here, the UK figures are much more closely comparable (93.5 per cent of the younger group and 79 per cent of the older group).

Table 11.2 Success stories: percentage of the samples expressing comfort

	24 and younger		34 and older	
	Edmonton	Lincoln	Edmonton	Lincoln
Email	100	80	92	88
Searching the Internet	96	61	92	83
Online banking	84	26	75	71
Online greeting cards	68	19	41	21

Table 11.3 National similarities: percentage expressing comfort with DVDs in both countries

	24 and younger	34 and older
Edmonton	96	75
Lincoln	93.5	79

In both countries there were some larger discrepancies in relation to DVD, to which we shall return below.

One big success story in the UK clearly reflects the influence of societal structures in a very practical way. A total of 77 per cent of all British respondents were comfortable users of text-messaging via mobile phones, and the age-related figures show that 84 per cent of the younger group and 67 per cent of the older group are confident users of this medium. Interestingly, of the five young women who did not circle this item, four do use instant messaging, leaving just one young respondent who claimed not to use either. In Canada, however, the figures were 56 per cent for the younger group and just 17 per cent for the older students (Table 11.4).

European readers may find the totals for both older and younger Canadians surprisingly low. In fact, North Americans have less to gain economically by texting and use this technology much less frequently than much of the rest of the world; whereas the UK tariffs mean that texting is often the cheapest way to use the mobile phone. A 2004 Bell Canada survey 'found that 30 per cent of 13–24-year-olds [in Canada] use it at least once a week' (Markusoff, 2004: A4), a figure which brands our little

Table 11.4 National differences: percentage expressing comfort with text-messaging in both countries

	24 and younger	34 and older
Edmonton	56	17
Lincoln	84	67

group of 20–24-year-old pre-service teachers as early adopters by North American standards. But the elder group is clearly unconvinced by the merits of texting and has almost nothing to do with it.

The very high figures for texting in the UK may partially explain what otherwise seems anomalous: the lower figures for comfort with email among the younger British students (80 per cent described themselves as completely comfortable with email). If you are accustomed to mobile communication, resorting to a computer may seem a clunky way of making contact. It seems likely that instant messaging may similarly represent a threat to email usage among young people, but we do not actually have figures to back up this possibility.

These success stories offer an interesting insight into what we now take for granted. Even with this small sample, it was noticeable that more of the older Canadian group claim to be perfectly at home with email than with television (83 per cent of the older Canadians are comfortable with the basic TV channels versus 92 per cent who are comfortable with writing and reading emails – the younger students register 100 per cent in both cases). This particular finding is so striking that it should lead us to reconsider what media formats an educator might now consider to be 'basic' equipment for teaching. In fact, this result is so astonishing that it calls for further consideration; there is among teachers, in Canada at least, a small sub-group who not only have little to do with television but in fact actually resist it, bragging that they have never owned a TV, don't let their own children watch it, etc. It seems likely that one or two of this way of thinking skewed our small sample, and it is not surprising that the discrepancy comes with the older age group.

For this Canadian group, corresponding by email and searching the Web are clearly part of their daily life, a fact borne out in that everybody circled them to indicate complete familiarity. In the UK, however, television (particularly the terrestrial channels) is still the most universally comfortable medium, with 95 per cent circling this item. When we look at just the younger UK group, this figure actually rises to 100 per cent, with many also expressing complete confidence with satellite, cable and other forms of television services.

MAJOR DISCREPANCIES BETWEEN AGE GROUPS

Not all the distinctions between the younger and the older students manifested themselves in ways we had expected. For example, it is not surprising to discover that, in Canada, satellite and Internet radio are more familiar to the younger group (64 per cent and 76 per cent respectively) than to the older (33 per cent and 50 per cent). The UK figures reflect the same pattern, with 26 per cent of younger respondents and only 17 per cent of the older group confident with satellite and 67 per cent and 37.5 per cent respectively for Internet radio. However, the UK results reveal yet another difference in media usage across the Atlantic, with radio of all kinds totally unfamiliar to a surprising number of UK respondents overall; local and national radio over the airwaves is completely unfamiliar or unused by 30 per cent and 36 per cent of all UK respondents respectively. (In Canada, only 16 per cent of the younger participants and 8 per cent of the older group did not express complete comfort with radio, but even these small numbers are thrown into doubt when we look at what they had to say about music on the radio, where the comfort level ran at 96 per cent and 100 per cent for younger and older respondents respectively). Here again the limitations of space hide some of the more interesting variations between those who never seem to listen to the radio in any form and those who are confident with airwaves, satellite and Internet: variations found in each age group.

Nor is it startling to see a big difference in the use of text messaging (56 per cent for the younger group, 17 per cent for the older students) in Canada, but it is worth questioning why the gap is so much smaller in the UK (84 per cent for the younger group, 67 per cent for the older group). Domestic realities may account for the reduction in this generational gap in the UK where texting is more common. Since the tariff system encourages texting, and since texting also has attractions in that it is not so immediate a connection, British teenagers have taken the initiative in using texting to keep in touch with home. A quick message by text to say 'B back l8' is both quick and cheap to send and avoids the discussion of this announcement with parents – or at least transfers any subsequent voice call onto the parent's phone bill. Given the ubiquity of mobile phones in the UK and the wholesale adoption of texting by the younger generation, it is perhaps not so surprising that older women in the UK in particular use texting to keep in touch with far more regularity than in Canada and in North America more generally.

Computer games evinced less of a generational contrast than we might have expected in the Canadian group, with 68 per cent of the younger group and 58 per cent of the older group claiming comfort with such games played alone (it is certainly possible that games such as Solitaire and Tetris skewed these findings). Console games (PlayStation, Nintendo, etc.) and hand-held electronic games (GameBoy, etc.) drew a bigger gap: 52 per cent versus 33 per cent and 52 per cent versus 25 per cent respectively, the younger users representing the higher figure in each case. Younger users (48 per cent) expressed greater comfort than older ones (25 per cent) with cellphone games also (Table 11.5).

There is a much more marked contrast between the younger and older groups in the UK. The figures for the younger respondents are remarkably similar to those from Canada, but students in the older group have very little confidence. It was notable that ten of the older UK respondents (42 per cent) left every item related to gaming completely blank, indicating absolutely no experience in this area (Table 11.6).

However, even among the younger student teachers in both countries, the level of familiarity and comfort with console, arcade and cellphone games hovers at around the halfway mark.

For the purposes of local comparisons, we conducted a small-scale survey of 16 UK teenagers, the offspring of people working at the college attended by the student teachers of our British survey. Their attitudes to a variety of gaming situations, in contrast to the student teachers, reveal a markedly higher degree of comfort (Table 11.7).

In particular, the very low numbers with no experience for every category except massively multi-player online role-playing indicate the widespread presence of computer gaming in the assets of teenagers.

This discrepancy suggests that one territory with potential for large levels of incomprehension and alienation between teacher and pupil still remains. Since most of the teenagers (13 out of 16) who provided this information were male and most pre-service primary school teachers are female, there is another important tension here to address when we turn to the implications for the classroom.

Table 11.5 Percentage of the Edmonton sample expressing comfort with digital games

	24 and younger	*34 and older*
Computer games	68	58
Console games	52	33
Handheld games	52	25
Cellphone games	48	25
Massively multiplayer online role-playing games	8	8

Table 11.6 Percentage of the Lincoln sample expressing comfort with digital games

	24 and younger	*34 and older*
Computer games	67	29
Console games	55	8
Handheld games	35	8
Cellphone games	48	13
Massively multiplayer online role-playing games	10	4

Table 11.7 Lincoln teenage responses to questions about gaming, $N = 16$, with 13 male

	Completely confident	Some familiarity	No experience
Computer games played alone	75%	12%	12%
Computer games played against face-to-face opponent	81%	7%	12%
Computer games played online	56%	19%	25%
Massively multiplayer on line role-playing games	31%	12%	56%
Video games (PlayStation, Nintendo, etc.)	75%	12%	12%
Hand-held electronic games (GameBoy, etc.)	63%	25%	12%
Arcade games	34%	31%	25%
Cellphone games	38%	50%	12%

Another striking zone of considerable differentiation within our survey of initial teacher education students lies in the use made of DVDs and their extra tracks of background information, out-takes, extra scenes and so forth. In Canada, 64 per cent of younger viewers were comfortable with looking at production information (versus 25 per cent of older viewers). Seventy-two per cent of younger students were happy about accessing the director's commentary (versus 58 per cent of older students). Fifty-two per cent expressed comfort about using different soundtracks and 56 per cent about exploring different camera angles (versus 17 per cent in each case for the older viewers). When it comes to looking at out-takes and deleted scenes the discrepancy narrows to a certain extent (64 per cent to 41 per cent). A similar picture emerged in the UK, with 52 per cent of younger respondents (and 75 per cent of the men) identifying at least one added feature as something with which they were comfortable as against 17 per cent of the older group. Again it is tempting to hypothesize that a mature student, more likely to have children, has enough familiarity with the medium to play a DVD film, but less leisure to explore the additionality than younger students with less responsibility.

One possibly undervalued quality of DVD films is the huge potential for media education that they offer. The supplementary tracks offer access to levels of information about the crafting of movies that would have required specific media education courses not very many years ago. The findings of this particular aspect of the study indicate that younger teachers will find themselves equipped with considerable intuitive and implicit understanding of film-making as a result of living with DVDs. However, such familiarity is not the same thing as a critical education, and teacher educators should certainly not think that they can relax about this aspect of media literacy. DVDs mean that students (pre-service teachers as well as school pupils) come into the classroom with a much broader range of tacit information, but articulating and interrogating that experience will still require scaffolding.

TECHNOLOGIES FOR LIFE AND TECHNOLOGIES FOR TEACHING

The results above seem to demonstrate, not surprisingly, that we are best at becoming confident with the technologies which we find add most to our lives. For hard-pressed mature students with families, this may be online shopping or banking, or the technologies necessary to keep in touch with and entertain the family. For younger students, a more straightforward pleasure principle may be operating. (For school-age teenagers, however, our limited investigations seem to identify pleasure and connected to communication as even more compelling forces). We have shown that for younger pre-service teachers, the PC is at least as much a source of pleasure and communication as of work, and for the younger UK group in particular, there is not that high a level of confidence in the more work-based uses such as searching for key information and bookmarking important sites, particularly when compared to such uses as watching online streaming music video. This point raises some key questions about the nature of literacy learning across media and the relationship between pleasure, play and the assets acquired.

Meek (1982: 81–85) has argued that we need to see reading as deep play if we are to engage most powerfully with young learners. It is when we see reading as work, as merely transactional and functional, that we struggle most to become fully literate. The study of Verónica, a young Mexican child, referred to above (Robinson and Turnbull, 2005) showed how over the first six years of her life she learned from all kinds of experiences across a whole range of media. Using these media as part of her play, she soon grasped how to make meaning in a new situation and how to use new situations to develop her set of assets still further. For example, in her play with a large inflatable *Tyrannosaurus rex*, she drew on the discourse of playing with dolls and of childcare to enact cleaning the dinosaur's teeth and putting it to bed; the story of *Dinosaur*, her favourite film at the time, acted to prompt a retelling in dramatic play with the dinosaur in a starring role; and her factual knowledge of *Tyrannosaurus rex* led to other more aggressive play. Her response to any new dinosaur book was related to her past experience and knowledge drawn from all kinds of sources, so that *Dinosaurs and All That Rubbish* (Foreman, 1993) was at first rejected, since it challenged her knowledge that dinosaurs did not live at the same time as people, and then accepted as she adjusted her understanding of the nature of fiction to allow her to tolerate the two coexisting worlds of scientific understanding about dinosaurs and the alternative worlds permitted in fiction. All these assets came from her pleasure in dinosaurs, which was not prompted by any formal learning and was never seen as a requirement. At the age of six her choice of activity during the school holidays showed that reading and writing were clearly pleasurable in the same way as re-watching her newest video or drawing or playing on the computer, and just as likely to be chosen by Verónica herself as a way of spending time.

WORK AND PLEASURE IN THE CLASSROOM

Verónica demonstrates the power of playful fascination as a driver towards becoming fully literate, but adults may be most comfortable with those elements of new technology that fit into the work of their daily lives. This distinction, between learning about technology through play and learning about technology through enhancements to the work experience, may actually represent the most significant component of the generation gap around technology. But if our pre-service teachers become dismissive of the technologies of *pleasure* and focus only on the *utility* of new technology, we are in danger of perpetuating and extending the rift between the outside world and the world of school. If we are not only excluding the texts of popular culture from our classrooms (and Marsh, 2003 and chapter 10 in this volume, for example, shows how unlikely intending teachers in the UK are to use such texts in their teaching practice) but also focusing on the bits of kit or the specific uses of such kit that are least likely to provoke the *jouissance* of deep play (Barthes, 1973) – or even *plaisir* – then the world of school could feel very alien to large numbers of young people and the connections between the assets they bring from home and those needed in the classroom will be slight.

In this depressing scenario, it is not only the school pupils who find many of their most successful literacy experiences eliminated from the classroom – though the significance of that loss should not be underestimated. The youngest of our new teachers also run the risk of excluding most of their own genuine textual pleasures, leaving them at the classroom door, so to speak, in order to pursue only those technologies that enable task pursuit and schoolwork orientation.

LESSONS FOR THE CLASSROOM AND FOR PRE-SERVICE TEACHER EDUCATION

If we take on board Meek's distinction between reading as work and reading as play and extend the view of reading to encompass a wide variety of texts, we need to consider how best we can both inspire pupils to engage with new media technologies and how we can capitalize on the assets they bring with them to the classroom. Somewhat worryingly, in the UK at least, we found that many pre-service teachers had a very functional view of the place of new media technologies in the classroom. If our new and intending primary school teachers are making a separation between their own assets with new media and the way that such media might play a part in education, then there is a serious risk of a continued and widening schism between the work of the school and the world of life outside. We have claimed elsewhere (Robinson and Mackey, 2003) that for young children there is an increasing porosity between media, with the narrative or the content more significant than the medium of presentation in making meanings and connections.

Unless our pre-service education programmes explicitly address the interconnected nature of children's learning in a media-rich world, then our new teachers will continue to miss valuable opportunities for exploring what Dyson has called the 'constellation of communicative practices in children's multimodal, socioculturally complex worlds' (Dyson, 2003).

POINTS FOR CONSIDERATION

There are major questions that deserve further attention. One is the role of gender. It is accidental that our sample group of teenagers was largely male, less of a coincidence that our sample of intending primary school teachers (in both countries) was largely female. However, this accident highlights major differences between the two populations, and it is tempting to see gender as a major consideration in the development of these differences. If primary school teachers continue to be mainly female, those responsible for pre-service teacher education perhaps should consider whether there is a need for some kind of specific attention to this gender gap.

A second issue involves teacher awareness of children's implicit learning from their recreational texts. If teachers do not understand or respect some of the basic formats (such as games) from which children learn through their play about how to interpret forms of text, they risk creating a social gulf that may be difficult to cross in other ways. They also risk a substantial pedagogical gulf, particularly in respect of children's composition processes: writing, drawing, organizing text, etc. Philip Pullman (1989) describes how teachers may better understand what children are writing if they take account of the 'invisible pictures' in children's minds as they write. Guy Merchant (2004) similarly draws our attention to the ways in which children's writing develops out of the matrix of previous textual experience, including many forms of computer affordance. James Paul Gee (2003) talks about levels of learning with video games: active learning as players confront new game territories, critical learning in which gamers learn to think *about* the game domain 'at a "meta" level as a complex system of interrelated parts' (ibid.: 23), and innovative learning in which players learn to produce novel and/or unpredictable meanings.

The blankness of so many upcoming teachers on the subject of computer games is a liability if it causes them to misunderstand the ways in which their pupils are coming to terms with how a text can be put together. If student teachers are not arriving at their colleges and universities with a personal background in gaming, it behoves their instructors to find ways for them to consider the implications of that absence for their understanding of children's ways of making sense in light of experience.

The role of DVD is a reminder of a third major issue that arises out of the findings of our modest surveys. DVDs, websites, television programmes, magazine and newspaper articles – all devote much space and time to exploring the nuts and bolts of how texts of popular culture (especially films) are put together. Yet much of this detailed technical explanation arises out of explicit commercial *celebration* of the film under consideration. A DVD 'extra' demonstrating, for example, how a soundtrack is composed from separate elements can be a useful teaching tool; but teachers should be mindful of the need to add a component of critical awareness to such use of the excellent instructional material now so readily available. Finding ways to augment the valuable information on DVDs (something as simple as having pupils create a more critical audio track, for example) is a teaching challenge that needs to be made visible to intending teachers.

CONCLUSIONS

The range of textual possibilities in contemporary society is large and bewildering; finding a productive and positive route through the maze of format and content options is a challenge that daunts even the most confident teachers, let alone those who are finding their teaching feet. We suggest that one very productive starting point would be for teachers to administer the kind of simple survey we used for our small study to their own school classes. Having some specific sense of what assets each pupil is bringing into school is a major advantage. Finding ways to discuss differences among teachers and pupils (as long as that conversation does not *a priori* disadvantage some formats and unduly valorize others) opens doors to ways of making fruitful progress, both in terms of skill development and also in terms of critical analysis.

The same starting point would be a valuable beginning to any pre-service teacher education. Once we are aware of the assets being brought to the situation by intending teachers, we can plan how to address any differences between the experiences of teachers and pupils and suggest appropriate strategies to intending teachers. At the same time, regular use of a survey such as the one presented below would be a reminder to those of us who work in teacher education that our own asset sets – and consequent assumptions about the nature of literacy today and tomorrow – may also be rather different from those of the people we are preparing for work as teachers as well as from those of Rheingold's early adopters and their younger siblings.

Even with their manifest limitations of size and scope, our little surveys demonstrate very vividly that we are in a time of flux. Finding creative ways of teaching through flux is a challenge for everyone – younger, older, pre-service teacher, in-service teacher and teacher educator alike. Denial and the deficit model do not help us to meet this remarkable challenge; exploring and extending the assets of teachers – including the essential asset of being able to reflect on the critical implications of all these rapid changes – is the only realistic route to developing a vital pedagogy for the twenty-first century.

APPENDIX   *AN ASSET MODEL OF CONTEMPORARY LITERACY EXPERIENCES*

AGE (in years)_____ GENDER (m/f)_____

Text on paper

- novels
- short fiction/poetry/drama
- information books
- newspapers
- magazines
    - arts/entertainment
    - fashion/self-help
    - sports/games/hobbies
    - general information/news
    - other – specify
- comics
- graphic novels
- zines
- picture books
- computer manuals
- games manuals/help books
- posters
- other – specify

Audio

- radio
  - local
    - airwaves
    - satellite
    - Internet
  - national
    - airwaves
    - satellite
    - Internet
  - international
    - satellite
    - Internet
  - music
  - talk
  - sports
- audiocassette/minidisc
  - music
  - spoken word
- CD
  - music
  - spoken word
- MP3, iPod, or other form of online sound
  - music
  - spoken word
- other – specify

Audiovisual

- television
  - basic channels
  - satellite
  - cable
  - digital cable
  - pay-per-view
- video
  - taped TV programs for later or more convenient viewing
  - movies
- DVD
  - movies
    - online features
    - alternative tracks

           production information
              special effects
              director's commentary
              trailers, etc.
           alternative playback
              different soundtracks
              different camera angles
              out-takes/deleted scenes, etc.

- music
  - video
  - DVD
    personal recording (movies, etc.)
- other – specify

• personal video recorders (TiVO)
• movies at the cinema
• online (streaming video)
  - music videos
  - movies
  - television clips
  - original shorts
  - flash movies
  - CNN clips
  - other – specify

Wireless text

• text messaging
• other – specify

Electronic images

• computer games
  - played alone
  - played against face-to-face opponent
  - played online
  - massively multi-player on line role-playing games
• video games (PlayStation, Nintendo, etc.)
• hand-held electronic games (GameBoy, etc.)
• arcade games
• cellphone games

- cellphone photo images
- watching movies/TV/music videos on line
- gaming on line
- other – specify

Electronic text

- e-books
- PDAs (personal data assistants such as Palm Pilot)
  - with built-in telephone
  - with gaming features
- on-screen readers such as Adobe PDF
- email
  - writing
  - reading
  - sending attachments
    - text
    - audio
    - moving images
- CD/DVD-ROM information texts
- blogs (weblogs)
- literary hypertext
- online magazines
- e-zines
- e-cards
- other – specify
- online commerce
  - banking
  - shopping
- online reading
  - surfing/browsing websites
  - searching for specific information
  - revisiting bookmarked sites
  - lurking on listservs
  - reading listservs as contributor
  - lurking in chatrooms
- online producing
  - visiting chatrooms
    - related to specific topics
      computer games
        in role
        as a player
      television programs
      movies

       particular hobbies
       other – specify
    – general chatrooms
    – other – specify
- instant messaging
  - with personally known friends
  - with Internet-only friends
- writing to listservs
  - specific topic-related
  - general
- blogging (web logging)
  - on a specific topic
  - general
- creating websites
  - personal – e.g. home page
  - topic-related
    - text-only
    - text and still image
    - text and moving image
    - audio
- contributing to other websites
  - in writing
    - opinions
    - fan fictions
    - other – specify
  - in visual forms
    - still images
    - moving images
- online learning
  - using WebCT
  - other – specify
- online – helping others
- online – other – specify
- using HTML/XML/VRML/etc.
- programming

ACKNOWLEDGEMENTS

We gratefully acknowledge the help of Clare Smith (UK) and Sarah Mackey (Canada) in tabulating the results for us with cheerfulness, accuracy and dispatch.

REFERENCES

Barthes, R. (1973) *Le Plaisir du Texte*. Paris: Editions du Seuil.

Barton, D. and Hamilton, M. (1998) *Local Literacies: Reading and Writing in One Community*. London: Routledge.

Dyson, A.H. (2003) Keynote address at UKRA annual conference, University College Chester, UK.

Foreman, M. (1993) *Dinosaurs and All That Rubbish*. London: Puffin Books.

Gee, J.P. (2003) *What Video Games Have to Teach Us about Learning and Literacy*. New York: Palgrave Macmillan.

Mackey, M. (2002) 'An Asset Model of New Literacies: A Conceptual and Strategic Approach to Change', in R.F. Hammett and B.R.C. Barrell (eds), *Digital Expressions: Media Literacy and English Language Arts*. Calgary: Detselig, pp. 199–215.

Markusoff, J. (2004) 'Vowels are for Losers in a 155-Character World', *Edmonton Journal*, A4. 8 June.

Marsh, J. (2003) 'Tightropes, Tactics and Taboos: An Enquiry into the Attitudes, Beliefs and Experiences of Pre-Service and Newly-Qualified Teachers with regard to the Use of Popular Culture in the Primary Literacy Curriculum', unpublished PhD thesis: University of Sheffield.

Meek, M. (1982) *On Being Literate*. London: The Bodley Head.

Merchant, G. (2004) 'The Dagger of Doom and the Mighty Handbag', in J. Evans (ed.), *Literacy Moves On: Using Popular Culture, New Technologies and Critical Literacy in the Primary Classroom*. London: David Fulton, pp. 59–75.

Pullman, P. (1989) 'Invisible Pictures', *Signal 60*: 160–86.

Rheingold, H. (2003) *Smart Mobs: The Next Social Revolution*. Cambridge, MA: Perseus.

Robinson, M. and Mackey, M. (2003) 'Film and Television', in N. Hall, J. Larson and J. Marsh (eds), *Handbook of Early Childhood Literacy*. London: Sage, pp. 126–41.

Robinson, M. and Turnbull, B. (2005) 'Veronica: An Asset Model of Becoming Literate', in J. Marsh (ed.), *Popular Culture, New Media and Digital Literacy in Early Childhood*. London: RoutledgeFalmer.

Tyner, K. (1998) *Literacy in a Digital World: Teaching and Learning in the Age of Information*. Mahwah, NJ: Lawrence Erlbaum.

Chapter 12

Transformative practitioners, transformative practice: teachers working with popular culture in the classroom

Elaine Millard

In developed Western and Anglophone societies, the space of education has become subjected to an increasing network of disciplining regulation and control. As in the case of Foucault's (1977) nineteenth-century prisoners controlled by the gaze from the central panopticon, teachers experience their professional lives as under constant surveillance – a surveillance which has been internalized into external constraints. For, alongside an ever-increasing growth in affluence and influence of the Western powers, there has come an accompanying anxiety about the capacity to retain and monopolize that power as governments begin to compete within a global market for their national interest. Globalization begins then to exert its pressures on the youngest members of the community on school entry with the push from policy-makers for a highly educated workforce with developed technical competencies. Education has assumed a neo-Gradgrindian[1] face so that what counts as relevant are work-related skills, which always include some version of literacy. Governments seek to accomplish their educational goals through imposed national curriculum strategies that emphasize central regulation, high-stakes testing and over-determined pathways to accreditation. In England, these strategies are identified with a complexity of prescribed courses of training and professional development, whose aim is to chivvy teachers along predetermined pathways to agreed systems of values. Imposed national programmes (DFEE, 1998; 1999) have led commentators to remark on the disempowerment of the teaching profession through the intensification and proletarianization of their work (Hargreaves, 1994).

Michael Fullan gives expression to many teachers' perceptions of external pressures in posing the question: 'What does the outside look like to schools?' and responding:

> Essentially, it is a sea of excessive, inconsistent, relentless demands. Policies are replaced by new ones before they have had a chance to be fully implemented. One policy works at cross-purposes with another one.

> Above all, the demands of various policies are disjointed. Fragmentation, overload, and incoherence appear to be the natural order.
>
> (Fullan, 2000: 582)

In the United Kingdom it is the teachers of English and the primary language curriculum who have been most subjected to such 'relentless demands'. At the same time as these pressures on teachers' conditions of employment, there have come equally transformative changes to academics' understanding of the ways in which both adults and children develop effective learning strategies and, indeed, the very notion of what it is to be appropriately literate. The New Literacy Studies (NLS) (Street, 1984; Gee, 1996, 2000; Barton, 1994; Barton and Hamilton, 1998; Barton *et al.*, 2000) emphasize that literacy is not a series of skills to be transmitted but is shaped as a social practice and linked to larger social structures. Globalization is just one such structure, creating what Appadurai (1996) has described as 'borderless flows and scapes' of not only bodies and capital but also of information and images, constantly introducing new sites for the creation of new ways of making meaning.

The British government's response to the global changes which impinge on literacy practices has been an attempt to hurry reform through rigidly time-constrained interventions with externally imposed targets and programmes of training, focusing largely on patterns of testable language skills. This is, *par excellence*, an autonomous model of literacy (Street, 1984) which appears to allow little space for local initiative and indeed stifles a demand for continuous professional development (CPD) that is not directly relevant to implementing government-driven reform. Such strongly framed national initiatives are often preoccupied with pedagogical method and over-focused on basic skills, a state of affairs equally applicable to American and Australian reforms as those currently being undertaken in England. Here, government training, it has been argued, has been taken up uncritically by a 'supine' profession (Marshall, 2002) that has had most of the stuffing knocked out of it by the conditions which Fullan, quoted above, described as 'fragmentation, overload, and incoherence'. It is not surprising then, that many English teachers and primary language specialists have found themselves at odds with a strategy for developing literacy in which they seem to have been given little agency.

There is little space in this chapter to expand on what constitute two enormously complex areas of debate. On the one hand stand questions of teacher status and professional autonomy; on the other, the very definitions of what it is to be properly literate and how a 'new' literacy should be 'taught' or 'delivered' in schools. Nevertheless, these debates form the political and educational backdrop to the work described below, in which teachers were engaged in research projects drawing heavily on the use of children's cultural interests in the classroom. It was the period in England in which the National Literacy Strategy was being implemented and in which the nature of English was being strongly debated by the profession in polarities which suggested that established English teaching and literature-focused work were creative and good, whilst the literacy strategy, with its language-focused work, was stultifying, oppressive and bad.

My own stance is located within a paradigm of reflective practice and practitioner research that stresses teacher agency in bringing about peda-gogical change; for without teachers' attention to the demands of their local context and sensitivity to their students' world-view, all classroom-based work can too easily become an autonomous 'schooled' practice (Street, 1993). However, despite the many predictions of gloom and anxiety about the 'dulling and dumbing' of the profession through these measures, teachers, and arguably English teachers and primary language specialists in particular, continue to report that their motivation for entering and staying in the profession is influenced to a great extent by an individual sense of being able to make a difference and bring aspects of their own interests and identity into play when working with children (Ellis *et al.*, 2002). Such was the motivation of all the teachers engaged in the literacy research projects described below.

PARTICIPANTS IN THE STUDY

The six teachers whose projects I have observed closely, in three cases as a participant observer, have arrived at a view of the imposed curriculum objectives of the English Literacy Strategy as something that at best enables their work, at worst must not be allowed to obstruct a view of learning which is most important to them. All had chosen at different times to become involved at different levels with ongoing work within the Sheffield Literacy, Language and Culture Research Group, which seeks to understand the place of children's own cultural interests in motivating achievements in the literacy curriculum. It has become increasingly difficult for many teachers to see such interests as part of the concerns of the classroom because of curriculum objectives which privilege works of literary merit and often sideline children's own cultural preferences (Marsh and Millard, 2000, 2003). Moreover, teachers often feel a discomfort bordering on an aversion to interests brought in from home (Lambirth, 2003; Marsh, 2003).

Two of the participants, Harry and Paula, had worked with my col-league, Jackie Marsh, to explore the response of younger children to media texts, including comics, video and television. Both had had subsequent experience of disseminating their work locally and nationally. Three, Margaret, Fay and Teresa, had been involved in larger projects with LEA support for literacy development, which I had conducted in Barnsley, Ealing and Kirklees. The sixth, Rachel, was at that time a member of the staff of a Nottinghamshire primary school which concerns itself with a continuous review of its own practice. Four teachers from this school have worked regularly with me, contributing substantially to my own writing (Millard, 1994, 1997; Marsh and Millard, 2000, 2003; Millard and Marsh, 2001). I have spent much time in the school observing and recording children's responses for the work given them, and these observations have played a substantive role in shaping my own understanding of how pupils prioritize their engagement with schoolwork. In this chapter, however, it is with the teachers and how they reconcile the interests of their pupils with the increasingly formalized National Curriculum objectives that I am concerned.

WHAT KINDS OF TEACHERS ENGAGED IN DELIBERATE, RESEARCHED CURRICULUM CHANGE?

In some ways the teachers described in this study are 'special', in that they have become involved in work that has led them to collaborations beyond the classroom; on the other hand, their concerns mirror those of their colleagues and their work has found resonance within both their individual institutions and the wider community of practitioners. Within the group, there is an extensive range of experience, with all but one of them having taught for over 10 years: one is a head of a secondary English department, another the head of an inner city primary school (Table 12.1).

These particular teachers have been selected from the larger group for this study because they had all become increasingly confident in working with contested material in the classroom. I wanted to enquire into what characteristics, if any, they shared, and whether these characteristics were generalizable to other members of the profession, in other contexts. Although my initial intention was to conduct face-to-face interviews with all six participants, time and space intervened in the research time available. Four of the interviews, those with Harry, Paula, Teresa and Rachel, were conducted in this way, but the responses of Fay and Margaret are drawn from their evaluations and my research notes taken from the project data and therefore mediated through my own writing. It can be argued, in any case, that in selecting from the transcriptions of the other participants I have also imposed a personal vision. To avoid any personal distortion or misrepresentation I therefore ensured that all participants were able to comment on my writing and make any changes where necessary.

The first finding from the interviews was that all the participants were already experienced and confident practitioners with established careers in education prior to their work in popular culture (Table 12.2). Rachel, who had the least teaching experience, had already taught for eight years

Table 12.1 The research projects

Name (pseudonym)	Context of research	Experience (years)	Focus
Howard	Sheffield Primary School	16	Comic home lending library
Paula	Sheffield Community	13	Media boxes
Teresa	Kirklees J&I school	11	Writing at KS 2 Information texts, visual literacy, cartoon representation
Fay	Ealing Secondary School	12	Boys' writing project, researching and representing information
Margaret	Barnsley Primary School	12	Drama role-play, local histories, mysteries
Rachel	Nottingham Primary School	8	Narratives based on interactive problem-solving related to computer games

Table 12.2 Comparison of the participants' teaching roles and experience

Name (pseudonym)	Support for research	Experience (years)	Position
Howard	Sheffield Primary School	16	Head teacher
Paula	Sheffield LEA	13	Community teacher
Teresa	Kirklees J&I School	11	KS 2 teacher, language coordinator
Fay	Ealing Secondary School	12	Secondary English teacher
Margaret	Barnsley Junior School	12	Y5 class teacher, with a special interest in drama
Rachel	Nottingham Primary School	8	Y4/5 teacher, Maths coordinator

in two contrasting institutions; Harry, with the most, for 16 years. All the teachers had engaged with the profession outside of the classroom. Harry, in his role as headteacher, had had many opportunities for working with others and disseminating his ideas; Margaret, a classroom teacher, had contributed to writing for her authority's dissemination of a drama project; Fay, a secondary head of an English department, had presented her findings within her authority and at National Conference; Paula had co-written a paper with Jackie Marsh (Marsh and Thompson, 2001); Rachel had presented nationally on several occasions with myself; and Teresa had submitted her work on popular culture as part of a Best Practice Scholarship scheme. All reported gaining professional confidence from their collaborations out of school.

WHAT MOTIVATIONS WERE SHARED IN MAKING CURRICULUM CHOICES?

All the teachers claimed that they enjoyed most of their teaching, felt confident in examining and developing their own practice, and were particularly interested in working with pupils who demonstrated a lack of enthusiasm for the conventional literacy curriculum. Teresa, for example, explained that much of her professional satisfaction came from helping children to develop a belief in their own abilities:

> I am most successful at helping alienated children to tune back into learning, which generally, though not always, means boys.

She had researched individuals' writing preferences in the context of their own cultural interests. Using individual interviews, she was able to learn more about her pupils' attitudes and this had prompted her to modify her marking practice:

> The children who took part in the interviews appeared to enjoy the opportunity to discuss their work in such depth. I have certainly stopped adding the 'buts' to the end of positive comments when I'm marking, which seems to have led to less obsession about the mechanics of writing amongst the children even though I still teach the mechanics, apparently from results, as successfully as I did before.

In working with her year 5 class, she had incorporated children's preferences for different modalities, such as cartoon imaging and the visual mapping of their ideas into their work. A group of three children in her class had produced their own comic at home, reflecting the class's current interests, and this was circulated in the classroom. The children's writing books were similarly dotted with cartoon images illustrating their narratives.

Paula's work was located within the community, rather than in an individual classroom, and had as much to do with adults' learning as with that of young children. In her early teaching she explained that she had been placed in a school which used rigid schemes of work. (It is worth noting here that the freedoms and state of autonomy, assumed by some teachers to have been in place before 1997, are often illusory).

> I felt, I remember that they had very rigid language schemes, you're talking 1987 and it was very, very rigid and the children were, you know, when you walked in you could see, totally switched off, weren't interested, you know, when you go and visit on your teaching practice and trying to be that student who goes and helps everybody. But you can't, they just weren't interested and particularly those, whereas a lot of the Maths and the languages were brought in just by being interested in looking at adverts and what they related to and things.

She is acutely aware of the importance of the local in her configuration of appropriate ways of drawing parents and children together in intergenerational learning and traces her own concern to working with children's cultural interests to her previous school experience:

> It was through a teaching practice in a particularly difficult third-year teaching practice where the children were seven- to nine-year-olds who the class teacher was struggling with and left me to do it. So I wanted something to hook the children in, so I did a topic on television.

Her memory of this initial work, which had taken place over 12 years ago, remained alive in her memory because it had given her her first taste of success:

> It was the way that I managed to hook the children in, because there seemed to be nothing that captured their interest, they were very disillusioned, it was, you know, very, almost an out-of-control school looking back on it, but it did hook the children in, so we did, I had a friend who made videos and held an editing suite. So we did lots of writing scripts and then we actually filmed them, my friend came in and filmed them, and then edited it for them and it had credits on and everything and then we had a big grand showing at the end of the teaching practice and it kind of hooked every subject in.

The work resonated with her own experience of popular culture's ability to cross class barriers, encountered when she had been a pupil:

> I went to a private school on a bursary, but that was a very difficult time because, of course, all my friends were going to the local comprehensive and [unclear] because you're coming back to that place where you live and everyone else is going to a different school and they

suddenly see you as different, 'Why are they going to that different school?' You go to that different school, which is a private school, but everyone knows you're in a bursary scheme 'cos you haven't got the money to go to the private school! (Laughing) So it was very interesting, I think I learned a lot from that kind of experience.

Her project focused on helping parents to construct media boxes to share narrative pleasures with young children based on their television and video consumption.

She connects her current practice with the knowledge she gained then of the power of shared cultural interests to bridge social differences:

> Sometimes things like television are common ground, they are across class, you know, something that you talk about as common ground and I think they're popular culture kind of ideas and I wasn't an ideal student ... not academic.

She uses this knowledge in her community role to make links with others, what she terms 'bridging the gap':

> I've been doing a lot more work with parents, you know, and that way of bridging the gap between people's different experiences and getting people to understand about their child and their child's learning and also, with the children, getting them excited about learning ... running from one thing to the next and that enthusiasm, that natural enthusiasm is often there anyway, and I'm capitalizing on that.

Rachel had also discovered that the children's knowledge of popular culture could be used to facilitate their learning. Her working context is a school with mainly comfortably-off, well-motivated working-class children who achieve well. She finds that popular culture provides a more relevant way into literacy for them:

> The children are involved, the fact that it stretches their imagination and their sort of verbal interaction with each other. The way that you can make it cross-curricular, so you could start with literature and, OK, you know, from your literature point of view you're getting written work and poetry and, you know, newspaper articles and those sorts of things out of it.

Her projects used the modalities of popular cultural forms such as computer games and cartoon films to produce interactive problem-solving texts where image and print were granted equal importance. Her latest work had involved using heroes and villains from the children's favourite popular culture narratives to support her class in writing chapters of an adventure story, based on *The Lion, the Witch, and the Wardrobe*. She had chosen this as her class novel. She commented:

> I think that it's a mixture of the fact that they can relate to aspects of it because they choose books, or literature, that has some sort of influence in their life, in the fact that aspects of it are popular at the time. They can relate to the baddies and the goodies and their characteristics, you know. They meet them every day in PlayStation games and comics and it's things that they relate to and understand. It relates to their world now because of media interest and that sort of thing, so they relate to it straightaway and I think it attracts their imaginations.

This is not as true of her experience of most books she has shared with them in school, although these are something she enjoys working with on a personal level:

> If you take some children's novels, the children just don't relate to them. They give a really old-fashioned image of school and they are either very middle-class in their ideas and children don't necessarily live in those environments any more. It's often the schooling of the teachers it appeals to.

In developing the children's writing she had drawn on aspects of the C.S. Lewis text to support their understanding of particular linguistic and narrative structures, while allowing free rein to their interests in such different characters as Cruella de Vil, Darth Maul and Voldemort to influence their composition.

WORKING WITH CHALLENGING CHILDREN

Margaret's school provides a more challenging context:

> My school is set in the most challenging area, with high levels of long-term unemployment and family break-up. Of the 33 children in my class, 17 are on the Special Needs register and many consistently demonstrate limited speaking and listening skills. All 15 boys in the group claim to dislike writing, although all the girls stated enjoyed writing narratives.

Her research used role-play to unlock children's enthusiasm for imitating the language of specific characters and later incorporating the language produced into extended writing tasks. She had devised a scenario based on a village community divided over the proposal to build a theme park on the site of an old manor house. She found that in creating dramatic characters they could draw from their understanding of popular characters found in newspapers, soap operas, films and videos. Their acting provided the stimulus for a range of writing tasks, for example, arguing a case in a letter to the council. She kept a detailed observation diary of their responses during her role-play sessions. Here are some of the comments they offered her in a thought-shower session in which they discussed how the role-play had helped with their written work:

- Gets your brain working
- Opens the idea drawer – the drawer opens and ideas fall out
- Makes me work faster and connects the wires in my brain
- Better ideas go round in your head
- Creates a screen in the mind that helps you write ideas down
- Makes writing easier 'cos it – lets me bring my voices out

A boy whom Margaret described as enjoying mimicry and giving impressions of others' voices had contributed the last comment. She said:

> He had the potential to be distracting in class but during the role-play sessions allowed the character he had adopted, a dignified elderly resident, to guide his concentration and he avoided 'playing the fool' throughout the unit of work.

Harry, the only headteacher, has also spent his career working in what many others would consider challenging circumstances:

> The majority of the time, I've worked in inner-city, multicultural schools and schools where there are, sort of issues if you like, around, well I suppose around deprivation, around some of the challenges faced by communities, I think I've got quite a – I've got quite an interest in the roles schools play in communities.

Like Paula, Harry had found popular culture to be at the heart of his school's culture, going as far as to say:

> I don't think there's many lessons go by when you can't refer to something on television or current film. I think that you can usually find something that says, you know, think about this, you know.

The project in his school had created a comic lending library where children were able to take home comics along with their reading books to share with other family members. It was found that many more family members were willing to engage with children's reading because of this, (Marsh and Millard, 2000). Children, he believes, benefit from developing a critical awareness of the media that surround them:

> We're in one of those settings where really, what we've got here are the people who can be manipulated by the media if we don't help them to understand and be more critical users of it...I want them to enjoy it to the full but I want them begin to be able to say, 'Yes, I love this but there is more to responding to this.' I don't, you know, want to stop at enjoyment.

A POWER TO CONNECT

Each of the interviewees emphasized their use of children's own interests in making connections with the materials and concepts found in the curriculum which were more culturally remote from them. Fay, when reporting her work to the LEA, suggested that her Year 7 (11-year-olds) pupils' ability to draw on their popular cultural knowledge had helped them make connections with the myths she wanted them to study in the context of the curriculum. She had asked them to design little books for younger children with facts about a variety of myths and legends they had found from computer searches and library reference books:

> The sense of ownership given by making the books was evident, as was the importance of the focus on greater visual stimuli. Equally important was the sense of fun engendered by my allowing them to include word searches, acrostics, quizzes, tricks and pop-ups. One boy used texting messages written across illustrations and continuous prose to focus the attention of his reader on particular aspects of his information text, which was written in more formal language. There were pullout sections; ancient scrolls maps, and portraits too.

She explained that by allowing them more time to manage their own learning, she had not only given them this autonomy but also provided herself with better opportunities to scaffold the learning for individual pupils:

> Throughout the entire making of the books there was a lot of collaborative talk going on in the classroom, much more than I would normally encourage. I stood back a great deal, allowing much more freedom than in the usual teacher-led lessons...

Teresa's support for her pupils' popular cultural interests has developed from her Year 5 class's independent work in lunch clubs and out-of-school activities such as the comic-making, as well as in her acceptance of their interests in the curriculum:

> The best things, in my opinion, that have taken off this year are two lunchtime clubs organized and run by children in my class. One is a Warhammer club which is based on the game and which is mostly enjoyed by Key Stage 2 boys. The second is an amazing story-telling club. This is organized by one of the boys who makes up fantasy stories which involve the audience slaying dragons and gaining special powers. It's a pleasure to observe, which I do as I quietly undertake my own work in the corner of the room.

For Paula, the use of popular culture enabled her to draw in both parents and children into a shared interest:

> They [the boxes] were based around what the children actually enjoyed watching, so *Bob the Builder, Tweenies, Teletubbies, Rosie and Jim* I think was one of them and *Toy Story 2* was out at the time as well and so they liked that very much. We got them to ask their children what they would probably like and they would suddenly start bringing in all the articles, a lot of MacDonald's toys and things like that. Parents learn very quickly whether they can mention what their children watch on television or whether they just keep quiet about things (laughing) because, you know, they've already had the health visitor visiting and some health visitors make derogatory comments about watching television.

Her last comment shows how powerfully the education agenda features in shaping attitudes in the community that are not always conducive to children's ability to bridge the home-school gap.

CONTINUITIES AND DISCONTINUITIES WITH THE OBJECTIVES AND TARGETS REQUIRED BY THE STRATEGY

Paula's community role means she did not have to work within an imposed literacy framework. However, there were internalized expectations of what might be appropriate work for liaison between parents and school, communicated by other teachers:

> There is a lot of pressure from Year 1 teachers, that they couldn't do stuff when they came into school. There is all of that kind of pressure and again you have to be planning, you know the planning, the Government tampering with planning and sending out these planning

proformas and all that. People get very confused, you know, really quality early years practitioners, so I would say that early years are more open to working with popular culture because there are less, or used to be less restrictions on them and it isn't as formalized as the Literacy and Numeracy hour etc., but there are still those constraints that they're dealing with.

It's different in early years again because it's very hard to validate what you do, that's terrible, but it's true. Although the school had an ethos of working with parents their actual idea of working with parents was that they could come in and do baking or help with the schoolwork. It wasn't a partnership, or it wasn't my idea of a partnership.

Here, Paula echoes Jackie Marsh's view that most parent–school liaisons involve only a one-way traffic, whereby teachers ask parents to imitate school practices without understanding the literacy practices of the home (Marsh, 2003).

The teachers of older primary children had all experienced some sense of limitation and unwanted control. For example, Teresa explained that her frustrations stemmed not from the changes to the content or structure of the curriculum but from a lack of perceived governmental trust in the professionalism of teachers, reflected back sometimes by parents. She explains:

It feels like monitoring gone mad. Unfortunately, the constant need to prove improvement has led to a system which actually makes developments much more difficult than they need to be. It has also led to a devastating distortion and narrowing down of the curriculum. I am very frustrated by the narrowing of the curriculum.

While acknowledging the benefits she had taken from the NLS (DFEE, 1998), Rachel has also experienced aspects of the strategy as a limitation:

The Literacy Strategy and the Numeracy Strategy are very helpful in some respects in the fact that it ensures that you cover a wider variety of genres that you might not have covered before the strategy came out. However, if it's followed to the letter it can be very restrictive as far as cross-curricular work is concerned. It's much easier to inspire children's literacy across the curriculum rather than stick to set genres at set times and set year groups.

Teresa sees the emphasis on results and testing as a factor in some boys' lack of interest in their schoolwork:

At the same time, the obsession with testing is, I believe, closely related to the rise in anti-swot subcultures, which are currently been blamed for the underperformance of boys. It seems to me that this subculture might actually be seen as a healthy response to children being asked to compete in an academic race which holds little meaning for them.

Fay, in her secondary school, also imagines the strategy managers breathing down her neck as she moves away from what she perceives as the 'recommended' structures of lessons:

> My lessons moved away from the Literacy Strategy three-part formats, as the pupils concentrated on making their books. I stood back a great deal, allowing much more freedom than in the usual teacher-led lessons. Although I felt that I had stepped outside the Literacy Framework by abandoning the desired lesson format, it was clear that the focus on developing writing skills comes directly from its concerns.

Margaret had had what she called a disconcerting interview with one of the managers of the Literacy Strategy, who had commented that her children's writing skills were so poorly developed that they should concentrate on improving these *before* she let them get involved with drama and role-play.

Only Harry expressed unqualified ease with the workings of the Strategy:

> I think since 1997 this has been a better thing to be doing, teaching, education has become better since there's been this emphasis on getting money and specific projects in there, to actually structure some of the things that we've all seen as needing doing.

This is probably a reflection of the confidence he experiences as the senior manager, rather than classroom practitioner, in implementing the work. He feels he is able to appropriate structures and resources and use them for his own purposes. He says of Local Authority-sponsored projects and initiatives: 'We grab these things and make the most of them, they will work'.

Through this confidence in his own management of a wide range of media-related activities he experienced no conflict with curriculum developments:

> I think the Literacy Strategy used well has not been, has not presented a problem to media education. I think if anything it has presented a really good basis on which to do some good-quality media education.

COLLABORATION BUILDS CONFIDENCE

Nevertheless, even Harry can recall as a young teacher his then headteacher being anxious about him choosing to work on film:

> She was a long experienced headteacher, retired shortly after, and in fairness to her, she just tested me on it, and when I could demonstrate why she was very, very happy. She just wanted to be sure that it was not going to dull them down, that was her nervousness.

He acknowledges that an involvement with a university project helps to gain 'respectability' for his popular cultural preoccupations:

> I think it's been different in different schools, but if you're a class teacher and want to use a snatch of video or if you're a class teacher and want to use comics, to a certain extent, an outside agency is almost like your licence to do it. Say the University of Sheffield coming down, you know it helps if you've got a recognized body working with you.

All the other teachers reported how being able to develop their classroom practice collaboratively with other colleagues and university support had increased their confidence. Teresa expressed this most eloquently when she suggested:

> If we are to truly develop our understanding of teaching and of learning, then we must take time to research and to reflect upon what we are doing and upon the children's responses to our interventions. I found the opportunity to take part in the research both refreshing and enlightening and I would certainly recommend it to others.

Work in collaboration with others had prompted in all of them a more careful consideration of their children's development. Margaret commented:

> The project enabled me to see the children in a different light. I recorded in my journal many occasions when individuals bonded with people they would not naturally choose to partner.

Rachel confessed to some initial difficulty in relaxing her anxieties about the 'quality' of the fictions drawn on by the children. In our discussions, I was reminded of the prevalence of accusations of 'dumbing down' levelled at those who use popular cultural modalities in the classroom. One incident we discussed was her response to a boy who wanted to use James Bond villains in the story he was composing. Initially Rachel had rejected his contribution and it was only later, when we held a class discussion about how enemies could be defeated without killing or 'zapping' them, that she allowed him to describe the fracturing of a glass floor with a diamond ring, taken from one Bond episode. It fulfilled all our criteria for a defeat that did not involve overt violence, but cunning, as in the best folk tales. We decided that his contribution, and similar uses of the 'horror' genre in other children's work, showed that the class could be trusted to select from their repertoire of popular culture material that fitted appropriately into their school work.

Once the project was completed, Rachel continued to draw energy and ideas from collaboration with others through her role in disseminating her work:

> I've led some workshops in connection with Sheffield University and I found that experience extremely satisfying talking to other teachers, because sometimes you're in your own little bubble and you do your own, own little thing and you're really pleased with your children but you don't have any idea how you can sort of send it, you know, globally, and it was really nice to talk to other teachers about the work that we've done and they were really quite inspired.

A LITERACY OF FUSION

There has been in England, a trend in professional development away from participatory change towards the 'delivery' of acceptable 'good practice' by consultants and experts. In contrast with this transmission model, each of these Sheffield projects enabled practitioners to scrutinize the outcomes of each other's work in detail and adapt their own practice and planning as a consequence. None of them had rejected the current Framework for literacy as irrelevant, but recognized the importance of widening children's experience from a local to a more globalizing focus; all, however, welcomed an opportunity to challenge its applicability to their own situation.

Here is Margaret once more, discussing the effect of sharing a localized experience with others:

> It enabled me to learn from others. I have listened carefully to others' work and want to use some aspects in my own planning in the future.

In working with particular aspects of popular culture to promote literacy, all these practitioners were involved in fusing the demands of what at times appeared a very rigid eternally framed framework with children's own intents and motivations. Interestingly, these interests were also located in more autonomous literacy related to globalized markets, such as the film industry and computer gaming. Each teacher therefore engaged in the fusion of local, national and globalized literacies to enable their students to become more critical of the strategies of the powerful, through a variety of tactics brought in from the children's lives.

I have elaborated the tactics necessary for creating a pedagogy of fusion, that is, teacher interventions which allow children's cultural interest to be merged with school and external curriculum requirements. Elsewhere (Millard, 2003). Such a fusion seems to me to be of crucial importance in an age where the central modes of communication are in a rapid stage of development and multimodality is now the norm for creating messages outside of the schoolroom or the essayist traditions of the academic world. As Kress argues, it may be important that learners are able to access traditional modes of reflective text production, but only as one of many ways of making meaning and not '*the* form of reading that defines what reading is' (Kress, 2003: 175).

All six teachers reported that, when they began to reflect on the work they were involved in for the projects, they had found that the externally imposed literacy objectives were readily covered and sometimes subverted. As Lankshear and Knobel (2002) have suggested, in the context of student's imaginative subversions of cultural productions:

> The broad orientation we want to take today is that we should be looking ever more intently to find ways of 'drawing out' and encouraging the development of certain things learners already know and enact. These are things that have the capacity to resist and subvert, to prey upon, spoof and exploit, and – en masse – to gradually wear away at the world.

Each differently focused, small-scale, research project had enabled its participants to make these kinds of interventions in their own planning and to hand on these tactics to their pupils. I am reminded in particular of one of Teresa's 10-year-old boys who, when asked to make notes of his research on plant reproduction, drew cartoons, derived from his love of comics. They featured anthropomorphic images of plants with faces, arms and legs, cavorting about, to show wind dispersal and the use of animal vectors. One small flower held a grenade to indicate the explosion of its pods, another was peeing into a flowerpot with a censored sign covering the imagined organ, another waving goodbye to a mother plant as it sailed out of sight for water dispersal. The effect was subversive, but all relevant facts had been recorded and were made memorable.

Each of the projects I have described engaged the teachers in looking for ways in which they could draw from students' own 'funds of knowledge' (Moll *et al.*, 1992) to make their children's learning memorable, whether this was in terms of the ideas themselves, or alternative ways of recording them.

DISCUSSION

Each of the projects adopted a methodology that involved teachers negotiating the development of their emerging understanding with their classes, while sharing their work and recording observations within a loose framework evaluated externally by the University. This ensured that specific aspects of teaching and learning which the participants themselves had identified as important were followed through. Indeed, I would go so far as to claim that it is only a teacher with a knowledge of a particular class, an understanding of preoccupations and a grasp of the different modalities in which communication can be shaped, who is effective in creating opportunities to bring local and global issues into play in the classroom.

The teachers involved in the Sheffield projects consistently described how their concern for, and engagement with, their students' particular cultural interests provided a very productive way of reconciling teacher and student priorities for communicating meaning. In teaching particular genres they were more open to allowing their pupils to make individual 'design decisions' (Kress, 2003). In this they satisfied not only their pupils' but also their own creative needs and gave a lie to the charge that all those who engage with the literacy strategy are uncritical and dull. The implications of their work seem very clear. Teachers deserve to be trusted and in turn they need to trust their pupils. Curriculum change that helps to develop all pupils' literacy within the modes that are appropriate to the task in hand is in the interest of both teacher and taught. What is required is a sympathetic orchestration of change which will enable teachers to reclaim ownership of the curriculum, shaping its form in relation to their students' needs while preparing them for the world beyond the classroom.

NOTE

1 Mr Gradgrind was the retired manufacturer, member of Parliament and educational reformer from Dickens's *Hard Times* (1854), who demanded that schools should teach nothing but facts. In Dickens's working notes for the novel the name 'gradgrind' is associated with the mechanical, repetitive drudgery of the factory system. Mr Gradgrind represents rationalism, self-interest, and cold, hard fact. He is an 'eminently practical' man, and he tries to raise his children also to be practical by forbidding the development of their imaginations and emotions. By the use of Gradgrindian, I imply that much current emphasis in education has been on 'basic' skills and employment-related competences.

REFERENCES

Appadurai, A. (1996) *Modernity at Large: Cultural Dimensions of Globalization.* Minneapolis, MN: University of Minnesota Press.

Barton, D. (1994) *Literacy: An Introduction to the Ecology of Written Language.* Oxford: Blackwell.

Barton, D., and Hamilton, M. (1998) *Local Literacies: Reading and Writing in One Community.* London: Routledge.

Barton, D., Hamilton, M., and Ivanic, R. (eds) (2000). *Situated Literacies: Reading and Writing in Context.* London: Routledge.

Department for Education and Employment (DfEE) (1998) *The National Literacy Strategy: Framework for Teaching.* London: HMSO.

Department for Education and Employment (DfEE) / Qualifications and Curriculum Authority (QCA) (1999) *The National Curriculum Key Stages 1 and 2.* London: HMSO.

Ellis, V., Furlong, T., and Grant, G. (2002) *The English Teacher Recruitment and Retention Project. First Report: Factors Affecting the Decision to Train to Teach.* Sheffield: NATE.

Foucault, M. (1977) *Discipline and Punish: The Birth of the Prison.* Harmondsworth: Penguin.

Fullan, M. (2000) The three stories of education reform, *Phi Delta Kappan.* Bloomington, IN: 581–84.

Gee, J.P. (1996) *Social Linguistics and Literacies: Ideology in Discourses* (2nd edn). London: Falmer Press.

Gee, J.P. (2000) New people in new worlds: Networks, the new capitalism and schools. In B. Cope and M. Kalantzis (eds), *Multiliteracies: Literacy Learning and the Design of Social Futures* (pp. 43–68). London: Routledge.

Hargreaves, A. (1994) *Changing Teachers, Changing Times: Teachers' Work and Culture in the Postmodern Age.* London: Cassell.

Kress, G. (2003) *Literacy in a New Media Age.* London: Routledge.

Lambirth, A. (2003) 'They get enough of that at home': understanding aversion to popular culture in schools. *Reading, Literacy and Language,* **37** (1): 9–14.

Lankshear, C. and Knobel, M. (2002) Steps toward a pedagogy of tactics, Keynote paper prepared for the National Council of English Teachers' Assembly for Research. New York.

Marsh, J. (2003) One-way traffic? Connections between literacy practices at home and in the nursery, *British Educational Research Journal,* **29** (3): 369–82.

Marsh, J. and Millard, E. (2000) *Literacy and Popular Culture: Using Children's Culture in the Classroom.* London: Paul Chapman.

Marsh, J. and Millard, E. (2003) *Literacy and Popular Culture in the Classroom,* Reading: Reading and Language Centre Publications.

Marsh, J. and Thompson, P. (2001) Parental involvement in literacy development: Using media texts, *Journal of Research in Reading,* **24**: 266–78.

Marshall, R. (2002) Editorial: Revolting Literacies, *English in Education,* **36** (2): 4–5. Sheffield: The National Association for the Teaching of English.

Millard E. (2003) Transformative pedagogy: Towards a literacy of fusion, *Reading, Literacy and Language,* **37** (1): 3–9.

Millard, E. (1997) *Differently Literate: Boys, Girls and the Schooling of Literacy*. London: Falmer Press.

Millard, E. (1994) *Developing Readers in the Middle Years*. Buckingham: Open University Press.

Millard, E. and Marsh, J. (2001) Sending Minnie the Minx home: Comics and reading choices, *Cambridge Journal of Education*, **31** (1): 25–38.

Moll, L.C., Amanti, C., Neff, D., and Gonzalez, N. (1992) Funds of Knowledge for Teaching: Using a Qualitative Approach to Connect Homes and Classrooms, *Theory Into Practice*, **31** (2): 132–41.

Street, B. (1984) *Literacy in Theory and Practice*. Cambridge: Cambridge University Press.

Street, B. (ed. 1993) *Cross Cultural Approaches to Literacy*. Cambridge: Cambridge University Press.

Street, B. (2003) What's New in New Literacy Studies?, *Current Issues in Comparative Education*, **5**(2).

Afterword: popular literacies in an era of 'scientific' reading instruction: challenges and opportunities

Donna E. Alvermann

> To read a good book, Japanese pull out their cell phones.
> (Kageyama, 2005)
> 'Go to your room!' sends many kids to multimedia hub.
> (Armas, 2005)
> ... today's students have grown up in a deregulated attention economy and have been living by its rules.
> (Lankshear and Knobel, 2003)

Imagine trying to reconcile the gist of the foregoing references to popular culture, media, and new information communication technologies with the current definition of what constitutes 'scientifically based' reading instruction in the USA. When I initially agreed to take on such a challenge by writing a short chapter that would examine the themes raised in *Popular Literacies, Childhood and Schooling* from a US perspective, the impact of the federally legislated No Child Left Behind (NCLB) Act (2001) had yet to be felt – at least not widely. Since then the critique of this piece of legislation and its narrow definition of what counts as reading has reached epic proportions, with a broad array of newspapers, professional journals, organizational newsletters, and reports from state legislatures (NCSL Task Force, 2005) drawing attention to the difficulties associated with implementing NCLB.

My focus here is not with the critique itself, but rather with an examination of the challenges and opportunities which present themselves in the course of introducing textual practices in popular literacies to classroom teachers – specifically, to literacy teachers in the USA whose every lesson must now pass the litmus test of 'scientific' reading instruction. That this examination has implications beyond the NCLB Act of 2001 goes without saying. For, even if some of its sanctions were lifted in the foreseeable future, the fact remains that educators in the USA have been (at best) lukewarm to the idea of connecting students' popular literacies with language arts curricula (Alvermann and Xu, 2003; Hagood,

2003; Short *et al.*, 2003). That this is not a phenomenon peculiar to the US seems evident in many of the chapters in *Popular Literacies, Childhood and Schooling*.

Why this is so, in my view, is largely attributable to what Dyson (2003) has described as 'the "nothing" assumption – the decision to make no assumption that children have any relevant knowledge' (p. 101) when it comes to knowing things that are pertinent to literacy-learning outside an idealized, print-centred environment. At a time when reading a book on one's cellphone, or being sent to one's room, is no longer viewed as a punishment but as an opportunity to engage with media of various kinds, the notion of an idealized, print-centred existence seems an anachronism. A holdover from earlier times, the printed word will survive and right-fully so, but it is quickly becoming just one among several other textual practices vying for children's attention. As Heim (cited in Lankshear and Knobel, 2003) puts it,

> [the] word now shares Web space with the image, and text appears inextricably tied to pictures. The pictures are dynamic, animated, and continually updated. The unprecedented speed and ease of digital production mounts photographs, movies, and video on the Web. Cyberspace becomes visualized data, and meaning arrives in spatial as well as in verbal expressions.
>
> (Ibid.: 170)

POPULAR LITERACIES AND THE CHALLENGES THEY PRESENT

What are the textual practices of popular literacies, what distinguishes them from conventional forms of literacy, and what challenges do popular literacies present in an era of 'scientific' reading instruction? Readers need but skim the chapter titles and contents of the present volume to answer the first of these questions. The second and third questions, however, deserve attention here. In my view, the main distinguishing characteristic of textual practices of popular literacies is the association of these practices with low culture. As I have discussed elsewhere (Alvermann *et al.*, 1999; Alvermann and Xu, 2003), traditionally the idea of low culture, as con-trasted with high culture, serves to identify what people think of as appealing to the masses, or common people. Low-culture textual practices are thought to have a coarseness that makes them undesirable (at least among high-brow elites). It is this presumably that sets them apart from certain kinds of paintings, books, music and the like that are dubbed high culture.

A second distinguishing characteristic is the association of popular literacies with mass media. As Hagood (2001) has noted, those who find a culprit in the intersection of mass media and the textual practices of popular culture believe that 'the culture industry socializes people in common ways by exposing them to mindless drivel' (ibid.: 254). This perception of popular literacies tends to propagate the notion that people (and especially children) lack the ability to interpret for themselves the messages that mass media produce; in short, that they are consigned to a lifetime of engaging in substandard textual practices which, in addition to duping them, will do little to improve their minds or status in society. Although I personally do not subscribe to this view, the fact remains that it has a large and vocal group of supporters among those who advocate for 'scientific' reading instruction as defined under the NCLB Act of 2001. And, understandably so, especially if the assumption is that popular literacies are somehow inferior to traditional print literacy and thus best ignored – a perspective that is challenging and troubling for the very reason described next.

One of the goals of NCLB is that *all* children, regardless of skin colour, ethnicity, disability, immigrant status and wealth, will make annual yearly progress at a rate determined sufficient for producing a society in which everyone is educated to her or his full potential. A noble goal on the surface, but it has its darker side. For example, when the 'all' children are in Dyson's (2003) terms 'almost always syntactically linked or semantically associated with that other category, the "different" children – not middle class and not white' (ibid.: 100), then there is cause for concern. This is especially the case when teachers act on 'the assumption that "diverse" children come to school without literacy [and in effect ignore] the resources they bring from popular media texts' (Dyson, 2003: 1–2).

A third challenge, one that will grow in magnitude as NCLB-driven policies make their weight felt increasingly at the middle- and high-school levels, is how to reconcile the narrow definition of 'scientific' reading instruction with the need to develop older students' critical awareness as they engage in textual practices that make use of popular literacies. A review of the literature on new information communication technologies among secondary students in the USA (Alvermann, forthcoming) revealed only a handful of studies that analyzed in depth how young people develop a sense of critical awareness about their own implication in the production and consumption of popular literacies.

With few exceptions (e.g. Dillon and O'Brien, 2001; Chandler-Olcott and Mahar, 2001; Kamberelis and Dimitriadis, 1999; Moje, 2000; Myers *et al.*, 2000), researchers in the United States interested in adolescents' critical awareness have worked in classrooms where the curriculum is primarily print driven and necessarily constrained by school-based norms for teaching and learning. Thus, it remains unclear as to whether developing students' critical awareness of textual practices that employ conventional print within the confines of a school curriculum will transfer to textual practices that make use of popular literacies outside of school.

OPPORTUNITIES FOR CHANGE

Do the opportunities that popular literacies present in an era of 'scientific' reading instruction outweigh the challenges? I believe they do, and for the following reasons. First, I sense that there are several motivating factors for taking into account textual practices in popular literacies and that these factors will increasingly find their way into US teacher education programmes, professional journals, and eventually into mainstream thinking about instruction in grades K through 12. One such factor is the massive, multimedia realm of digital information communication technologies that is all pervading and shows no sign of abating. As Lankshear and Knobel (2003) have cogently argued, this realm of ICTs troubles the very notion that knowledge is primarily conveyed through printed words and

> makes *normal* the radical convergence of text, image, and sound in ways that break down the primacy of propositional linguistic forms of 'truth bearing.' While many images and sounds that are transmitted and received digitally still stand for propositional information, many do not... Meaning and truth arrive in spatial as well as textual expressions.
>
> (Ibid.: 171)

Not trusting to theory alone, literacy scholars with a background in public schooling are gradually beginning to locate their work in spatial theories of young people's digital practices, For instance, Leander (2002, 2003) and his colleagues (Leander and McKim, 2003; Leander and Sheehy, 2004) are making use of current thinking in the fields of social and cultural geography to generate insights for imagining the place of ICT-related literacies within a school's curriculum. Their work represents an important shift in the study of online literacies among US youth, both in and out of school. It also represents richness and complexity in what can be learned by moving away from a fixation on technology as a tool toward using it to map what Lemke (2000) refers to as ecosocial systems – that is, digital spaces in which learners produce and perform new literate identities.

A second factor that may motivate US educators to explore more aggressively the potential connections between popular literacies and the language arts curriculum is the research on popular culture coming out of Australia, Canada and the UK. In these countries, especially, there is a growing trend among some educators to view popular culture as folk culture, wherein common people are indeed capable of making their own meanings of popular literacies – meanings, however, that are never entirely devoid of what mass media producers may have intended as the message. There is also some evidence that in acknowledging the appeal of popular literacies in children's everyday lives, parents (Guzzetti and Gamboa, 2005) perhaps more so than teachers (Xu, 2004) in the USA, are beginning to recognize that these literacies are not something to be shunned, set aside, or kept at a distance. At the same time, textual practices that position children as simultaneously incorporating both pleasures and critiques in their use of popular literacies (see Hagood, 2003; Marsh and Millard, 2000; Tobin, 2000) are finding it a bit more difficult to gain a foothold within the narrow definition of 'scientific' reading instruction that currently prevails.

Whether (or more likely to what degree) US educators will take up Hull and Schultz's (2002) call 'to think again and anew about teaching and learning in the schoolroom' (p. 3) is open for debate. Views vary about what constitutes valuable use of classroom time and how much time should be spent in 'scientific' reading instruction. For example, in NCLB-backed Reading First schools a minimum of 135 minutes of 'scientific' reading instruction is required each day. Often this leads to shortchanging the time spent in teaching other subjects – a reality which in some states has led to the discontinuation of student assessments for writing, social studies and science (Rado, 2005).

Despite one's personal view about the emphasis currently placed on 'scientific' reading instruction, it is encouraging to note that textual practices in popular literacies are not limited to decoding the printed word. In popular literacies, the ability to analyze media messages presumes that one is at least visually (if not sound) literate. Becoming visually literate involves expanding print literacy skills by developing a greater awareness of how things come to have the meaning that they have and why those meanings vary from one individual to the next. As Muffoletto (2001) explained, 'Being "visually literate" means more than having the ability to produce/ encode and read/decode constructed visual experiences; it . . . is to be actively engaged in asking questions and seeking answers about the multiple meanings of a visual experience'.

Strangely enough, visual literacy is one of the new literacies that 'scientific' reading instruction and the Institution of Old Learning (IOL) – a tongue-in-cheek term coined by O'Brien and Bauer (2005) to denote historically situated practices and rigid organizational structures of US schools – largely ignore. Pre-dating the No Child Left Behind Act and 'scientific' reading instruction by nearly one hundred years, the IOL attempts to fit new information communication technologies into its century-old rigid structures and goals. And, while it is easy to critique the IOL in relation to popular literacies, it is quite another matter to loosen its stranglehold on US educators at large. Perhaps the best course of action presently is to conduct inquiries of popular literacies within the IOL, as O'Brien and Bauer (2005) urge, in order to 'gain and maintain the insider status that we need to inspire ourselves, our preservice teachers, our school-based colleagues, and future students in gradually transforming the IOL' (p. 130). Toward this end, I can think of no better place to turn initially than to the chapters in *Popular Literacies, Childhood and Schooling*. By offering insights into the importance of popular culture, media, and new technologies for contemporary children and young people's literacy education, the chapter authors have in effect joined O'Brien and Bauer in the call to transform the age-old Institution of Learning. A question that remains for us, the readers, is this: are we prepared to heed that call?

REFERENCES

Alvermann, D.E. (forthcoming). Technology use and needed research in youth literacies. In M. McKenna, L. Labbo, R. Kieffer and D. Reinking (eds), *Handbook of literacy and technology* (2nd edn). Mahwah, NJ: Lawrence Erlbaum.

Alvermann, D.E., Moon, J.S. and Hagood, M.C. (1999). *Popular culture in the classroom: Thinking and researching critical media literacy*. Newark, DE: International Reading Association and the National Reading Conference.

Alvermann, D.E. and Xu, S.H. (2003). Children's everyday literacies: Intersections of popular culture and language arts instruction. *Language Arts*, 81: 145–55.

Armas, G. C. (2005, 10 March). 'Go to your room!' sends many kids to multimedia hub. *The Seattle Times*. Retrieved 20 March 2005 from http://archives.seattletimes.nwsource.com/cgi-bin/texis.cgi/web/vortex/display?slug=mediakids10anddate=20050310andquery=Armas

Chandler-Olcott, K. and Mahar, D. (2001, November). Considering genre in the digital literacy classroom. *Reading Online*, 5 (4). Retrieved 10 March 2003 from http://www.readingonline.org/electronic/elec_index.asp?HREF=hillinger/index.html

Dillon, D.R., and O'Brien, D. G. (2001, April). *Reconceptualizing 'at-risk' adolescent readers as literate intellectuals*. Paper presented at the meeting of the American Educational Research Association, Seattle, WA.

Dyson, A.H. (2003). Popular literacies and the 'all' children: Rethinking literacy development for contemporary childhoods. *Language Arts*, 81: 100–109.

Guzzetti, B.J. and Gamboa, M. (2005). Zines for social justice: Adolescent girls writing on their own. *Reading Research Quarterly*, 39: 408–36.

Hagood, M.C. (2001). Media literacies: Varied but distinguishable. In J.V. Hoffman, D.L. Schallert, C.M. Fairbanks, J. Worthy and B. Maloch (eds), *Fiftieth yearbook of the National Reading Conference* (pp. 248–61). Chicago: National Reading Conference.

Hagood, M.C. (2003). New media and online literacies: No age left behind. *Reading Research Quarterly*, 38: 387–91.

Hull, G. and Schultz, K. (eds) (2002). *School's out: Bridging out-of-school literacies with classroom practice*. New York: Teachers College Press.

Kageyama,Y. (2005, 19 March). Literature on the move. *The Post and Courier*, p. B9.

Kamberelis, G. and Dimitriadis, G. (1999). Talkin' Tupac: Speech genres and the mediation of cultural knowledge. In C. McCarthy, G. Hudak, S. Miklaucic and P. Saukko (eds), *Sound identities: Popular music and the cultural politics of education* (pp. 119–50). New York: Peter Lang.

Lankshear, C. and Knobel, M. (2003). *New literacies: Changing knowledge and classroom learning*. Buckingham, UK: Open University Press.

Leander, K.M. (2002, December). *Situated literacies, digital practices, and the constitution of space-time*. Paper presented at the annual meeting of the National Reading Conference, Miami, FL.

Leander, K.M. (2003). Writing travelers' tales on new literacyscapes. (RRQ Online Supplement). Retrieved 7 October 2004 from http://www.reading.org/Library/Retrieve.cfm?D=10.1598/RRQ.38.3.4andF=RRQ-38-3-Hagood-supp_3.html

Leander, K.M. and McKim, K.K. (2003). Tracing the everyday 'sitings' of adolescents on the Internet: A strategic adaptation of ethnography across online and offline spaces. *Education, Communication and Information*, 3: 211–40.

Leander, K. M. and Sheehy, M. (eds) (2004). *Spatializing literacy research and practice*. New York: Peter Lang.

Lemke, J.L. (2000). Across the scale of time: Artifacts, activities, and meanings in ecosocial systems. *Mind, Culture, and Activity*, 7: 273–92.

Marsh, J. and Millard, E. (2000). *Literacy and popular culture: Using children's culture in the classroom*. London: Paul Chapman.

Moje, E.B. (2000). 'To be part of the story': The literacy practices of gangsta adolescents. *Teachers College Record*, 102: 651–90.

Muffoletto, R. (2001, March). An inquiry into the nature of Uncle Joe's representation and meaning. *Reading Online*, 4 (8). Retrieved 25 February 2003 from http://www.readingonline.org/newliteracies/

Myers, J., Hammett, R. and McKillop, A.M. (2000). Connecting, exploring, and exposing the self in hypermedia projects. In M.A. Gallego and S. Hollingsworth (eds), *What counts as literacy: Challenging the school standard* (pp. 85-105). New York: Teachers College Press.

National Conference of State Legislatures (2005, February 23). *NCSL Task Force on No Child Left Behind Report: Executive Summary*. Retrieved 11 March 2005 from http://www.ncsl.org/programs/press/2005/NCLB_exec_summary.htm

No Child Left Behind Act of 2001. PL 107–10, 115 Stat.1425, 20 U.S.C. 6301 *et. seq.*

O'Brien, D.G. and Bauer, E.B. (2005). New literacies and the institution of old learning. *Reading Research Quarterly*, 40: 120–31.

Rado, D. (2005, March 17). Illinois cuts testing on 1 of 3 R's. *Chicago Tribune*. Retrieved 24 March 2005 from http://www.chicagotribune.com/news/local/lake/chi-0503110251mar11,1,759825.story

Short, K.G., Schroeder, J., Kauffman, G. and Kaser, S. (2003). Thoughts from the editors. *Language Arts*, 81: 99.

Tobin, J. (2000). '*Good guys don't wear hats*': *Children's talk about the media.* New York: Teachers College Press.

Xu, S.H. (2004). Teachers' reading of students' popular culture texts: The interplay of students' interests, teacher knowledge, and literacy curriculum. In J. Worthy, B. Maloch, J.V. Hoffman, D.L. Schallert and C.M. Fairbanks (eds), *53rd yearbook of the National Reading Conference* (pp. 417–31). Oak Creek, WI: National Reading Conference.

Index

acquisition metaphor 64
adolescence 3–4, 164–5, 201, 209
advertising 166
Animated English Project 152, 154
animation 4, 16–19, 150, 153
appropriation and recontextualization 59
Art Attack 60, 85
Arts Council England 150, 152
authenticity 111–12

'Babyz Community' ('The BC') 166–71
Bear Hunt 65
Bentham, J. 194; *see also* Panopticon
Beyblades 66
big book scenario 185, 188, 190, 192
blogs *see* weblogs
Blue Peter 60
Bob the Builder 232
boys and alienation 226, 233–4, 237
British Film Institute (BFI) 151, 152
Bulger, J. 192

Canada 5, 202, 244
CD-ROM 15, 123
cell phones *see* mobile phones
Centre for Research on Literacy and the Media 150
chatrooms 97, 117–18
children's knowledge 56
Cinderella 77
comics 223, 225, 230, 235, 237
computer games 72, 118, 138, 140, 208–9, 228
    focus group 74–6
    gender distinction 74, 180, 209, 213

Crash Bandicoot 32, 38
culture, popular 2, 11, 29, 54
    in the classroom 221
    as folk culture 245
    and literacy 179
    problems of definition xvii–xviii
    teachers' attitudes 179–80, 190, 193, 196
    vs 'high culture' 242
curriculum xx, 5, 121–3, 172, 179, 185–6, 196, 231, 233, 238
    National 155, 157, 224
    new challenges 145–7

Dahl, R. 74
Dickens, C. xviii, 221, 238
digital divide 111, 121
dinosaurs 211–12
discussion boards 100, 105
disengagement 111
Disney films 180
DVDs 205–6, 210–11, 214

early years practitioners 233
ecards 205
Eliot, T. S. 59
email 1, 16, 96, 103–5, 113, 118–19, 121, 161, 204, 207

football 66, 74, 146
Foucault, M. 186, 194–5, 221
frame narratives 77–81

Gameboy 19, 162, 208, 210
globalization 221–2
Goldilocks 67

Harry Potter 74, 165, 229
home 29–52, 111, 119, 224, 232–3
Home–School Knowledge Exchange
    Project 54, 68
horizontal and vertical discourse 130
Horowitz, A. 152
horror videos 129, 133–4, 138, 146, 236

iMovie 152
information and communications
    technology (ICT) 118, 154, 160–1,
    173, 244
instant messaging (IM) 97, 106, 113,
    118–21, 206
Institution of Old Learning (IOL) 245–6
Internet xvii, xx, 4, 16, 111–12, 115,
    116, 118–20, 166, 172, 200, 204

James Bond 235–6
Jordan, Michael xviii
Just William 77

King, M. L. 104–5
Koala Trouble 16–19, 22

language
    changes in use 153
    metafunctions 154–5
laptops 120–1
Lara Croft 3, 77–90
Lewis, C. S. 229
literacies 150, 241
    asset model 200, 209, 211–15
    conservative attitudes 200
    criteria for defining 155, 158
    informal vs schooled 139–41
    National Literacy Strategy (NLS)
        185–7, 223, 233–4
    New Literacy Studies 163–4, 171–2,
        222
    and popular culture 179
    print 150
    progressive attitudes 201
    and social class 128, 140–5, 147, 228,
        243
literacy learning 54
    'top–down' models 151, 154

Mandela, N. 104–5
Matilda 77
meaning-making xviii, 1, 31, 52, 160

media
    boxes 228
    comfort and competence 111, 145,
        202
    explicitness of moving image 156–7
    inside and outside school 128–47
    studies 131–2, 134–5, 138–40
metaphors for learning 63–5
Mickey Mouse xviii
Mr Naughty Man 55–62, 65
mobile phones 15, 98, 162, 206
Montessori system 180

narrative forms 153
National Grid for Learning 103
Ninja Turtles 184, 191–2
Nintendo 19, 180, 208, 210
No Child Left Behind (NCLB) Act 241,
    243, 245
normalization process 195

oral history 123–5
'outsider'/'insider' mentality 162, 171,
    246

Panopticon 194–6
participation metaphor 64
patterns of play 73
pedagogies 121–3, 138, 144, 157, 158,
    172, 179, 215, 222, 237
    competence- and performance-based
        131
Personal Digital Assistant (PDA) 94
phones see mobile phones
phonics teaching 151
Piaget, J. 155
picture messaging 97, 98, 202, 242
PlayStation 31, 35, 208, 210, 229
poetry 152, 153, 157, 171, 192,
    228
Pokémon xviii, 19–24, 30, 32, 42–44,
    195–6
popular culture see culture, popular
popular literacies see literacies
PowerPoint 113–15
print literacy see literacies
Pullman, P. 213

race and ethnicity xix, 33, 47, 104–5,
    179, 184, 243
radio 207–8
rap 171, 192

Red Riding Hood 3, 77–90
Rowling, J. K. 74; *see also* Harry Potter

'savvy' 122–3, 201
school-defined purposes 112, 118–20,
    125–6
Schwarzenegger, A. 58
Scooby Doo 57, 65, 67
self-efficacy 189
self-selected purposes xix, 112, 118–20,
    125–6
Shakespeare, W. xviii, 143–4; *King Lear*
    58
Sheffield Literacy, Language and Culture
    Research Group 223
Simpsons, The 54, 61–64, 115
'Smartmob generation' 204
SMS *see* text messaging
'snail mail' 98
soap operas 133, 138
Sonic Adventures 81
Space Jam 36–37
Special Needs 229
Spice Girls 184, 191
Superman xx
Super Mario 32, 35–42, 51
Sweet Valley High 133, 140

talk about text 129–30
teachers
    engaged in curriculum change 224
    in-service 5
    pre-service 5, 160, 181–2, 187–94,
        201, 227, 246
    young xxi, 162, 201
technokids 12–13
technology 12
    its influence 12–15
    in schools 116

of work and pleasure 212
of writing 93–5
Teletubbies 66, 184, 232
television 128–9, 172, 181, 200, 207,
    223, 227–8, 230, 232
text messaging 15, 95, 98–9, 172,
    206–8
Thomas the Tank Engine 30, 43, 44,
    47–51
timescales for play 50–52
Toy Story (2) 42, 232
traditional tales 77
Tweenies 232

university projects 123, 235

video diaries 54, 123
video games xix, 100, 122, 200, 213
virtual learning environments (VLEs)
    106

webcam 97, 124–5
WebCT 204–5
weblogs 95, 99–100, 105, 119, 124
Wilson, J. 74
World Wrestling Federation (WWF)
    133, 134–8, 144
writing xix, 68, 102
    children's 156
    and computer (narrations) 72
    digital 3, 93–5, 120
    learned by 'apprenticeship' 103–6

youth 3–4, 164–5, 209; *see also*
    adolescence

Zone of Proximal Development 157